Creative Intuition in Art and Poetry

CREATIVE INTUITION IN ART AND POETRY

by Jacques Maritain

THE A. W. MELLON LECTURES

IN THE FINE ARTS

Meridian Books
THE WORLD PUBLISHING COMPANY
Cleveland and New York

M

A MERIDIAN BOOK

*Published by The World Publishing Company
2231 West 110 Street, Cleveland 2, Ohio
First printing December, 1954
Tenth printing April, 1961*

*Copyright © 1953 by the Trustees of the National Gallery
of Art, Washington, D.C.*

*Published for Bollingen Foundation Inc., New York, N.Y.
by Pantheon Books Inc., New York, N.Y.
First printing March 1953
Third printing January 1955
This is the first volume of the A. W. Mellon Lectures in the
Fine Arts, which are delivered annually at the National
Gallery of Art, Washington.*

*Library of Congress Catalog Card number: 55-5167
Printed in the United States of America*

Acknowledgments

This book grew out of six lectures given at the National Gallery of Art, Washington, in the spring of 1952. I appreciate very much the honor of having been invited to deliver there the initial series of the A. W. Mellon Lectures in the Fine Arts. I would like to express my sincere thanks to the lectureship committee; to the National Gallery of Art and its director Mr. David E. Finley; and especially to Mr. Huntington Cairns, chairman of the lectureship committee, whose enlightened and generous assistance was invaluable to me. I also thank cordially Mr. Macgill James, assistant director of the National Gallery of Art, and Mr. Raymond S. Stites, curator in charge of education, for their gracious help in the preparation of the slides shown during the lectures; without Mr. James's precious and untiring co-operation the illustration of the book would have been impossible.

I am greatly indebted to Mr. Francis Fergusson, who, as director of the seminars in literary criticism at Princeton University, gave me the opportunity for an indispensable preparatory phase of research, and whose friendly insistence is responsible for the essay on Dante which I wrote both as a contribution to the *Kenyon Review* and as the central part of the last chapter of this book. To him and to Mr. Allen Tate I owe my having become more familiar with the remarkable work done by contemporary American criticism, and with the perspectives and problems it has elucidated. Mr. Edward Toner Cone, associate professor of music at Princeton University, was kind enough to provide me with several texts from letters of great composers. Mrs. E. B. O. Borgerhoff was for me, regarding research work as well as my effort to achieve exact expression in a language which is not my native tongue, a collaborator for whose spirited attention, discerning competence, and congenial understanding I have deep gratitude.

Raïssa, my wife, assisted me all through my work—I do not believe that a philosopher would dare to speak of poetry if he could not rely on the direct experience of a poet.

J. M.

Publisher's note

Acknowledgment is gratefully made to the following publishers and persons for kind permission to include copyright material, as follows: Burns, Oates and Washbourne, Ltd., London, and Sir Francis Meynell, for passages of prose and poetry from the *Works* of Francis Thompson; Mrs. Ananda K. Coomaraswamy for a passage from her late husband's *Introduction to Indian Art;* The Cummington Press, Cummington, Mass., for two poems of R. P. Blackmur; J. M. Dent and Sons, Ltd., London, for passages from the Thomas Okey translation of Dante; Harcourt, Brace and Co., New York, for poetry of T. S. Eliot and Robert Lowell, a passage from Eliot's *Selected Essays,* and a poem of Heine, trans. Louis Untermeyer; Harvard University Press for passages from the H. R. Fairclough translation of the *Aeneid* of Vergil; Henry Holt and Co., New York, for passages from Cleanth Brooks and Robert Penn Warren, *Understanding Poetry,* Lionel de Fonseka, and for poetry of Robert Frost and E. E. Cummings; Houghton Mifflin Co., Boston, for poetry of Archibald MacLeish; Alfred A. Knopf, Inc., New York, for poetry of John Crowe Ransom; Little, Brown and Co., Boston, for a poem of Emily Dickinson; Liveright Publishing Corp., New York, for poetry in the *Collected Poems of Hart Crane;* The Macmillan Co., New York, for poetry of Marianne Moore and William Butler Yeats; New Directions, New York, for poetry of Thomas Merton, Dylan Thomas, and Robert Fitzgerald, and a passage from Djuna Barnes, *Nightwood;* Random House, New York, for a passage from Gertrude Stein, *Selected Writings,* and the Stephen Potter edition of Coleridge's selected poetry and prose; Charles Scribner's Sons, New York, for poetry of John Peale Bishop, and Allen Tate and a passage from John Crowe Ransom, *The World's Body.*

Jacques Maritain

Jacques Maritain was born in Paris in 1882. One of the major Christian thinkers in the world today, Maritain seeks, through the reconsideration of the philosophy of Saint Thomas Acquinas, to interpret anew the bases of modern thought. Since the war, Maritain has lived with his wife, the poet, Raissa Maritain, at their home in Princeton.

His works in English include: *The Degrees of Knowledge; True Humanism, Art and Scholasticism; Existence and the Existent;* and *Creative Intuition in Art and Poetry.*

Contents

Preliminary Note

A few indications may be given about some of the characteristics of this book.

I. The material of the quotation is principally English and French. Many excerpts from French authors (especially poets), have been cited in the original, not only because it is almost impossible, except for a poet, adequately to translate poetry (especially modern French poetry), but also, and first of all, because this book—in its perspective, if not in its subject matter—is concerned with comparative poetry. In the view of its author, it is a kind of joint tribute to British and American and to French poetry.

II. In the original edition (Bollingen Series, Pantheon), the book comprises on the one hand a number of pictorial illustrations (a Frontispiece in color and sixty-eight plates in black and white), and on the other hand various literary excerpts (Texts without Comment)—"pure texts" for "pure reading,"—which come in addition to nine chapters. In the present edition it has been necessary to omit all of the pictorial illustrations, and the Texts without Comment (except for Chapters IV and VIII), as well as a great many footnotes and references.

III. Finally, I might mention here that while I cite the existing English translation of my books and give page references where required, I have exercised the privilege, occasionally, of revising the language.

Creative Intuition in Art and Poetry

ONE

POETRY, MAN, AND THINGS

Preliminary Remarks

1. Art and poetry cannot do without one another. Yet the two words are far from being synonymous. By Art I mean the creative or producing, work-making activity of the human mind. By Poetry I mean, not the particular art which consists in writing verses, but a process both more general and more primary: that intercommunication between the inner being of things and the inner being of the human Self which is a kind of divination (as was realized in ancient times; the Latin *vates* was both a poet and a diviner). Poetry, in this sense, is the secret life of each and all of the arts;[1] another name for what Plato called *mousikè*.

Art and poetry—one of the main purposes of this book is to try to make clear both the distinction and the indissoluble relationship between these two strange companions.

Another main purpose has to do with the essential part played by the intellect or reason in both art and poetry, and especially with the fact that poetry has its source in the pre-conceptual life of the intellect. I use the words intellect and reason as synonymous, in so far as they designate a single power or faculty in the human soul. But I want to emphasize, from the start, that the very words reason or intellect, when they are related to that spiritual energy which is poetry, must be understood in a much deeper and larger sense than is usual. The intellect, as well as the imagination, is at the core of poetry. But reason, or the intellect, is not merely logical reason; it involves an exceedingly more profound—and more obscure—life, which is revealed to us in proportion as we endeavor to penetrate the hidden recesses of poetic activity. In other words, poetry obliges us to consider the intellect both in its secret wellsprings inside the human soul and as functioning in a nonrational (I do not say antirational) or nonlogical way.

If, in the course of my discussions, I refer especially to the art of the painter and the art of the poet, it is not that I consider the other arts to be less significant. Music is perhaps the most significant of all. But music, I think, requires a separate, quite special analysis. Furthermore, this book is in no way a treatise on the arts; I am neither a historian nor a critic of art. My inquiry is a philosophical inquiry. I need examples which are closest at hand for everybody. Examples are only an inductive or instrumental way to get at ideas and to check ideas.

2. The first two chapters in this book are, to a certain extent, introductory chapters. This first chapter, although mainly occupied with broad considerations about plastic arts, is concerned in reality with poetry—poetry in the universal sense I just mentioned a moment ago—but it is concerned with poetry from a still external, merely descriptive point of view. Its aim is only to bring us, through an inductive way, to confront some basic facts and state a basic problem. The problem will be scrutinized later.

The second chapter deals with art, in the strictly determined sense which must be given to this word. Its aim is to establish a certain number of fundamentals, which are needed for further investigation, especially when it comes to the crucial point: the relationship between art and poetry.

Nature and Man

3. As soon as beauty is involved, the prime fact that is to be observed is a sort of interpenetration between Nature and

Man. This interpenetration is quite peculiar in essence: for it is in no way a mutual absorption. Each of the two terms involved remains what it is, it keeps its essential identity, it even asserts more powerfully this identity of its own, while it suffers the contagion or impregnation of the other. But neither one is alone; they are mysteriously commingled.

Man, when he feels the joy of beauty, does not only enter with the things of nature into that relationship of intentional [2] or spiritual identification which constitutes knowledge—"to know is to become another in so far as it is another." Man is seduced by Nature (metamorphosed as Nature may be when the object contemplated is a work of art). To some extent Nature enters his own blood and breathes his own desire with him. Whether art, in its beginnings in mankind, always had some magic purpose is a questionable assumption. But in a deeper though improper sense, art by itself involves a species of magic, which has become purified in the course of centuries, and is pure, and purely aesthetic, when the invasion of man by Nature pertains exclusively to the joy of a vision or intuition, that is, of a purely intentional or suprasubjective becoming.

Conversely, in connection with aesthetic feeling there is always, to some degree, a sort of invasion of Nature by man.

Take the objects of aesthetic delight which are the most completely remote from any impact of humanity: say, either a beautiful mathematical demonstration—or, in the domain of art, a beautiful abstract arrangement, an Arabic mosaic or piece of stuccowork;—or a shining flower, a gleaming sunset, a tropical bird;—or any of the great spectacles offered by wild Nature, desert, virgin forest, mountains, or those big noisy waterfalls which offer innumerable families of tourists the thrill of the sublime. Everywhere, in reality, man is there, under cover. Man's measure is present, though hidden. All these nonhuman things return to man a quality of the human mind which is concealed in them: intellectual proportion and consistency in the case of a beautiful or "elegant" mathematical demonstration, or in the case of a beautiful abstract arrangement. In the case of that beauty which simply delights the senses, number or proportion is there again, and makes the senses rejoice in a property of their own; and as to physical qualities themselves, if a beautiful color in its relation to other surrounding colors "washes the eye," as Degas put it, it is because it corresponds in things to the need of the eye for rhythmical concentration and release, and to that immaterial transparency through which the inner operation of the sense reaches fulfillment.

Finally, what about the great spectacles of wild Nature? Something of man is still involved—this time a certain feeling (related of itself to no aesthetic perception, I would say a brute feeling, or a merely subjective feeling) which is produced in us, and projected by us into things, and reflected upon us by them: especially, with respect to Nature in her own fierce or solitary, unpierceable selfhood, the feeling of an infinite disproportion between Nature and man: this is not simply crushing and astounding, it also stirs in us, obscurely, vague and indeterminate heroic potentialities—we wonder in the dark through what kind of frightful experiences we might possibly overcome the very disproportion. Hence an impression both of awe and of challenge, which causes, I think, the sensation of the sublime, but which makes this sensation far distant from the pure perception of beauty and, I would say, defective in aesthetic value. (Not to speak of the fact that what is called sublime by tourists, sometimes by philosophers, is often simply what causes them to be in a daze.)

4. Yet what I should like to emphasize now has nothing to do with the category of above-mentioned cases, where the object of aesthetic perception, though implying some inherent relationship to man, was as separate as possible from human life. My contention is that, apart from these particular cases, the beauty of Nature is all the greater, the aesthetic delight or perception in the face of Nature is all the purer and the deeper, as the impact of human life upon Nature is more profound and extensive.

This may come about through the power of imagination.

(Thus do the slow clouds moving in the sky, or the immensity of the sea—*"Homme libre toujours tu chériras la mer"*—speak endlessly to man of the human soul.)

And it may come about in actual existence. Nature happens to be invaded by man in her own physical and spiritual reality, I mean, by this last expression, in her inner power of significance. And then her own beauty is best revealed. The bay of Rio de Janeiro, immense, luminous, exquisitely delineated, is one of the most rightly admired natural sites. But how much more beautiful, how much more moving—I mean moving the very sense of beauty—is the entrance, at nightfall, into the port of Marseilles, as it opens its man-managed secretive basins one after another, in a forest of masts, cranes, lights, and memories! When you drive along the Hudson River or through the hills of Virginia (it is not a question of walking, Americans do not know this meditative pleasure), imagine for a moment that the country you contemplate is still populated with Indian warriors and tents: then the beauty of Nature will awake and make sense all of a sudden, because the relationship between Nature and man has been re-established; modern inhabitants have not yet had the time to permeate the land with the form of man. But look at the violent forms, laden with human labor, that have been here and there planted in fields or along rivers by industry: here the relationship is established, Nature avows a new beauty. How is it that when coming from the ocean you pass the Pillars of Hercules and enter the Mediterranean, the beauty of the airy shores and lifelike sea bursts into a song, a triumph? How is it that the simple curves of the Campagna fill you with a plenitude of emotion which seems inexhaustible? If not because of Vergil and the Greek heroes (though you don't actually think of them), and the impalpable breezes of memory which freshen your face. These places on the earth have been impregnated with man's intelligence and toil. It is through history that the union of Nature and man is accomplished. As a result Nature radiates with signs and significance, which make her beauty blossom forth.

From this analysis we may draw two conclusions. First: Nature is all the more beautiful as it is laden with emotion. Emotion is essential in the perception of beauty. But what sort of emotion? It is not the emotion which I called a while ago brute or merely subjective. It is another kind of emotion—one with knowledge: because, like the emotion produced by all those signs and that significance with which Nature invaded by man abounds, and which I just pointed out, it constitutes or integrates a delight involved in a vision. Such an emotion transcends mere subjectivity, and draws the mind toward things known and toward knowing more. And so induces dream in us.

Second: The signs and the significance I just pointed out remain, as a rule, virtual or latent, at least at that very moment when the wanderer on the earth is struck by the impact of beauty. No particular recollection, no particular idea, is expressed in consciousness. Yet, for all that, these signs and this significance do not lose anything of their power with respect to the experience of beauty. Let us remember this fact, to which we shall have to return later. Unexpressed significance, unexpressed meanings, more or less unconsciously putting pressure on the mind, play an important part in aesthetic feeling and the perception of beauty.

Following the same line of reflection, we also see that Oscar Wilde's saying, Nature imitates art, is but an obvious truism, as far as our perception of the beauty of Nature is concerned. For man's art and vision too are one of the ways through which mankind invades Nature, so as to be reflected and meant by her. Without the mirrors worked out by generations of painters and poets, what would our aesthetic penetration of Nature be? Only after Giotto had replaced by peaks and mountains the gold backgrounds of early medieval art did we[3] become aware of the beauty of mountains. When you are walking in Rome, part of your joy depends on Piranesi; it depends also on the mirror of theater: yellow-ocher palazzi, stores, and workshops open as a grotto, people at home in old streets, are there to offer you the charms of the stage. Let us look at human faces as if they were pictures, then the pleasures of our eyes will be multiplied. An epicurean of art traveling in New York subways enjoys a ceaselessly renewed exhibition of Cézanne's, Hogarth's, or Gauguin's figures, offered free of charge by nature, or of Seurat's when all the lights are on.

Things and the Creative Self

5. It is not enough to consider the mutual entanglement of Nature and man in relation to aesthetic feeling or the perception of beauty. What matters to us is the mutual entanglement of Nature and man—let us say, the coming together of the World and the Self—in relation to artistic creation. Then we truly enter our subject matter. And then we have to do with Poetry.

But while standing on the threshold I cannot help, first, complaining about human vocabulary. I need to designate both the singularity and the infinite internal depths of this flesh-and-blood and spiritual existent, the artist; and I have only an abstract word: the Self. I need to designate the secretive depths and the implacable advance of that infinite host of beings, aspects, events, physical and moral tangles of horror and beauty—of that world, that undecipherable Other—with which Man the artist is faced; and I have no word for that except the poorest and tritest word of the human language; I shall say: the things of the world, the *Things.* But I would wish to invest this empty word with the feelings of primitive man looking at the all-pervading force of Nature, or of the old Ionian philosophers saying that "all things are full of gods."

The Things and the artist's Self: what can we learn on this subject from the typical forms in which the creative effort of man's eyes and hands has manifested itself in the course of centuries?

I do not like generalizations and bird's-eye views. Yet I am constrained to resort to them by the method I am trying to follow in this chapter. I hope I can attach myself to broad characteristics simple and evident enough to avoid too great a risk of arbitrary interpretation.

The crucial fact with which we are confronted is, it seems to me, the contrast and opposition between the approach and spirit, the poetic perception, of the Orient, and the approach and spirit, the poetic perception, of the Occident, as regards the relationship between Things and the artist's Self.

In a general way it can be said—and it is strongly emphasized by Oriental writers—that the art of the Orient is the direct opposite of Western individualism. The Oriental artist would be ashamed of thinking of his ego and intending to manifest his own subjectivity in his work. His first duty is to forget himself. He looks at Things, he meditates on the mystery of their visible appearance and on the mystery of their secret life force, he reveals both in his work, either for the pleasure of man and the ornament of human life, or for the sacred rites of prayer and worship. But because Oriental art is essentially religious or religious-minded, this art is in communion with Things not for the sake of Things but for the sake of some other—invisible and adorable—reality whose signs Things are, and which, through Things, art reveals together with Things. In actual fact religion, not art, has lifted art to that level of life which is the very life of art, basically needed for its own truth and greatness, and which is the life of symbols. Oriental art is only intent on Things; but, like every genuine art, it loathes realism.

Now there are two specific features which must be pointed out, and which help us to realize why Things and the pure objectivity of Things, not man and human subjectivity, hold sway over Oriental art.

On the one hand, as everywhere where the religious instinct in mankind has not been transfigured by the Gospel, the various religions with which Oriental art is connected are primarily bound to keep and protect the human community through the social, legal, ritual efficacy of the sacred functions. Accordingly, Oriental art is primarily concerned with the universe of objects involved in rite; it turns away from Man to look for the sacred things meant by Things and the sacred faces mirrored in the world—a mythical universe which is extraneous to Man, suprahuman, sometimes ferociously antihuman. How could idolatry not lie in wait for such an art? As long as God has not assumed flesh, and the invisible made itself visible, man is prone to adore, together with the invisible powers, the Signs and the Things through which his art brings them to his eyes; he is all the more prone to do so as his art is more profoundly art, or endowed with a stronger symbolic virtue.

On the other hand art, for Oriental thought, does not stop at the work done. Better to say, a work of art is not simply an object fashioned by the artist and existing on its own. The work is brought to completion, the work *exists,* only when it is seen—as a meeting place where two minds (the artist's and the beholder's) join one another: it veritably exists only as a vehicle of actual ideal communication. As a result, not only is the Oriental artist entirely intent on Things, but on Things such as to be made communicable to the minds of others. And this (together with the related ascendancy of traditional disciplines) is a further obligation for him to depart from himself and make self-forgetfulness his primordial virtue.

6. Such is, it seems to me, the general picture, as concerns the Orient and the poetic approach of Oriental art. But let us examine things at closer range. Asia "is nothing, if not spiritual," Okakura Kakuzo said, and her unity is the unity of a single spirit. Yet there is diversity in this unity. A look at the difference between the major types of Oriental art offered by India and China may help our analysis reach more definite conclusions.

In what way is Indian art entirely intent on Things? I would say that this art is captured by Things; it means a giving up of the soul to the life-giving violence which dwells in Things and ripens into sense-striking luxuriance.

No doubt Indian art, like Indian philosophy, is permeated with spiritual practical purpose. What is done by the artist is less a work of art than an instrument for some invisible result to be produced within the mind. I am thinking not only of those hieratic diagrams which are, so to speak, ecstatic gadgets of yoga; but also of the spiritual expression and smile through which so many images of Buddha aim to induce peace and contemplation in the beholder.

Yet on the one hand everything which is not the Absolute is illusion; and on the other hand this very illusion is a manifestation of the Absolute, not as participated in by a created reality, but as mirrored in a dream;—and the only Self is the Absolute. Let us say, then, that this dream is sacred: just as the pure flower of the lotus resting on the surface of the water, so the mud from which it arises is sacred; everything is sacred. There is no ascetic purification of the senses, but rather self-expansion and self-evolution of a life-power which is indivisibly sensual and spiritual—until final liberation from that very life-power, and from any sensible or intellectual representation.

And there is no ascent to the Absolute through created realities (since there are no created realities). How could the figures of the dream be of use to point to reality, the supreme, the Unique Reality? The wise man looks for pure aloofness, and turns only to his own inner self. There is no spiritualization of visible things (except in certain works of the Greco-Buddhist school). Art has its dwelling place in maya, and in the realm of senses. It depicts a mirage,[4] but it is delivered over to the mirage, and to the unbridled exuberance of sense-captivating forms. And such a process is all the more irresistible as the prime duty of the artist, in the Oriental conception, is to identify himself with that which he has to express. Try as he may to reach beyond Nature, he can only succeed in identifying himself with the very life-force, the ferocious eros which carries the dream of the world along to ceaseless births and renewals and swarming productivity. He is vanquished by Nature, and the implacable fecundity of Becoming.

Thus it is that Indian art, while always looking for the hidden meaning of Things, is captured by Things, as I said a moment ago, and gives itself up to their inner vital violence and outer vital luxuriance. Busy with their *nine flavors*, it offers us a profusion of dancing and moving, happy, poignant, heroic or pathetic, sometimes provocative, sometimes savage forms, of exquisite details, or of majestic stone outgrowths which seem enormous vegetable productions shaped from within by the soul of tropical vines and forests. It bursts forth into a riot of ornaments and embellishings. It makes us wonder whether the conviction of the illusory nature of everything proffered by the senses does not result from, and counterbalance, a most profound sensual vitality.

So richly beautiful an art does not seek after beauty. It always remains a vehicle at the service of some practical effect, either erotic, magic, or religious. Even in its most splendid achievements it remembers the impermanence of the wooden or clay materials it used originally, as well as the impermanence of Nature (a century ago Father Huc still had the opportunity of admiring in Tibet statues carefully carved in butter). This art is not interested in the beauty of the human figure. The human figure, for it, is only a part of cosmic appearances and one of the shadows cast by the dance of Shiva.

7. Chinese art also is entirely intent on Things: but in a way typically different from the Indian way. It is not captured by Things; rather does it capture them, in the light of a sort of animist transnaturalism. This art is a contemplative effort to discover in Things and bring out from Things their own encaged soul and inner principle of dynamic harmony, their "spirit," conceived as a kind of invisible ghost which comes down to them from the spirit of the universe and gives them their typical form of life and movement.

Here we have no dash for the Absolute, the supreme, and unique Self. We have a cosmic faith, a sacred veneration for Tao, the primal source,[5] and for heaven, in which the spirits of all that is visibly shaped pre-exist, and from which they come down into Things to hide in them and shape and move them from within. And Things exist, be it in a fleeting manner—this native, deep-seated Chinese feeling has possibly been invaded, but has never been effaced by Buddhist irrealism; Things are not a dream, they have their own reality. Then Things themselves (since they are real participations in being) can be spiritualized—in other words the spirit they conceal can be discovered and set free by our contemplative grasping. And senses, through which Things are reached, can be purified too. Such a process describes the primary intent of Chinese art. What does the first of the famous six canons of Hsieh Ho prescribe?—To have life-motion manifest the unique spiritual resonance that the artist catches in Things, inspired as he is by his communion with the spirit of the cosmos. The second canon is no less significant. If the brush strokes which render bone structure have primacy among all means of execution, to the point of making painting, so to speak, a branch of calligraphy, it is because the very vigor and alertness of these touches (together with the quality of the ink tones) express the movement of life perceived in things and its structural harmony (and they are, at the same time, a token of the value of the artist's inspiration).

The Chinese contemplative painter becomes one with Things, not to be carried along by their generative torrent, but to seize upon their own inner spirit. He draws them in; he suggests their spiritual meaning, leaving aside the whole glut of sense-satiating, flesh-and-blood forms and colors, luxuriant detail, or ornament; he endeavors to make Things more impressively themselves, on his silk or his paper, than they are in themselves, and to reveal at the same time their affinities with the human soul; he enjoys their inner beauty, and leads the beholder to divine it. Thus it is that he is busy with capturing Things, as I said a moment ago.

A second typical difference from Indian art appears in the major importance given by the Chinese artist to empty spaces, to silent times: because what matters above all is the power of suggestion of the work, and because, in the Taoist view, the nonexistent has as much significance as the existent. This makes Chinese painting particularly akin to music, where rests are as important as sounds—whereas the works of Indian art are filled up, packed with the irresistible off-spring of life and with expressive forms that saturate the eye. There is no more anatomical science or concern in China than in India. But a running Chinese horse is the very spirit of the horse's powerful movement, while Indian horses and elephants, dancers, and dryads are sense-astonishing or en-rapturing spokes of the wheel of Nature. The flowing quality of Chinese art is more of a melody, that of Indian art, of a brimful river.

Finally, as concerns the attitude of art with regard to beauty—a difficult subject, which I now only touch upon —I have already noted that Indian art is not directly con-cerned with beauty. Distinguishing between the conscious purpose of the artist and the vital dynamism of the virtue ot art which is at work in him, one might say, more precisely, that neither Indian *art* (except by stealth) nor the Indian *artist* seeks after beauty, I mean for beauty's sake.

Nor does the Chinese artist—any more than our medieval craftsmen—seek after beauty for beauty's sake; but Chinese art, like our medieval art, seeks indeed after beauty, as its supreme, transcendent end. In other words the search for beauty does not haunt the consciousness of the Chinese or medieval artists, who enjoy the beauty of things but want only to make a "good" work, and to make it a vehicle of spiritual instruction. But the search after beauty for the sake of beauty, or as supreme, transcendent end, is present and paramount in the unconscious, intrinsic dynamism of Chinese art, and of medieval art as well; whereas the dyna-mism of Indian art itself tends, I would say, to a supreme end which is not beauty, but praxis, practical use, especially spiritual experience, either of the devouring impermanence of Becoming, or of the power of divinities. This virtue of art finds beauty by the way, without looking for it. Chinese art, however, despite its interest in portraiture, has not yet perceived the privileged beauty of the human figure. It is less interested in the beauty of the human body than in the beauty of landscapes, birds, and flowers.

Some of the traits I just pointed out make Chinese art, in one sense, nearer than Indian art to our own art. It remains, nevertheless, dominated by the supremacy of Things over the human Self which characterizes Oriental art in general. According to this tendency toward sheer objectivity, the motion-giving and life-giving spirit on which Chinese art is intent in Things was to become a kind of typical formula assigned once and for all to the various categories of things. Even the Chinese passion for codification, canonic rules, and recipes, as well as the Chinese cult for masters in whose footprints disciples must follow, and whom they must piously copy, has made Chinese art liable to the temptation of an academicism which is no less boring than our own: hence those bamboos invariably stern in their never-yielding flex-ibility, those plum trees invariably courageous because they blossom in winter, those orchids invariably pure because they display their beauty in solitude, those chrysanthemums invariably noble because they have the mind of a hermit, those mountains invariably smiling in spring and sleeping in winter, those farmers invariably rustic, those ladies invariably refined, and those generals invariably brave.

8. To what purpose did I submit these observations about Indian and Chinese art? What is the conclusion they lead us to?

The typical difference between Indian art and Chinese art does not proceed from the Things that man contemplates. It proceeds from men who contemplate Things. All the distinc-tive features on which I have laid stress are but an expression of the invisible human fabric, spiritual and carnal, religious, intellectual, or emotional, depending both on nature and history, on conditioning and freedom, which is rooted in the subjectivity of the Indian people and the Chinese people. What makes Oriental art either typically Indian or typically Chinese is the fact that the particular poetic approach em-bodied in Chinese or Indian art—while, in both cases, turning away from the human ego to look only at Things—conveys to the work, in reality, not only an obscure revelation of Things, but also—in an involuntary, reluctant, and masked manner—an obscure revelation of the human Self as well, the collective Indian Self or collective Chinese Self.

Furthermore, let us now take into account the great diversity of schools and styles into which both Indian and Chinese art have divided, in the course of centuries burdened with an extraordinary succession of human events, changes, and experiences. The poetic approach peculiar to each one of these schools conveyed to the works issuing from them, as well as an obscure revelation of Things, an obscure revelation of a particular collective subjectivity.

And lastly let us look at the individual works themselves, at the great works which, traveling through the ages, bring to us the impact of some unforgettable creative intuition. In and through the admirable disinterestedness of the Oriental artist, in and through his pure effort toward Things to be revealed in their pure objectivity, it is also his individual soul, the unique quality of his singular emotion, the secret night of his own singular subjectivity, which are, despite himself, obscurely revealed to us, and which strike us in the dark. The more the personality of the Oriental artist succeeds in forgetting itself and immolating itself in Things, the more, in point of fact, it is present and revives in the work.

Here is, then, the conclusion we may retain (a partial conclusion, since it refers only to the art of the Orient): it is that Oriental art is the opposite of Western individualism and never says "I." It endeavors to hide the human Self and to stare only at Things. It is primarily directed toward communion with and expression of the transnatural, particularly the sacred content which is meant by Nature and by Things. But to the very extent to which it reveals the secret meanings of Things, Oriental art cannot help obscurely revealing also, despite itself, the creative subjectivity of the artist.[6] The more the poetic perception which animates art catches and manifests the inner side of Things, the more it involves at the same time a disclosure and manifestation of the human Self.

The same conclusion holds true for Greek art. I observe, parenthetically, that it is not invalidated by Islamic art, which being forbidden the representation of figures (at least in public edifices), developed along the lines of a purely abstract objectivity. Islamic art is intent on mathematical harmony and rhythmic order, and yet with all its rosettes and arabesques, garlands, palm leaves, and floral tendrils, and its delight in color, it involuntarily betrays the vivid sensuousness, burned by the intellect's refined fire, of the creative subjectivity from which it proceeds.

As regards Hellenic art, we know (this is a commonplace observation, yet true, to be sure, and sufficient for our purpose) what testimony it affords of the "Greek miracle" as an epiphany of human reason. Man and reason stand facing the crushing impetus of cosmic powers and the traps set by the shrewd ruthlessness of the gods: they are set on understanding the mystery of that implacable Nature within which they remain encompassed and of that life to which it would have been better not to be born. Armed with invisible ideas they struggle with Things. Orpheus charms the beasts and is torn by Maenads. Fate and freedom are face to face. Art, then, while being aware of the suprahuman, divine or magic or dionysian power inherent in Things, strives after the intelligibility of Things and intends to bring out their connivance with Reason.

It was when such conflict and tension made the enigmatic and threatening significance of Things still present in the victory of reason that Greek art reached its unique, everlasting splendor. Later on, it luckily preserved in a host of incomparable works its genuine poetic approach, but it was finally to succumb to the lies both of imitation and idealism. In its period of decadence it deteriorated through submission to the separate authority of a thing-in-itself to be copied, and to the search after the canons of ideal beauty of this very thing. It became self-satisfied with those perfectly rationalized but deaf-mute melting shapes, imprisoned in themselves and mirroring nothing, which Praxiteles offers to the admiration of the historians of art.

Contrary to what we have noticed apropos of Chinese art, not only Greek art but the Greek artist himself sought after beauty, and in the most conscious and purposeful manner. This was a great event in the spiritual history of mankind: a liberation of the transcendent value of beauty, which is a participation in divine attributes, and, at the same time, an invaluable step (though naturally pregnant with those "beautiful dangers" that Plato cherished) in the progress of the human spirit in self-awareness. By the same stroke, Greek art perceived the privilege of man in the objective realm of beauty; it realized that the human body is the most beautiful object in nature: a revelation which was too much for it. Greek art bent in adoration before the human figure. Thus it was in the long run doubly vanquished: by nature and by the figure, by aesthetic submission to the external thing-in-itself and by idolatrous worshiping of the human body.

In concluding these brief remarks, we must observe that beneath all essential differences, Greek art and Oriental art have a basic characteristic in common: like the art of the Orient, Greek art is entirely intent on Things; it is against the grain of this fundamental tendency that creative subjectivity is disclosed and manifested in the work, without the artist willing or knowing it. In struggling with Things and Nature, Greek art is always turned toward them. Man, privileged as his figure may be, remains an object in Nature and a thing in the cosmos, subordinate to the perfection and divinity of the universality of Things. A certain individualism starts to assert itself, it is true, but only as to the artist's individual talent or mastery, not as to his individual self-interiority. The Greek artist had less self-forgetfulness, perhaps, than the Chinese, but only in so far as he was concerned with his own excellence in the face of beholders or competitors, rather than with his own inwardness in the face of Things. The inner mystery of personality was not yet revealed to man.

The Advent of the Self

9. It is in a theological form, and at the peak of the most abstract conceptualization, that the notions of person and personality were first explicitly offered to the human mind: namely, in the dogmatic formulas concerned with Christian faith in the divine Trinity—one Nature in three Persons—and in the Incarnation of the Word—a divine Person assuming human nature. At the same time the human mind was confronted with a new idea of man—the Gospels and St. Paul disclosed to it the prevalence of the internal man over the external man, of the inner life of the soul over legal or exterior forms—and it could contemplate in the Son of Man crowned with thorns the abysmal depth of the most living and mysterious Self.

How, then, was art to go its way through the centuries dating from the birth of Christ? To make a long story short, I would say that in the course of its extraordinarily diversified evolution, our Western art passed from a sense of the human Self first grasped as object, and in the sacred exemplar of Christ's divine Self, to a sense of the human Self finally grasped as subject, or in the creative subjectivity of man himself, man the artist or the poet.

Shall I indicate in a most diagrammatic way the main essential phases of this evolution as I see it? In the first phase the mystery of the Person comes into sight as a mere object, in the world of Things but transcending Things. Man emerges above Nature and has vanquished the world. Here we have Byzantine art—so close, in one sense, to Oriental art, though freer from Things—with its glorious and royal, not suffering Christs; and Rome's basilicas, and their grand mosaics, more radiant with spirituality in the barbarous centuries than at the time of Roman classicism; and Ravenna; and further Romanesque art. The immense reality of the human soul is more and more present, but not revealed, even in the manner of an object; it remains veiled behind the intellectual and universal, dogmatic significance of sacred symbols and figures. The divinity of Christ soars over everything.

In the second phase the mystery of the Person still comes into sight as a mere object, in the world of Things though transcending Things. But now—in Gothic architecture's times, and especially after St. Francis of Assisi—this mystery discloses its more human depths. This is the age of Duccio, Giotto, Angelico, of French and Spanish *Pietà*'s, and, in its final ardor, of Grünewald. Art is still dominated by sacred inspiration, and Christ is still at the center. But this time it is Christ in His humanity, in His torment and redeeming Passion—and around Him the Virgin in compassion and all the saints with their individual features and adventures, and mankind with all the characters who play their part in human life, and all nature reconciled with man in the grace of the Gospel. The human soul gleams everywhere through the barred windows of the objective world, the human Self is more and more present on the stage, in the manner of an object which art offers to our sight. Soon it will feel lost in its human loneliness, when the sacral order of old Christendom dissolves and man begins seeking on a hostile earth a place for his newly discovered autonomy. And we shall contemplate the dances of the dead, and the great "existentialist" distress of the later fifteenth century.

10. I would submit that in the third phase the sense of the human Self and of human subjectivity enters a process of internalization, and passes from the *object* depicted to the *mode* with which the artist performs his work. Then occurs the outburst of individualism commonly pointed out apropos of the Renaissance, baroque art, and our classical art. Here we have not only—together with a *prise de conscience* of the intellectual energy or virtue of art—a *prise de conscience* of the working ego, exceedingly stronger than in the Greek artist. This is what happened at first—a sudden beholding of the sublimity of the artist's calling and of the new power and ambition afforded to him by science, by anatomical

knowledge, mathematics, perspective, and the discovery of three-dimensional representation in painting, which intoxicated with glory the great Italians of the second *Rinascimento*. But I think of something much more profound, which was to last and develop in subsequent centuries, namely the fact that the unconscious pressure of the artist's individuality upon the very object he was concerned with in Nature came to exercise and manifest itself freely in his work.

No doubt the old illusion in which Leonardo himself (as a philosopher, I mean, not as an artist) believed when he praised painting as the art of offering the eye perfect simulacra of natural objects remained in the ideological background. But the fact gave it the lie. Painters did not strive for external resemblance. The external form was not to be copied, but to be interpreted—thus Michelangelo's precept, to give moving figures the form of the flame of fire, was long an accepted maxim. Over and above all, natural appearances, though still treasured and lovingly revered, were caught and carried along in the freedom of imagination fecundated by nature. "We painters take the same liberties as poets and madmen take," Veronese said.[7] Speaking of Titian, Tintoretto, Veronese: "They addressed themselves," Allston rightly observed,[8] "not to the senses merely, as some have supposed, but rather through them to that region (if I may so speak) of the imagination which is supposed to be under the exclusive dominion of music, which, by similar excitement they caused to team with visions that 'lap the soul in Elysium.' In other words they leave the subject to be made by the spectator, provided he possesses the imaginative faculty; otherwise they will have little more meaning to him than a calico counterpane."

Nature, then, with her sensible forms, always confronts the artist as a separate thing-in-itself. And the artist, it is true, no longer looks at her to draw from her symbols of supernatural realities, as the Middle Ages did, he no longer believes with Michelangelo that "good painting is nothing but a copy of the perfections of God and a recollection of His painting." (He added, and this is singularly close to modern consciousness: "It is a music and a melody which only intellect can understand, and that with great difficulty." [9] But the artist is now very far also from seeking in Nature, as Greek classicism did, the ideal beauty of a given object grasped by the senses. Nature for him is the inspirer of an imaginary world which he draws from Things with her assistance and collaboration. And the *subject* on which he is intent is a fruit of imagination born of nature and permeated with nature, which he tries to make present to our eyes. Thus on the one hand he remains submitted to the primacy of the object—become, in the sense I just specified, the "subject represented." But on the other hand he definitely imprints on it the mark of his own individuality, of his own style, even if it is true that he aspires to achieving "style" rather than to "having a style." [10] The work bears more openly than ever, it bears of necessity, by virtue of the typical relationship prevalent in those times between the artist and Nature, the imprint of its maker.

An external manifestation of this fact is the multiplicity of contrasting schools and techniques from the early sixteenth century on. Even the individual factor in the mode of performing the work becomes so powerful that the greatest artists cannot actually understand each other's art. Michelangelo was singularly hard on Flemish painting, "which attempts to do so many things that it does none well," and El Greco said that Michelangelo "was a good man but did not know how to paint." When, in the seventeenth and eighteenth centuries, the perfect economy of intelligence and the creative order of a reason admirably sensitive and respectful of intuition gained prevalence, the free assertion of the artist's personality was not effaced, at least in the great achievements of classical art. Such an art has become purely human, it has got loose from sacred inspiration. But not only in Rembrandt, Zurbarán or Georges de Latour, say, in Velásquez' portraits or Vermeer's figures, in Poussin's or

Claude's landscapes or Watteau's tragic games and ballets as well, it remains open, one way or another, to that kind of religious gravity which emanates from any spiritual depth.

Yet we know too well how our classical art was threatened by the perennial enemies of creative reason: naturalism academicism, adoration of the perfection of means. The end came when the sense of the Sign got completely lost in corrupted classicism. But even in the great epoch the dominant concern—regarded as inherent in the very essence of art— with the subject treated and the rational consistency, the objective intelligibility of the spectacle offered to sight, continued to repress or control to a large extent creative subjectivity and obliged poetry to pass through a permanent obstacle, perhaps for a greater blessing in disguise and a more powerful assertion of its native freedom.

It is curious to notice that in the last years of the eighteenth century, Chardin (in words perhaps retouched by Diderot's pen) already gave expression to that awareness of the artist's tragic condition which later the Romantic muse was to make general. Yet he had in view more the ill-effects of academic training than the inner ordeal of creative freedom. "When we are seven or eight years old," he said in his address to the jury of the Salon of 1765, "a pencil is put in our hands. We begin to draw from the cast eyes, mouths, noses, ears, and afterwards feet and hands. . . . After having withered for days and nights before immobile and inanimate nature, we are presented with living nature, and suddenly all the preceding years seem wasted: we were no more at a loss the first time we held a pencil. The eye must be taught to look at nature; and how many have never seen and will never see it! It is the agony of our lives. We have been kept thus far five or six years before the model when we are delivered over to our genius, if we have any. Talent does not declare itself in an instant. It is not at the first attempt that one has the honesty to admit one's inabilities. How many attempts, now happy, now unhappy! Precious years have flown before disgust, lassitude, and boredom overcome the student. . . . What shall he do, what shall he become?

He must throw himself into one of those low conditions whose doors are open to misery, or die of hunger. He chooses the first alternative, with the exception of some few who come here every two years to expose themselves to the beast; the others, unknown and perhaps less unhappy, wear a plastron on their chests in some fencing school, or a musket on their shoulders in some regiment. . . . He who has not felt the difficulties of his art does nothing that counts; he who . . . has felt them too soon does nothing at all. . . ."

11. The fourth phase of the evolution I am analyzing coincides with the latest great epoch of modern painting. It began, in rough outline, after the Romantic preparations, with the second half of the last century, and it seems to be entering a serious crisis in our day. In this phase, the process of internalization through which human consciousness has passed from the concept of the Person to the very experience of subjectivity comes to fulfillment: it reaches the creative act itself. Now subjectivity is revealed, I mean as creative. At the same time and by the same token is also revealed the intuitive, and entirely individualized, way through which subjectivity communes with the world in the creative act. While being set free, the basic need for self-expression quickens and makes specific the new relationship of the artist to Things. The inner meanings of Things are enigmatically grasped through the artist's Self, and both are manifested in the work together. This was the time when poetry became conscious of itself.

We shall have to discuss in other parts of this book the spiritual event which I am pointing out. It is more clearly analyzable in the poet than in the painter, for the painter, whatever happens, remains completely held in the world of the eyes. Let us indicate only a few points. It has become a commonplace to observe that modern painting has freed itself from the dominion of the subject (be it the imaginary spectacle of which I spoke a moment ago) and, by the same token, from the requirements for objective and rational consistency in the externals of the things shown. The object henceforth is uniquely the work. Painting is concerned with painting, and not with measuring itself to anything possessed of a separate value-in-itself.[11]

All that is true, but it is only a half-truth. For what do we see in great modern painters? Men more intent than ever on Nature, though otherwise; men who seeking after themselves are by the same stroke carried along beyond the natural appearances of Things, in desperate search of they don't know what deeper reality that is obscurely meant by Things in a different way for each particular searcher. The conquest, by brush and palette, of this unnamable something is enough of a man to offer up his entire life and energy and to run any risk. It is so because creative subjectivity cannot awaken to itself except in communing with Things. Thus the relationship with Nature has been changed, but has not been abolished. Nature, for the painter, is no longer a separate thing-in-itself, but Nature, in some of her inner aspects, has reached the heart of creative subjectivity, as a germ of that object which is the work to be born. Accordingly, the painter (who henceforth is simply nothing if he lacks poetic vision) sees deeper into Things, though in the dark of Things and of his own Self. He grasps enigmatically an aspect or element of the mystery of the universe of matter, in so far as this aspect or element is meant to fructify into a construction of lines or colors.[12] And because subjectivity has become the very vehicle to penetrate into the objective world, what is thus looked for invisible Things must have the same kind of inner depth and inexhaustible potentialities for revelation as the Self of the painter. As a result, modern painting at its best attains, while remaining strictly painting, to a sort of ontological vastness, and to a superior—though paradoxical for logical reason—degree of intellectuality.

So the sign and token par excellence of the advent of the Self in modern painting is the very fact that, whatever the price paid, modern painting in its heroic period (which is perhaps now behind us) is pledged to reveal in Things not simply, as Chinese painting, a life-giving ghost concealed in them, but a much vaster and more real immanent unknown

—namely some of the infinite inner aspects of visible matter and of the infinite meanings they convey, which are caught in and through the sovereign awakening of creative subjectivity to itself, according to any direction whatever in which an act of spiritual communication with the Things of the world can be brought about, and which can be expressed only by recasting those Things into a new visible fabric.

It is permissible to regard Piero della Francesca and Hieronymus Bosch as forerunners of this full liberation of the poetic sense in painting. The great witness of it remains Cézanne. More, to be sure, than Manet or any other, he has been the liberating figure in contemporary art: precisely because he was so totally, he seemed so obdurately and desperately intent on that bound, buried significance of visible Things, which he felt perpetually escaping him in proportion as he took hold of it. Hence his abiding dissatisfaction with his work, his so typical desire to *refaire Poussin sur nature*— recreate Poussin by painting from nature—his longing for a consubstantial order and harmony emerging from the brute universe of the eye in the act of seeing, and that quality of emotion, echoing both being and man, which the least landscape or still life painted by him awakes in us.[13]

Cézanne imposes his style on Nature all the more forcefully as he was not concerned with inventing a style, but with discovering in Nature, in that world of thick, voluminous matter permeated with light and color that is the very world of the painter, a working secret as singular as his own Self. I am willing to insist that any of Cézanne's paintings is (as André Malraux says of van Gogh's *Chair*) but an ideogram of himself.[14] Yet I should not like to forget—such an omission mars a good part of contemporary artists' most brilliant ideology—that it is also, and indivisibly, an ideogram of some invaluable real aspect, seized only by him, in the mystery of corporeal being, so as to convey to our eye and our heart what no word can express—yet let me try to say, though how inadequately!—the architectural authority with which Things *exist* and, at the same time, the austere serenity with which they confront our dreams.

Thus it is that, by carrying to achievement the progressive advent of the Self in art, the great modern painters brought about a revolution, but did not break their bonds with the great painters of the past. The poetic sense, which they set free—and the joint revelation of Things and creative subjectivity in the work, which they cleared of age-old adventitious burdens—have been at play throughout the perennial effort of art, and have animated in every time everything it has done worth remembering.

12. I do not know what the future of modern painting is, or what the next phase in the evolution of art will be. What interests me is the fact that as a given moment modern painting, in the Occident, has offered the characteristics I just tried to point out. The great protagonists of modern painting, each in his own way, Manet or Whistler, Monet or Bonnard, van Gogh or Henri Rousseau, Seurat, Renoir, Matisse, Braque or Picasso, Rouault or Chagall, give in this connection a similar testimony. For a period of about eighty years, starting in the second half of the nineteenth century, painting attained an extraordinary point of splendor and truthfulness—tearing aside one veil after another in order to become more aware of its own essence, and disclosing with unprecedented freedom its inherent poetic power. In contemplating the canvases of Cézanne or Rouault, van Gogh, Henri Rousseau, Braque, Chagall, or, to cite less resounding names, Odilon Redon, Toulouse-Lautrec, Utrillo, La Fresnaye, Jean Hugo, Marin, or Paul Klee, our feeling that we are in the presence of an exceptionally great epoch comes from the fact that on the one hand never was painting so purely painting, and on the other hand never in painting was such poignant humanity united with such powerful penetration of visible things, through the simultaneous manifestation of the painter's creative Self and of the occult meanings grasped by him in reality.

We are, then, confronted with the second half of the conclusion I should like to make clear: as opposed to Oriental art, Western art has progressively laid stress on the artist's

Self, and, in its last phases, has plunged more and more deeply into the individual, incommunicable universe of creative subjectivity. Disclosure of the Self has entirely superseded in point of importance the portrayal of external beauty. But to the very extent to which art has been really able to reveal and express creative subjectivity, to that extent it also, and by the same token, has been busy revealing and expressing the secret aspects and infinitely varied meanings of Things, whose visibility conceals but can, by virtue of man's spiritual power, reveal the ocean of being. Is it not in the very release of the transapparent reality and objective meanings inherent in Things that we just found the sign par excellence of the liberation of creative subjectivity in modern painting?

The integral conclusion must, therefore, it seems to me, be set forth as follows: On the one hand, as we have seen apropos of Oriental art, when art only intent on Things succeeds in revealing Things and their hidden meanings, it does also reveal obscurely, despite itself, the creative subjectivity of the artist. While endeavoring to catch and manifest what matters most in Things and the secret significance on which they live, the poetic perception which animates art does involve at the same time a disclosure and manifestation, unintentional as it may be, of the human Self. On the other hand, when art primarily intent on the artist's Self succeeds in revealing creative subjectivity, it does also reveal obscurely Things and their hidden aspects and meanings—and with greater power of penetration indeed, I mean into the depths of this Corporeal Being itself and this Nature that our hands touch. While endeavoring to disclose and manifest the artist's Self, the poetic perception which animates art catches and manifests at the same time what matters most in Things, the transapparent reality and secret significance on which they live.

What does this mean? What is the philosophical impact of this factual conclusion? Our descriptive and inductive inquiry suggests that at the root of the creative act there must be a quite particular intellectual process, without parallel in logical reason, through which Things and the Self are grasped together by means of a kind of experience or knowledge which has no conceptual expression and is expressed only in the artist's work. Are we to think—but how can this be possible?—that in such an experience, creative in nature, Things are grasped in the Self and the Self is grasped in Things, and subjectivity becomes a means of catching obscurely the inner side of Things? Are we confronted at this point with that poetic knowledge or poetic intuition which is the very subject-matter we shall try to elucidate in our further discussions?

Let us look at those deer and bison painted on the walls of prehistoric caves, with the admirable and infallible élan of virgin imagination. They are the prime achievements of human art and poetic intuition. By the virtue of Sign, they make present to us an aspect of the animal shape and life, and of the world of hunting. And they make present to us the spirit of those unknown men who drew them, they tell us that their makers were men, they reveal a creative Self endowed with immortal intelligence, pursuing deliberately willed ends, and capable of sensing beauty.

TWO

ART AS A VIRTUE OF THE PRACTICAL INTELLECT

The Practical Intellect

1. Before sewing one must cut. A philosopher who is in search of the nature of things is obliged to begin with sharp distinctions. These distinctions may seem brutal. They simply deal with certain essences taken in themselves: and how could we bring out otherwise the intelligibility of things from the confused flux of existence? To isolate an essence does not imply any disregard for the complexity and continuity of the real. It is indispensable in order to analyze this complexity and continuity in a correct manner—and finally to become aware of their very richness and meaning.

In this chapter I shall limit myself to the consideration of art—art in its most basic and primordial form, or in its fundamental nature, which is, in one sense, contradistinguished to poetry. For it is in the useful arts that we may discover the most obvious and typical characteristics of art in so far as it is art, and its most universal significance as a root activity of the human race. In prehistoric ages, it seems that the search for beauty and adornment was contemporary with the search for contriving tools and weapons, and that the painting and carving activity of the primitive man was not always, nor even from the very beginning, directed toward magical purposes.[1] The fact remains, nevertheless, that the "pleasure of imitation" and the poetic impulse were but one with the effort to satisfy some need of human life—even if it was the need for adornment and ornamentation, in which beauty is, no doubt, instinctively sought for but not for its own sake (the intended aim being to make woman more attractive or man more formidable, or the human dwelling place more stamped with the mark of man and of his vision). With regard to the natural development of its potentialities, art does not begin with freedom and beauty for beauty's sake. It begins with making instruments for human life, canoes, vases, arrows, necklaces, or wall paintings destined to subject, through magical or nonmagical signs, the human environment to the mastery of man. Art must never forget its origins. Man is *homo faber* and *homo poeta* together. But in the historical evolution of mankind the *homo faber* carries on his shoulders the *homo poeta*. Thus I shall point, first of all, to the art of the craftsman; and, secondarily, compare the universe of this art of the craftsman with the universe of the art of those for whom, since the Renaissance and its demi-gods, we reserve the name of artists.

2. Aristotle has shown—this is an example of an acquisition definitively made by philosophy (at least, if philosophers were aware of their own treasures)—that the absolutely first and primordial division to be recognized with respect to the activity of the intellect is the division between the speculative or theoretical intellect and the practical intellect. This does not mean a distinction between two separate powers but a distinction between two basically different ways in which the same power of the soul—the intellect or reason—exercises its activity.

The speculative intellect knows only for the sake of knowledge. It longs to see, and only to see. Truth, or the grasping of that which is, is its only goal, and its only life.

The practical intellect knows for the sake of action. From the very start its object is not Being to be grasped, but human activity to be guided and human tasks to be achieved. It is immersed in creativity. To mold intellectually that which will be brought into being, to judge about ends and means, and to direct or even command our powers of execution—these are its very life.

Such a distinction does not deal with accidental circumstances. It is an essential distinction. For the entire dynamism of the intellect and its typical approach to its object depend on this very object, and they are basically different when the object is merely knowledge and when the object is action.

3. We see this more clearly if we take into account two fundamental points: first, the part played by the *appetite;* and second, the nature of *truth*—either when it comes to the activity of the speculative intellect or when it comes to the activity of the practical intellect. The difference between these two kinds of intellectual activity is so deep that neither the vital relation between the intellect and the appetite nor even what truth consists of are the same in the two cases in question.

In the case of the speculative intellect, the appetite—that is to say, the will, but not in the sense of a mere power of decision, rather in the larger sense of man's energy of desire and love, intent on some existential good—the appetite intervenes only to bring the intellect to the exercise of its own power, say, to embark on and pursue a mathematical problem or an anthropological inquiry. But once the intellect is at work, the appetite has nothing to do with this work, which depends only, as far as normal knowledge through concepts is concerned, on the weapons of reason.

On the other hand, in the case of the practical intellect, the appetite plays an essential part in the very work of knowledge. In one way or another, and to quite various degrees (for practicality admits of a vast scale of varying degrees), reason, then, operates in conjunction with the will. For the intellect taken in itself tends uniquely to grasp Being; and it is only as permeated, in one way or another, by the movement of the appetite toward its own ends that the intellect concerns itself, not with Being to be grasped, but with action to be brought about.

As a result, truth, in speculative knowledge, is the adequation or conformity of the intellect with Being, with what things are. But in practical knowledge how could this be so? In practical or creative knowledge there is no previously existing thing with which the intellect can make itself consonant. The thing does not yet exist, it is to be brought into being. It is not with being, it is with the straight tendential dynamism of the human subject with regard to this thing not yet existing, but to be created, that the intellect must make itself consonant. In other words, truth, in practical knowledge, is the adequation or conformity of the intellect with the straight appetite, with the appetite as straightly tending to the ends with respect to which the thing that man is about to create will exist. This statement, basic in Thomist philosophy, applies to the various fields of practical knowledge in the most diversified ways, and in an analogous, not univocal manner. But it holds true for the whole realm of practical knowledge.

The Virtue of Art

4. Now there is a second essential division to be taken into consideration, this time in practical knowledge itself. The activity of the practical intellect divides into human actions to be done (within the universe of man's destiny) and works to be made (by man, but within the universe of things, outside the universe of man's destiny); in other words, it divides into moral activity and artistic activity.

Morality is concerned with what the Schoolmen called *agibilia,* or what pertains to doing: that is, the very use of human free will, on which depends the fact of a man's being good or bad. Art is concerned with what the Schoolmen called *factibilia,* or what pertains to making: that is, the making of a work, on which depends the fact of this very work's being good or bad.

Thus prudence, the moral virtue par excellence (I mean old *prudentia* in its genuine sense, practical wisdom at the highest degree of practicality, the virtue through which the Bold make an infallible decision, not our bourgeois and timorous prudence)—prudence is the straight intellectual determination of actions to be done. Art, on the contrary, is the straight intellectual determination of works to be made.[2]

Art resides in the soul and is a certain perfection of the soul. It is what Aristotle called an ἕξις, in Latin a *habitus*, an inner quality or stable and deep-rooted disposition that raises the human subject and his natural powers to a higher degree of vital formation and energy—or that makes him possessed of a particular strength of his own: when a *habitus*, a "state of possession"[3] or master quality, an inner demon if you prefer—has developed in us, it becomes our most treasured good, our most unbending strength, because it is an ennoblement in the very kingdom of human nature and human dignity.

Art is a virtue—not a moral virtue (it is contradistinguished to moral virtues). Art is a virtue in the larger and more philosophical sense the ancients gave to this word: a *habitus* or "state of possession," an inner strength developed in man, which perfects him with regard to his ways of acting, and makes him—to the extent to which he uses it—undeviating in a given activity. The virtuous man is not infallible, because often, while acting, he does not use his virtue; but virtue, of itself, is never wrong. The man who possesses the virtue of art is not infallible in his work, because often, while acting, he does not use his virtue. But the virtue of art is, of itself, never wrong.

Art is a virtue of the practical intellect—that particular virtue of the practical intellect which deals with the creation of objects to be made.

We see, then, how essential is the relationship between art and reason. Art is intellectual by essence, as the odor of the rose pertains to the rose, or spark to fire. Art, or the proper virtue of working reason, is—in the realm of making—an intrinsic perfection of the intellect. Not in Phidias and Praxiteles only, but in the village carpenter and blacksmith as well, the Doctors of the Middle Ages acknowledged an intrinsic development of reason, a nobility of the intellect. The virtue of the craftsman was not, in their eyes, strength of muscle or nimbleness of fingers. It was a virtue of the intellect, and endowed the humblest artisan with a certain perfection of the spirit.[4]

5. But, in contradistinction to prudence, which is also a perfection of the practical intellect, art is concerned with the good of the work, not with the good of man. The ancients took pleasure in laying stress on this difference, in their thorough-going comparison of art and prudence. If only he contrives a good piece of woodwork or jewelwork, the fact of a craftsman's being spiteful or debauched is immaterial, just as it is immaterial for a geometer to be a jealous or wicked man, if only his demonstrations provide us with geometrical truth. As Thomas Aquinas put it, art, in this respect, resembles the virtues of the speculative intellect: it causes man to act in a right way, not with regard to the use of man's own free will, and to the rightness of the human will, but with regard to the rightness of a particular operating power. The good that art pursues is not the good of the human will but the good of the very artifact. Thus, art does not require, as a necessary precondition, that the will or the appetite should be undeviating with respect to its own nature and its own—human or moral—ends and dynamism, or in the line of human destiny. Oscar Wilde was but a good Thomist when he wrote: "The fact of a man being a poisoner is nothing against his prose."

Here we are confronted with a problem which is beyond the subject of this book, but about which it is perhaps not irrelevant to say a few words, parenthetically. As I observed at the beginning, the prime obligation of philosophy is to bring out and circumscribe the nature or essence of the given thing, taken in itself, which it considers: for instance the nature or essence of art taken in itself or in its own basic and constitutive requirements. Yet the trouble is that in actual existence we do not deal with essences taken in themselves, but with essences embodied in concrete reality. Art in itself pertains to a sphere separate from, and independent of, the sphere of morality. It breaks into human life and human affairs like a moon prince or a mermaid into a custom office or a congregation; it will always make trouble and arouse suspicion. But art exists in a human being—the artist. As a result, though the fact of a man's being a poisoner is nothing against his prose, the fact of a man's being a drug addict can be, in the long run, something harmful to his prose. Baudelaire himself has warned us against the exclusive passion for art, which progressively destroys the human subject and finally—through an indirect repercussion, owing to material or subjective causality—destroys art itself: for once a man is through, his art is through also.

But things are still more complicated, because of the fact that the artist is aware of this kind of impact of his own moral life on his art, and therefore is tempted, when he totally yields to his cherished demon, to develop, for the sake of his art, a peculiar morality and peculiar moral standards of his own, directed to the good of the work, not of his soul. Then he will endeavor to taste all the fruits and silts of the earth, and will make curiosity or recklessness in any new moral experiment or vampiric singularity his supreme moral virtue, in order to feed his art. And the undertaking will finally prove to be a miscalculation, for in this adventure he will warp in a more subtle manner—and in a manner more closely connected with the sphere of creativity—that general temperament of thought and sensibility, and that general relationship of the sense and the intellect to reality, which are the human ambiance of the activity of art.

Yet he can still remain an artist—even a great artist, however injured in some respects: the fact is that his very being has been offered in self-sacrifice to the all-devouring glory of art;—well, to the glory of this world also, and to our own delights, and to the spiritual welfare of mankind. For St.

Teresa of Avila said that without poetry life would not be tolerable—even for contemplatives. We do not have to judge him. God will work it out with him, somehow or other.

Useful Arts and Fine Arts

6. It is a basic maxim in Aristotelian philosophy that the practical intellect works always, in one way or another, in conjunction with the will, and that, in practical knowledge, truth is the conformity of the intellect with the straight appetite. This statement applies to art and prudence in totally different manners. In the case of prudence, it is in so far as the appetite tends to the ends of human life that it plays an indispensable part in practical knowledge; and truth is conformity with the straight will or appetite in so far as the appetite has been made straight by moral virtues.

But in the case of art, the will plays its part in so far as it tends to the work; and the fact of the will's or appetite's being straight means that it tends to the good of the work as it is to be brought into existence by means of the rules discovered by the intellect; so that the judgment of the artist about each of the movements his fingers have to make is true when it is in conformity with the appetite straightly tending to the production of the work through the appropriate rules born out of the intellect. Thus, in the last analysis, the main part is played by the intellect, and art is much more intellectual than prudence.

Let us think (purposely using an oversimplified imagery) of the first boat invented by men, on a day when neither the word nor the idea of boat yet existed. Nothing was present except a will to satisfy a certain need—the need of crossing a river or an arm of the sea. This need to be satisfied —this was the only rule or ruler for the operation of the inventor's intellect. When, by using certain bits of knowledge previously acquired (men had seen trunks of trees floating on the water), and by putting them together into a newborn idea, the intellect contrived a first appropriate means, its judgment was true because it was in conformity with the first rule.

The first contrived raft was probably something quite defective and clumsy. It had to be improved. Now the intellect had to heed two rules: the first and primary rule (the need, grasped by the intellect, the satisfying of which was wanted by the appetite), a rule in conformity with which the first raft had been contrived; and a second rule, the newborn rule of making which the intellect had just discovered in the very process of creating the first raft. The second raft was thus contrived in conformity with these two rules; and at the same time a third newborn rule of making, dealing with the improvement brought about in the making of this second raft, was discovered—and kept in memory. And so the process continued, both by the intellect heeding previously discovered rules, and discovering newborn rules. We have the same story with the invention and progressive improvement of the airplane, the cyclotron, the calculating machine, etc.

I hope I shall be pardoned the excessive simplicity of the example I have just used. It helps us to bring out some truths which are also quite simple indeed, but basic for our purpose. The first one is that even in the useful arts, the rules are not ready-made recipes, taught by professors in schools and museums, but vital ways of operating discovered by the creative eyes of the intellect in its very labor of invention. Once discovered, they tend, it is true, to become recipes; but then they become obstacles as well as aids to the life of art.[5]

Another basic truth is that whatever the more and more refined and more and more ingenious rules discovered by the craftsman may be, his primary obligation remains to obey the primary rule—the need to be satisfied, toward which, from the very start, his will basically tends.

Finally, to sum up, let us say that in the useful arts, what the will or appetite demands is the satisfying of a particular need; and the straightness of the appetite means that it tends to the satisfying of this particular need by means of the rules discovered by the intellect, the first of which is this very need as grasped by intelligence.

7. Now what about those arts which are designated (I shall say later on why I distrust the expression) as the fine arts? Here I would say that in the fine arts what the will or appetite demands is the release of the pure creativity of the spirit, in its longing for beauty—for that enigmatic beauty whose love affairs and quarrels with poetry will occupy us in a further chapter.

And the straightness of the appetite means that it tends to this aim as to be achieved by means of the rules discovered by the intellect, the first of which is the creative intuition from which the whole work originates. Creativity, or the power of engendering, does not belong only to material organisms, it is a mark and privilege of life in spiritual things also. "To be fertile, so as to manifest that which one possesses within oneself," John of St. Thomas wrote, "is a great perfection, and it essentially belongs to the intellectual nature." [6] The intellect in us strives to engender. It is anxious to produce, not only the inner word, the concept, which remains inside us, but a work at once material and spiritual, like ourselves, and into which something of our soul overflows. Through a natural super-abundance the intellect tends to express and utter *outward,* it tends to sing, to manifest itself in a work. This natural desire, because it goes beyond the boundaries of the intellect, can be implemented only through the movement of the will and the appetitive powers, which make the intellect go out of itself—in accordance with its own natural aspiration—and which determine thereby the operative practicality of intelligence, in its most primordial and general impulse.

This creativity of the spirit is the first ontological root of the artistic activity. And in fine arts it is pure, cleared of all adventitious elements. And the pure creativity of spiritual intelligence tends to achieve something in which spiritual intelligence finds its own delight, that is, to produce an object in beauty. Left to the freedom of its spiritual nature, the intellect strives to engender in beauty.[7]

Such is, in its longing for beauty, that pure creativity of the spirit, to the release of which the appetite basically tends, together with the intellect, in the vital dynamism of fine arts.

Here we do not have a demand for the satisfying of a particular need in human life. We are beyond the realm of the useful. The need is not extraneous to the intellect, it is one with the intellect. We have a demand for the participation, through the object created, in something which is itself spiritual in nature. For beauty, which is of no use, is radiant with intelligence and is as transcendental and infinite as the universe of the intellect. Thus the very end—transcendent end —intended pertains to the realm of the intellect, of its exultation and joy, not to the world of utility, and the intellectuality of art is in the fine arts (though more bound there with the sensitive and emotional powers) at a much higher degree than in the arts of the craftsman. The need of the intellect to manifest externally what is grasped within itself, in creative intuition, and to manifest it in beauty, is simply the essential thing in the fine arts.

From this point of view we may perceive how short of the mark inevitably fall all the explanations and theories of art offered by psychological or sociological, materialist, empiricist, logical-empiricist, or pragmatist positivism, or by those who, as Allen Tate[8] puts it, explain to us "how the *stimuli* of poems elicit *responses* in such a way as to *organize our impulses* toward action," and who tell us that "poetry is a kind of applied psychology," or else (this is logical positivism) that it is "only *amiable insanity*," because "it 'designates' but it does not denote anything *real*."

8. Let us come now to that with which the creative judgment, if it is true, comes into accordance, namely the rules— or the straight appetite tending toward beauty to be participated in by a work produced according to the appropriate rules.

This very notion of rule, in the fine arts, is transfigured, through the impact of beauty on the activity of art.

First, the rules, in fine arts, are subjected to a law of perpetual renewal infinitely more exacting than in useful arts.

They must be perpetually newborn rules, not only with respect to a given object—boat, vase, or calculating machine—to be improved, but with respect to beauty to be participated in; and beauty is infinite. Outside any particular style or lineage of masterworks, there is always an infinity of other ways to achieve participation in beauty. No form of art, however perfect, can encompass beauty within its limits. The artist is faced with an immense and desert sea,

> . . . *sans mâts, sans mâts, ni fertiles îlots,*

and the mirror he holds up to it is no bigger than his own heart. He is bound to go hunting a new analogate, a new typically different participation in beauty; and this new participation in beauty will involve and require new ways of making—either a new adaptation of the fundamental and perennial rules, or the use of rules not hitherto employed, which are simply new, and which at first disconcert people. It seems relevant, moreover, to lay stress at this point on the spiritual universality of what I just called the fundamental and perennial rules of art—or, better, the eternal laws of art. These eternal laws of art are not to be found at the level of the particular rules of making, say, the famous Golden Number. They exist only at the supremely universal level of philosophy, and of that wisdom (more lived than conceptualized) which is concealed in the roots of the virtue of art. They are in the artist the spiritual, and general, foundations of his intellectual virtue, prior to any particular, technical manifestation of this virtue. And it is through an infinite diversity in application that they are exemplified by the great works of any epoch and any style.

In the second place, the work to be made, in the case of the fine arts, is an end in itself, and an end totally singular, absolutely unique. Then, every time and for every single work, there is for the artist a new and unique way to strive after the end, and to impose on matter the form of the mind. As a result, the rules of making—which, as concerns art in general, are fixed and determined, as opposed to the rules used by prudence—come in the fine arts to share in the infinite suppleness and adaptability of the rules used by prudence, because they deal every time with the utter singularity of a new case, which is, in actual fact, unprecedented. It is, then, with prudential rules not fixed beforehand but determined according to the contingency of singular cases, it is with the virtues proper to prudence—perspicacity, circumspection, precaution, industry, boldness, shrewdness, and guile—that the craftsmanship of the artist succeeds in engendering in beauty.

In the third place, and also because the work to be made is an end in itself and a certain singular and original, totally unique participation in beauty, reason alone is not enough for the artist to form and conceive this work within himself in an infallible creative judgment. For, as Aristotle put it, "as everyone is, so does the end appear to him." Everyone judges of his own ends, when they engage his own self, in accordance with what he himself actually is. And since the final transcendent end is beauty—not a particular need to be satisfied, but beauty to be seduced—such a spiritual and transcendental, self-sufficient, absolute, all-exacting end demands that the very self and subjectivity of the artist should be committed to it. As a result, in order for the artist to form and conceive his work within himself in an infallible creative judgment, it is necessary that his subjective dynamism, his will and appetite straightly tend to beauty. At this point the statement that the truth of the practical intellect consists in conformity with the straight appetite takes on a new meaning. And we see that the fine arts, though they are more fully intellectual than the useful arts, imply, however, a much greater and more essential part played by the appetite, and require that the love for beauty should make the intellect co-natured with beauty. Because, in the last analysis, in art as in contemplation, intellectuality at its peak goes beyond concepts and discursive reason, and is achieved through a congeniality or connaturality with the object, which love alone can bring about. To produce in beauty the artist must be in love with beauty. Such undeviating love is a supra-artistic rule—a precondition, not sufficient as to the ways of making, yet necessary as to the vital animation of art—which is presupposed by all the rules of art.

9. The most significant point remains to be made. In speaking of the useful arts, we have observed that however important and necessary the secondary, more and more refined rules discovered by the craftsman may be, his primary obligation is to the primary rule, which is, in his case, the satisfying of a certain need, toward which, from the very start, his will basically tends. A splendid house with no doorway is not a good piece of architecture.

Now what is this primary rule in the case of the fine arts? I have said that in this case the appetite, together with the intellect, basically tends to the release of the pure creativity of the spirit, in its longing for beauty. Consequently, the primary rule is the vital actuation or determination through which this free creativity of the spirit expresses itself first and foremost—and to which, therefore, the mind and the hand of the artist must first of all be loyal.

Thus for the apprentice as a painter or as a composer the primary rule is to follow purely the pleasure of his eyes or ears in the colors or sounds he will be responsible for; to respect this pleasure, and pay total attention to it; at every instant to produce nothing but what the senses are fully pleased with. For the creativity of the spirit, in its longing for beauty, passes through the senses, and is first vigilant in them, in a fragile way. Moreover, as soon as a tyro begins to discover, or to be taught, a particular rule of making, he happens more often than not to lose these fragile, inchoate awakenings of art, because he lacks the inner strength to master the particular rule in question, which then becomes a recipe and mars, along with his fidelity to his pleasure, the primary rule of art.

But with all that the threshold of art has not yet been crossed. It is crossed when the making of a work passes under the regime, no longer of the pleasure of intelligence-permeated senses, but of the creative intuition, which is born in the deepest depths of the Intellect. For the really genuine vital actuation through which the free creativity of the spirit expresses itself first and foremost is this creative or poetic intuition, to which the entire work to be engendered in beauty, in its perfect singularity as a kind of unique cosmos, is appendent. I shall have to discuss creative intuition in a subsequent chapter; I am only mentioning it now.

What I should like to stress is the fact that in creative intuition we have the primary rule to which, in the case of the fine arts, the whole fidelity, obedience, and heedfulness of the artist must be committed. I also should like to stress the fact that between this primary, primordial, primitive rule and all the other rules of making, however indispensable they may be, there exists an essential difference, so to speak infinite, as between heaven and earth. All other rules are of the earth, they deal with particular ways of operation in the making of the work. But this primary rule is a heavenly rule, because it deals with the very conception, in the bosom of the spirit, of the work to be engendered in beauty. If creative intuition is lacking, a work can be perfectly made, and it is nothing; the artist has nothing to say. If creative intuition is present, and passes, to some extent, into the work, the work exists and speaks to us, even if it is imperfectly made and proceeds from a man

c'ha l'habito de l'arte e man che trema,

—who has the habit of art and a hand which shakes.

At the summit of artistic activity, and for the one who has long traveled along the road of the rules, finally there is no longer any road. For the sons of God are under no law. Just as finally the unique law of the perfect soul, according to the saying of St. Augustine (not literally of him, but it does not matter), is *"ama et fac quod vis"*—love and do what you want—so the unique rule of the perfect artist is finally: "Cling to your creative intuition, and do what you want." "This kind of excellence . . . we recognize in a person in whom we are aware of a rare presence, a pure creative force, or an untrammeled spirit." [9]

Transcendence of the Fine Arts

10. The division between the useful arts and the fine arts must not be understood in too absolute a manner.[10] In the humblest work of the craftsman, if art is there, there is a concern for beauty, through a kind of indirect repercussion that the requirements of the creativity of the spirit exercise upon the production of an object to serve human needs. Furthermore, especially in works produced by our industrial age, in the various kinds of machines, or machinelike objects, contrived by the art of engineering or by our modern engineering-minded arts, the mere search for the pure technical exigencies of the utility, the solidity, and the good functioning of the thing made, without any search for beauty, naturally results in a beauty of its own. Our modern steamships, constructed only with a view to speed and utility, do not need the ornamentation of ancient galleys to provide a joy of the eyes and the mind by their perfect shape. I do not think that Brooklyn Bridge was built with any intention of beauty; and it was able to stir the deepest emotions of Hart Crane, and is bound forever to his lines. The chaos of bridges and skyways, desolated chimneys, gloomy factories, queer industrial masts and spars, infernal and stinking machinery which surrounds New York is one of the most moving—and beautiful—spectacles in the world.

All that is true. But for all that I consider the theories of Le Corbusier to be faulty dogmatism, and any system of aesthetics which gets clear of beauty for the sake of mechanical adjustment to be puritanism of forms and spurious austerity. For the kind of beauty I just described exists indeed: but as an accidental occurrence, a quite peculiar case in the whole universe of art, and I even wonder whether the delight we find in it does not flatter, perhaps, some perverse instinct of our too civilized eyes. In actual fact, nature does not follow the teachings of Le Corbusier. Flowers, insects, and birds are not constructed with a view to the mere necessities of living; they display an amazing extravagance of ornament and luxury. And the beauty of the baroque also exists. And finally the same concern for beauty which was present in the craftsman, the same repercussion of the requirements of the creativity of the spirit, surreptitiously creeps into the very construction of machines and the very art of engineering. The beauty of the lines of an automobile is not indifferent to the engineers who draw its blueprint. And I doubt whether the engineers who built the George Washington Bridge or the Delaware Memorial Bridge were mere puritans of utility.

As to the great artists who take pleasure in describing themselves as mere engineers in the manufacturing of an artifact of words or sounds, as Paul Valéry did, and as Stravinsky does, I think that they purposely do not tell the truth, at least completely. In reality the spiritual content of a creative intuition, with the poetic or melodic sense it conveys, animates their artifact, despite their grudge against inspiration. And they are well aware of the vital value of this God-given element. But because it is scanty in them, or arises only from some secret stir in the working reason of a touchy Muse, they make good this very aridity, and manage to sidetrack us, by magnifying it, so as to glory in what they falsely describe as a total lack—lack of a quality that Plato has supposedly invented, and which is nothing, they say, for real art. For all that, Stravinsky is not a narcissist but a genuine creator, "a ferocious intellect which has fallen in love with the song of the daughters of man." 11

11. Now the essential thing I should like to point out in our present comparison between useful arts and fine arts is contained in this twofold assertion: First, the fine arts, because of their immediate relation to beauty and to the pure creativity of the spirit, are free—with the very freedom of the spirit. They belong, therefore, in actual fact, to the world of liberal arts: a truth which the ancients did not recognize with respect to most of the fine arts, because any manual labor bore in their eyes the stamp of the servile condition. And this spiritual freedom of the fine arts causes them to dwell in a place which admits of no common, univocal meas-

ure with the useful arts. Everything said about art in general is to be transfigured when applied to them. They are virtues of the practical intellect; but, as we shall see in our further chapters, the intellect or reason which plays the principal and royal part in them is not conceptual, discursive, logical reason, nor even working reason. It is intuitive reason, in the obscure and high regions which are near the center of the soul, and in which the intellect exercises its activity at the single root of the soul's powers and conjointly with them. Thus it is that the fine arts are transcendent with regard to the useful arts.

Yet—this is my second point—the fine arts, from the very fact that they belong in the generic nature of art, participate in the law of the useful arts. Thus the conceptual, discursive, logical reason, or better (since we are in the practical order), the working reason, plays an essential and necessary— though secondary—part in the fine arts. This part, which relates to the particular ways of the making of an object, and of the realization of a creative intuition in matter, is an instrumental part: not only secondary, but merely instrumental. As soon as it gets the upper hand, the work is but a corpse of a work of art—a product of academicism. But when the resourcefulness of discursive reason, and the rules involved—which I called a moment ago the secondary rules—are used as instruments of a master *habitus,* and as the fingers, so to speak, of creative intuition, they compose the indispensable arsenal of prudence, shrewdness, and cleverness of the life of art. Degas pointed at all that when he said: "A painting is a thing which requires as much cunning, rascality, and viciousness as the perpetration of a crime." [12] To make fun of the rules, in proclaiming the liberty of art, is just an excuse provided by foolishness to mediocrity. "It is clear," Baudelaire wrote, "that systems of rhetoric and prosodies are not forms of tyranny arbitrarily devised, but a collection of rules required by the very organization of the spiritual being: never have prosodies and systems of rhetoric prevented originality from manifesting itself distinctly. The opposite would be far more true, that

they have been a help to the blossoming forth of originality." [13] And Coleridge's sentence is still more to the point:
"As it must not, so genius cannot, be lawless; for it is even
this that constitutes it genius—the power of acting creatively
under laws of its own origination." [14]

12. Two final remarks must be made. I have tried to
bring out, and to lay stress upon, the pure essentials of art in
its very nature, as operative virtue of the practical intellect.
But obviously no virtue of the intellect can live in isolation.
Since art is a virtue of the intellect, it demands to communicate with the entire universe of the intellect. Hence it is
that the normal climate of art is intelligence and knowledge:
its normal soil, the civilized heritage of a consistent and integrated system of beliefs and values; its normal horizon, the
infinity of human experience enlightened by the passionate
insights of anguish or the intellectual virtues of a contemplative mind. The worshiping of ignorance and rudeness is for
an artist but a sign of inner weakness. Yet, the fact remains
that all the treasures of the earth are profitable to art only if
it is strong enough to master them and make them a *means*
for its own operation, an aliment for its own spark. And not
all poets have the strength of a Dante.

On the other hand, the intellect is reflective by nature; so,
no virtue of the intellect, even practical virtues, can genuinely develop in its own particular sphere without a more or
less simultaneous development of reflectivity. Now what is
the name of reflective intelligence in the domain of art? Its
name is critical reason. Baudelaire wrote in this connection:
"It would be quite a new departure in the history of the arts
for a critic" (Baudelaire meant a critic who is born with
only the gifts of a critic—which is, in my opinion, a nonsen-
sical assumption) "to turn poet, a reversal of all psychological laws, a monstrosity; on the contrary, every great poet
becomes naturally, inevitably, a critic. I am sorry for poets
who are guided by instinct alone; I consider them incom-
plete. In the spiritual life of great poets a crisis infallibly
arises, in which they want to reason out their art, to discover

the obscure laws by virtue of which they have produced, and to derive from such a scrutiny a set of precepts whose divine aim is infallibility in poetic production. It would be a prodigy for a critic to turn poet and it is impossible for a poet not to contain a critic within himself." [15] These views are, I think, simply true as regards the poet. As regards the critic, they must be qualified, as we shall have an opportunity to see in a further chapter.

To conclude, let us observe that if it is true that art is a creative virtue of the intellect, which tends to engender in beauty, and that it catches hold, in the created world, of the secret workings of nature in order to produce its own work —a new creature—the consequence is that art continues in its own way the labor of divine creation. It is therefore true to say with Dante that our human art is, as it were, the grandchild of God—

Si che vostr' arte a Dio quasi è nipote.

THREE

THE PRECONSCIOUS LIFE
OF THE INTELLECT

Art Bitten by Poetry Longs to Be Freed from Reason

1. I have insisted, in the preceding chapter, that art is rooted in the intellect. Art is a virtue of the practical intellect; art is, and especially the fine arts are, to a considerable degree more intellectual than prudence: art is the very virtue of working reason. Now we are faced with a paradox, a fact which seems diametrically opposed to this contention: namely, the fact that modern art—I mean in its finest achievements, as well as in its deepest trends—modern art longs to be freed from reason (logical reason).

It is, of course, easy, too easy, to relate this fact to a much more general phenomenon, conspicuous enough indeed: what the French philosopher Blanc-de-Saint-Bonnet called the progressive weakening of reason in modern times. Then one would say, with some people inspired by a bitter zeal, that modern art suffers from the same general weakening of reason, or (and this would be perhaps a little more relevant) that modern art, being surrounded on all sides, and threatened, by modern reason—a so-called reason as afraid of looking at things as it is busy digging in all the detail around them, and as fond of illusory explanations as it is insistent in its claim to recognize only statements of fact, the reason of those who believe that poetry is a substitute for science intended for feeble-minded persons—modern art has endeavored to defend itself by seeking refuge in irrationalism.

Yet such an explanation would fall short of the mark and remain extraneous to the issue. For the yearning for liberation from reason of which we are speaking is in reality a phenomenon very much deeper and more significant. It has to do with a typical aspiration of art in its own line and inner life, in so far as it has become conscious of itself during the last century to an unprecedented degree, and has found, at the center of this self-awareness, poetry, naked and wild poetry. Modern art has been bitten by poetry. And that is the very cause of its estrangement from reason. I am not trying to discuss now what poetry is. I am only concerned with the effects that poetry produces.

Shall I try to describe, in a brief and, to be sure, oversimplified manner, the process, normal in itself and extraordinarily illuminating for the philosophy of art, which the evolution of modern art has enabled us to contemplate? I would say that all is appendent to the fact of art's becoming more and more fully aware—of its *freedom* with respect to everything which is not its own essential law—of the necessity which binds it to *master* everything which is not its own creative and engendering virtue—and of the kind of *loyalty to truth* which is required from the artist, and which is loyalty to his own singular vision. The formulas I just used have been the occasion for a swarm of inept claims and sickening commonplaces. They remain true in themselves.

I would also say that the process in question is essentially a process of liberation or enfranchisement, but liberation or enfranchisement of that intrinsic impulse, one with the nature of art, which requires it to *transform* the things it uses. For just as the art of the craftsman, while watching the natural properties of the materials it uses, deprives these materials of their natural form (I mean the form which wood is possessed of in trees, or metals in the mines of the earth) in order to bring them into a form born out of his mind, so the art of the painter or the poet, while watching the natural appearances of the realities of the world, deprives these realities of their own natural form and beauty, and the instruments of the mind of the age-old patterns of operation established by the common use of men, in order to produce a work invested with a new form and beauty born out of the artist's soul. Liberation and transformation, therefore, keep pace with one another.

Now it seems to me that three principal steps might be discerned in the evolution of modern art, especially modern painting and poetry.

First, it endeavors to free itself from nature and the forms of nature. It transforms nature, not only by carrying to extremes the law of deformation of natural appearances which painting has always brought into play, but also by causing another universe of forms and relations between forms—disclosing a deeper reality, more akin to our dreams, angers, anguish, or melancholy—to arise from nature in art's own fabric of colors or of words. And in great artists this in no way implies any contempt for or divorce from nature. They rather steal from nature its own secrets of poetry.[1]

The second step is liberation from and transformation of language, I mean rational language. Rational language is not cut out to express the singular, it is burdened with social and utilitarian connotations, ready-made associations, and worn-out meanings, it is invaded by the inevitable insipidity which results from habit. So it does not only interfere with poetry, it perpetually sidetracks it and makes poetry say something other than what poetry wants to say. The same observation can be made with regard to that intelligible discursus—organizing together, according to the accustomed patterns of the pleasure of the eyes or the ears, the movements of the design or the sounds of the melody—which is the rational language of painting and music. Why should we be surprised by the fact that modern artists struggle to free themselves from rational language and its logical laws? Never did they pay more attention to words, never did they attach greater importance to words: but in order to transfigure them, and to get clear of the language of discursive reason. Joyce creates with all the words of the earth a new language conveying an intelligible sense, but intelligible to himself alone. As a rule the other searchers conceal the logical or intelligible sense in a language made up of images, to the evocation of which the words are dedicated. The Impressionists and Neoimpressionists on the one hand, Cézanne, Gauguin, van Gogh on the other, are also more concerned than ever with the elements of the painter's language, its "words"—but in order to discover a new pictorial language liberated from that intelligible external consistency, that immediate rational legibility of visible aspects which was still present even in the drawings of a William Blake. Be it a poem or a painting, the work speaks: it speaks no longer in terms of logical reason.

Thus art enters the regions of obscurity. *"Je suis obscur comme le sentiment,"* I am obscure as feeling is, Pierre Reverdy said. This darkness grows deeper when we arrive at the third step in the process. Then art endeavors to get free from the intelligible or logical sense itself. Think of certain poems of René Char or Henri Michaux, Hart Crane or Dylan Thomas, or of certain cubist canvases. The work, more eager than ever to communicate an invaluable content, speaks no longer, as it were, seems mute. It strikes us at the heart through forbidden ways. Is it true that the logical sense has disappeared? No, that's impossible. But the logical sense has been digested, so to speak, by the poetic sense, it has been broken up, dislocated, to subsist only as a kind of variegated matter of the poetic sense. The poetic sense alone gleams in the dark. This poetic sense, which is but one with poetry itself, is the inner, ontologic entelechy of the poem, and gives it its very being and substantial significance. "It is in no way identical with the intelligible sense, as the soul of a man is in no way identical with his speech; and it is inseparable from the formal structure of the poetic work: whether the work is clear or obscure, the poetic sense is there, whatever becomes of the intelligible sense. The poetic sense is substantially bound to the form, immanent in the organism of words, immanent in the poetic structure as a whole." [2] In modern art it demands to be definitively freed, at any cost.

The process I just described is a process of liberation from conceptual, logical, discursive reason. Though it may entail accidentally a general disregard for the intellect, and a suicidal attitude of contempt for reason, it is by no reason, in its essence, a process of liberation from reason itself, if it is true that reason possesses a life both deeper and less conscious than its articulate logical life. For reason indeed does not only articulate, connect, and infer, it also *sees;* and reason's intuitive grasping, *intuitus rationis,* is the primary act and function of that one and single power which is called intellect or reason. In other words, there is not only logical reason, but also, and prior to it, intuitive reason.

> . . . *whence the soul*
> *Reason receives, and reason is her being,*
> *Discursive or intuitive.*[3]

Coleridge invoked the authority of Milton to confirm his own views on reason's intuitivity. He might also have invoked the authority of Aristotle. Already in the domain of speculative knowledge, science, and philosophy, intuitive reason is fundamentally at work: any demonstration finally resolves into first principles which are not demonstrated, but seen; and any discovery which really reveals a new aspect of being is born in a flash of intuitivity before being discursively tested and justified. But when it comes to poetry, the part of intuitive reason becomes absolutely predominant. Then, as our further analyses will show, we are confronted with an intuition of emotive origin, and we enter the nocturnal empire of a primeval activity of the intellect which, far beyond concepts and logic, exercises itself in vital connection with imagination and emotion. We have quit logical reason, and even conceptual reason, yet we have to do more than ever with intuitive reason—functioning in a nonrational way.

In all that I have just said, moreover, about the yearning for liberation from logical reason, I have tried, quite inadequately, I fear, somehow to disengage the pure meaning of the task progressively accomplished in the laboratories of modern poetry. It is an ideal line that I have tried to follow. In actual fact, the greatest among modern artists, though deeply involved in the general movement, never made for the extremes. They freed themselves from logical reason in the sense that they transformed the use of logical reason, not in the sense that they abolished it.

2. A process like the one we are discussing is of course full of serious dangers. The undertaking was heroical, it was paid for at the price of many casualties. The process took place, moreover, in a variety of ways, quite different in quality, in which genuine and spurious trends were in mutual contact, and sometimes intermingled. Now, to pursue our analysis, I should like to distinguish between three main lines of orientation, which, it seems to me, have passed, like arrows, through the whole process in question.

There has been a direction—the right one—which pointed straight to poetry itself. In the process of transforming nature, language, and the logical or intelligible sense, everything was directed, as to the final end, to the poetic sense itself: in other words, to the pure, free, and immediate passage, into the work, of the creative intuition born in the depths of the soul. Let us think, for instance of the artistic lineage composed of such men as Rouault and Chagall,[4] Satie or Debussy, Hopkins, Apollinaire, Hart Crane, Reverdy, T. S. Eliot, St.-John Perse (I name only the most significant), not to speak of the great originator, Baudelaire.

Another direction has pointed, I would say, to the pure creativity of art. The emphasis had shifted to something which was not the absolutely central element, yet was still essential. The creative power of the human spirit craved after pure creation—jealous, as it were, of God, Who was tactless enough to create before us. Poetry, and great poetry, was attained and seized upon but, so to speak, in addition, in a supererogatory manner. Let us think of Picasso. That's why he pushed forward along so many different ways of approach. Yet pure creation is not possible to man. Some inner content, received from elsewhere, is necessarily present. Picasso now gives expression to a bitter and desperate detestation of the world of today (after all, his distorted human faces are perhaps our true likeness, when we are seen by the angels). And contemporary abstract painting falls short of releasing a world of pure self-sufficient forms; it cannot help conveying symbolic meanings, only in a barer—and poorer—manner.

And there has been still another direction—an aberrant one, this time—which means in reality, despite all high ambitions, a diligent effort toward self-deception. For, here, the direction has been reversed; the supreme goal is neither the deliverance of the poetic sense nor even pure creation, but man's self-research through poetry. Narcissism was the beginning—entailing a search either for the subjective enjoyment of the poetic state itself (let us think of Rimbaud—a certain aspect of Rimbaud) or (let us think of Gide) for the bursting forth of a free or gratuitous act with no countenance, and of a power of choosing without making a choice, or (let us think of Mallarmé) for the elaboration of a pure and perfect artifact mirroring only the void, and exercising through the words a power of magic to transmute reality, at least as it exists in the souls of men. Then, narcissism gave place to a kind of Prometheism. Finally we had Surrealism, in which the meaning and direction of the impulse in question were revealed in full. With Surrealism the entire dynamism of deviated poetry tends, in the last analysis, to the liberation of the omnipotence of man or the conquest of infinity by man through the powers of unreason.

3. I think that particular attention should be paid to Surrealism, by reason of its exceptional significance for all the problems we are dealing with. I am interested in the Surrealists because there are real poets among them, and because I remember how they were able to awaken to poetry and to threaten with destruction some young people, now dead, who were among the most purely gifted and the most imperiled

in a period still capable of what Rimbaud called the *combat d'esprit.* First of all I have a respect, not for Surrealist bombast and sophistry, but for Surrealism as a spiritual phenomenon—of considerable intensity, in which we see high qualities of the spirit fall from above, and poetry fated to doom cast its last secret flame at the boundaries of death.

I do not intend to embark on a full discussion of this phenomenon. It is enough for my purpose to observe that with Surrealism we have no longer simply a process of liberation from conceptual, logical, discursive reason. We have a process of liberation from reason, absolutely speaking; a deliberate and systematic craving to deny the supreme autonomy of a power which is spiritual in nature, to reject everywhere and in every respect both the control of conscious reason and, even in its preconscious life, the superior intuitivity of the intellect, and to let loose the infinite powers of the irrational in man—with a view to setting free the *Übermensch* in man. This rejection of reason, this total breaking with reason, not only in its conceptual and discursive life but absolutely, marks the essential limit which separates Surrealism from all the other currents I previously mentioned.

André Breton's texts are quite significant in this regard. In the definition of Surrealism offered by him, the "absence of any control exercised by reason" is central, as well as the "pure psychic automatism"—which means a total release, entirely screened from any guiding activity of intelligence, of the wild powers of the unconscious and of an imagination *separated* from the intellect. "Automatic writing," therefore, becomes the ideal "limit toward which Surrealist poetry must tend."

Here we are faced with a basic illusion. For automatism "unbinds that which had been brought to the unity of life by concentration," and by that brooding repose of the soul which we call in French *recueillement.*[5] Automatism does not produce freedom, but only dispersion. Separated from intellectual light, the automatic life of the unconscious is fundamentally unable to reveal anything really *new*. To the extent to which there is genuine poetry in Surrealist poets,

they fall short of their own dogma, and obey despite themselves the secret music of intelligence.

Yet Surrealism in reality tends to aims which are quite
other than poetry. As Breton put it, it leaves aside "any aesthetic" as well as any "moral concern." The aim is to express
"the real functioning of thought." This, at first glance, seems
to be a sort of scientific aim, psychological in nature. In reality, such a formula is rather an esoteric one, and conveys
infinitely larger ambitions; it points to a kind of prophetic
revelation of the magic powers involved in human "thought"
as bound to the cosmic whole. Yet, in any case, whether we
have to do with experimental science or with gnosis, the aim
is beyond the province of poetry. Or else, if they say that poetry has no province of its own, and is as universal as
"thought," then poetry dissipates in the whole, and loses its
identity.

As a matter of fact, poetry has become for Surrealists a
mere instrument of prospecting, it has been made subservient
to all spiritual ambitions of man, it has been required to
provide man with deceptive and flashy substitutes for science,
metaphysics, mysticism, sanctity. All that poetry is permitted
to be is a hungry void, an altogether empty poetic perceptiveness, which satisfies itself *outside,* with the pseudo miracles
offered by chance or sorcery. We might expect as much: because poetry, in reality, is an end in itself, and an absolute.[6]
And for Surrealism there is and there must be no end in itself, and no absolute, except man himself in his possibilities
of development.

*Mania from Below and Mania from Above. The Pla-
tonic Muse*

4. The Surrealists have had no composers. They have had
painters, and good painters. Some particularly interesting observations may be made about these Surrealist painters. (I
mean orthodox Surrealist painters clinging to Breton's group
and ideology;[7] Miró, for instance, whose forms moving free
have such freshness, is not a Surrealist, any more than Cal-

der. Gargallo, who disclosed through the suggestions of the void a new poetry of sculpture, owed nothing to Surrealism.)

First, the Surrealist painters have restored in full the most baneful and antipoetic tenet of academicism, against which every genuine art, and modern art for its part, have waged war, namely the primacy of the *subject* represented. Now of course it was not a question of the beauty of this subject, but of its mysterious horror. The great trick was to represent things devised both to captivate the eyes and to wound and shatter at the same time the heart of the spectator, to disorganize him and destroy something in him, to catch him in a trap, by means of a certain monstrous contrivance suddenly revealed in the spectacle. Such a procedure, in which all the mystery, instead of deriving from the creative process itself, is demanded of the pictured subject, is the exact opposite of the nature-transforming expression of a creative vision. And in this return to the primacy of the subject represented, we have but a token of that displacement of poetry, transferred to the outside world, of which I spoke a moment ago.

After that, we must observe that the Surrealist painters made use of an extremely clever and reasoned-out art. With them we are very far from automatic writing and from that pure automatism which allegedly reveals the real functioning of thought. They know all the tricks and recipes of technique. Well, if our remark is true that Surrealism provides them only with an empty poetic perceptiveness mistaken for poetry, what will occur when they—anyway, those who have not received the gift of poetry on their own account—happen to fall out with the Surrealist group and Surrealist illusionism? They will simply appear as they are, shrewd craftsmen —sometimes doing their worst: Chirico, whom André Breton lauded to the skies as a revealer of deepest poetry and metaphysical emotions, has now dedicated himself to awful academic and pseudoclassical painting. I hope that Dali will not meet with the same adventure, thanks to the resources of his talented and well-calculated eccentricity.

In any case what I should like to retain is the fact that these madmen are crafty artisans. Here we are faced with a particular instance of that element of imposture and quackery which is so deep-rooted in Surrealism. Surrealism simply lies to us when it pretends to break with reason in the very field of art properly so called, or of *technè* in the Platonic sense: just as we lie to ourselves when we wish to think that *poièsis* proceeds in a rational way, and does not break with the measures of conceptual, logical, or discursive reason. For at this point we must recognize the importance of the task achieved by Surrealism in calling attention to many *invidiosi veri* which the rationalist bias of our everyday dealings, our classical teaching, our industrial civilization, and our moral prudery would prefer us not to see. The Surrealists were right in unmasking the part (not principal, but real indeed) played by the workings of the automatic or animal unconscious in the soul of the poet, and in emphasizing (as others had done before them) the longing for the world of the marvelous, the availability of sensitiveness to all the allurements of chance, the congeniality with the irrational, in short the element of madness which inhabits him. As William Blake put it:

All Pictures that's Painted with Sense and with Thought
Are Painted by Madmen, as sure as a Groat;
For the Greatest the Fool is the Pencil more blest,
And when they are drunk they always paint best.

(That's perhaps why the pencil of our dear Utrillo is less blest, now that he is a teetotaller.) "Great wits," Dryden had said, "are sure to madness near allied." [8] And Novalis, in much deeper terms: "The poet is literally out of his senses— in exchange, all comes about within him. He is, to the letter, subject and object at the same time, soul and universe." [9]

5. This element of madness Plato had seen before the Surrealists, and forcefully brought to light. They invoke him on this score, though in reality he is at the opposite pole from them.

The famous passages from the *Phaedrus* and the *Ion* about the poets have such lyrical brilliance that we risk not paying sufficiently serious attention to their significance in the systematic context of Plato's philosophy. For Plato the concept of the Muse is bound to passion, mania and madness, childlike play, and unconsciousness. He never tires of praising mania, or that enthusiasm which abolishes reflection and logical thought, as the finest gift of the gods to mortal beings. So there is no blame involved in his emphasis on the ignorance of poets, or in the lines of the *Apology* asserting that poets speak much and say fine things, but understand nothing of what they say. And he expresses a firm and reasoned-out conviction of his own, founded on his very dialectics, when he says that the poets are possessed and out of their senses, and carried along by passion and madness, that common sense is the greatest obstacle to poetry, and that neither concepts nor logic nor rational knowledge have any part in it. And not only the poets, but their listeners also, not only the poem, but also the delight and the contact with beauty that it brings to us, depend on an inspiration superior to reason; so that, for Plato, any effort of rational criticism remains inadequate if only rational, and necessarily presupposes the intuitive reception, in the unconscious of the soul, of the magnetic power conveyed by the poem. "The stone Euripides calls magnet," as he puts it in the *Ion*, "does not only attract iron rings, but it also gives them the power of attracting other rings as the stone itself does. . . . In the same way the Muse herself inspires the artists, and through their inspiration others are enraptured, and the line of the inspired is produced. . . . One poet is suspended from one Muse, another from another; he is said to be 'possessed.' . . . From these primary rings, the poets, others are in turn suspended, some attached to Orpheus, some to Musaeus, from whom they derive inspiration." [10]

When I said, a moment ago, that Plato was at the extreme opposite of Surrealism, I had two things in mind. First, contrary to Surrealism, poetry, for Plato, is appendent to a supreme end which is beauty; poetry conveys here below, and gives a body to, beauty, and beauty dwells in a world infinitely superior to man, the world of separate ideas, nay more, the world of the divine, where the Beautiful and the Good and the Wise and the True are united in harmony. Beauty, a sense-perceptible participation in which or a shadow of which human art affords us, is an absolute, a divine attribute, and it is because of its very transcendence that it requires madness from the poet, who is not concerned with truth, as the philosopher is, or with the just and the good, as the legislator is, but only with the beautiful (as reflected upon our shadowy world). Secondly, by the same token, the madness of the poet is madness from above, not from below. For there are various sorts of madness. Madness divides into human and divine madness, Plato explains in the *Phaedrus;* and divine madness into inspiring, mystical, poetic, and erotic madness. In the *Timaeus,* he tells us that because the desiring part of the soul is filled, night and day, with phantasms and fancies, the Maker of the world has planned for this, and put divination at the disposal of men, so that it becomes possible to improve this inferior part of ours, and bring us into contact with truth. Hence it appears, he goes on to say, that God gave inspiration to human unreason. Thus the poet is brought into contact with transcendent and divine truth, as descending to us in the specific line of sense-seducing beauty. Through mania, friendship between gods and men has become possible. And the madness of the poet reveals to us, not the "real functioning of thought," but our kinship with eternal things. That is why "a poet is a light and winged thing, and holy," [11] and "a tender and untamable soul," [12] which is seized hold of by the mania that proceeds from the Muses.

So the Platonic and the Surrealist notions of poetry are divided from one another, and diametrically opposed, as a philosophy of absolute transcendence is divided from and opposed to, a philosophy (Hegelian in its roots) of absolute immanence. Yet the fact remains that, like the Surrealists, though for opposite motives, Plato totally separates poetic inspiration from reason. The myth of the Muse signifies that the source of poetry is separate from the human intellect, outside of it, in the transcendent eternal fatherland of subsisting Ideas. A conception which is akin, in the realm of art, to the Averroistic conception of the separate Intellect in the realm of knowledge, and which is responsible for that detestable idealism which has for so long spoiled the theories of philosophers on beauty. And by virtue of this total separation between poetic inspiration and reason, the poets, for Plato as for Surrealism, simply belong to unreason. They got a good proof of this when Plato—executing another operation of dialectical division, and sacrificing that beauty of which poets are capable, and which they make into a seducer, to that justice which the legislator makes into the goddess of the city—drove Homer and his fellow madmen out of the state.

Here we meet, to be sure, with Plato's humor and his ironical ambiguity.[13] He spoke, moreover, to people who knew what's what, and we may question the irrevocable character of an exclusion performed with all the appearances of a lovers' row. But, after all, what has been ironically put forward to play a trick on the reader, must be seemingly accepted to the letter, to play a trick on the writer. Let us, then, accept in this way the notion that, although the mania of poets is divine, the only beauty they are able to provide the city with is sense-appealing beauty, moving in our earthly shadows and fond of lies, so that their mania finally makes them a nuisance for religion and morality, and for the order of the city: on this again we see Plato and the Surrealists in a sort of agreement. Either it is a duty for the good conscience and the good city to expel poetry, or it is a duty for poetry to disintegrate the good conscience and the good city.

Platonic dialectics succeeded in dividing; it was unable to unite. The sin of Platonism is separation, and a separatist conception of transcendence. Plato however did not manage totally to divide, as perhaps he would have wanted, poetry and art, *poièsis* and *technè*, from one another. But in distinguishing the one from the other, he did human thought an invaluable service, for which he is owed singular gratitude. "You know," he wrote in the *Symposium*, "that the word *poièsis* means many things: for every activity causing a passage from non-being to being is *poièsis*, so that the works produced by any kind of art are *poièseis,* and the workmen who achieve them are all *poiètai* or makers. You know, nevertheless, that they are not called *poiètai,* poets, rather they have other names; and only that portion of the whole *poièsis* (in the general sense of art) which is separated from the rest and is concerned with music (*mousikè*) and melodic measures, is called poetry, and those who share in its possession are called poets." [14] *Music,* thus, in Plato's vocabulary, does not mean only music, but every artistic genus which depends on the inspiration of the Muse. And he perceived that all the fine arts are the realm of *Mousikè,* and are appendent to poetry, which quickens painting or architecture as well as poetry in the strict sense of the word.

As to the madness of poets, I would say that Plato conceptualized what he felt about it in the too absolute perspectives of his system—but what he felt about it proceeded from the experiential awareness of a true lover of poetry. There is in the poet an element of madness (which of itself is in no way pathological, though of course it may happen to accompany really morbid states);[15] he obeys an all-conquering instinct which is free from and extraneous to logical and conceptual reason. Ben Jonson reminds us that according to Aristotle himself "there has been no great creative mind without a mixture of madness. Nor is the mind capable of anything grand, or of speaking above other men, if it is not stirred by some superior motion." [16] In point of fact this is a sentence attributed to Aristotle by Seneca. Yet Aristotle's *Poetics* tells us, in more moderate but no less significant terms: "Hence it is that poetry demands a man with a happy gift of nature, or else one with a strain of madness in him." And the *Rhetoric:* "Poetry is a thing inspired"; and the *Eudemian Ethics:* "As in the universe, so in the soul, God moves everything. The starting point of reasoning is not reasoning, but something greater. What, then, could be greater even than knowledge and intellect but God? . . . For this reason, those are called fortunate who, whatever they start on, succeed in it without being good at reasoning. And deliberation is of no advantage to them, for they have in them a principle that is better than intellect and deliberation. They have inspiration, but they cannot deliberate. . . . Hence we have the melancholic men, the *dreamers of what is true.* For the moving principle seems to become stronger when the reasoning power is relaxed." Not Romantic authors alone thought of the poet as a "dreamer of what is true," a man moved by "some breath, as it were, of insanity" [17] or frenzy.

> Lovers and madmen have such seething brains,
> Such shaping fantasies, that apprehend
> More than cool reason ever comprehends.
> The lunatic, the lover, and the poet
> Are of imagination all compact. . . .[18]

The Spiritual Unconscious or Preconscious

6. Is there, then, any truly philosophical solution to the debate of reason and poetry; is it possible to show that, in spite of all, poetry and the intellect are of the same race and blood, and call to one another; and that poetry not only requires artistic or technical reason with regard to the particular ways of making, but, much more profoundly, depends on intuitive reason with regard to poetry's own essence and to the very touch of madness it involves? The truth of the matter is neither in the Surrealist inferno, nor in the Platonic heaven. I think that what we have to do is to make the Platonic Muse descend into the soul of man, where she is no longer Muse but creative intuition; and Platonic inspiration descend into the intellect united with imagination, where inspiration from above the soul becomes inspiration from above conceptual reason, that is, poetic experience.

This is the very subject of this book. Here I should like only to outline the general philosophical framework needed for our considerations—in other words, to establish a first preliminary thesis, which paves the way for our further research, and which deals with the existence in us of a spiritual—not animal—unconscious activity.

It is difficult to speak of this problem without discussing

a whole philosophy of man. We risk, moreover, being misled by the words we use. I would observe especially that the word *unconscious,* as I use it, does not necessarily mean a purely unconscious activity. It means most often an activity which is *principally* unconscious, but the point of which emerges into consciousness. Poetic intuition, for instance, is born in the unconscious, but it emerges from it; the poet is not unaware of this intuition, on the contrary it is his most precious light and the primary rule of his virtue of art. But he is aware of it *sur le rebord de l'inconscient,* as Bergson would have said, on the edge of the unconscious.

My contention, then, is that everything depends, in the issue we are discussing, on the recognition of the existence of a spiritual unconscious, or rather, preconscious, of which Plato and the ancient wise men were well aware, and the disregard of which in favor of the Freudian unconscious alone is a sign of the dullness of our times. There are two kinds of unconscious, two great domains of psychological activity screened from the grasp of consciousness: the preconscious of the spirit in its living strings, and the unconscious of blood and flesh, instincts, tendencies, complexes, repressed images and desires, traumatic memories, as constituting a closed or autonomous dynamic whole. I would like to designate the first kind of unconscious by the name of *spiritual* or, for the sake of Plato, *musical* unconscious or preconscious; and the second by the name of *automatic* unconscious or *deaf* unconscious—deaf to the intellect, and structured into a world of its own apart from the intellect; we might also say, in quite a general sense, leaving aside any particular theory, *Freudian unconscious.*[19]

These two kinds of unconscious life are at work at the same time; in concrete existence their respective impacts on conscious activity ordinarily interfere or intermingle in a greater or less degree; and, I think, never—except in some rare instances of supreme spiritual purification—does the spiritual unconscious operate without the other being involved, be it to a very small extent. But they are essentially distinct and thoroughly different in nature.

7. It is not necessary to think of those high levels in spiritual life which are the domain of contemplation, of supernatural mystical experience, achieved beyond concepts through connaturality of love; or of that perfect freedom of which St. Paul speaks and in which the "sons of God" are moved by the Spirit of God in a manner which transcends the measures of reason. Nor is it necessary to think of the way in which the disciples in Emmaus recognized Christ when He broke the bread, or of that state of perfect prayer which occurs, according to the Fathers of the Desert, when a man does not even know that he is praying; or even of the natural mystical experience of a Plotinus or of Indian wise men, in which supreme intellectual concentration is attained by means of the void, and through the abolition of any exercise of conceptual and discursive reason.[20]

Nor is it necessary to think of the perception of, and delight in, beauty, which draws tears from the eyes of a man who does not know what has come about in his mind; or of all the examples of intuitive, nonconceptual knowledge that Bergson took pleasure in enumerating.

It is enough to think of the ordinary and everyday functioning of intelligence, in so far as intelligence is really in activity, and of the way in which ideas arise in our minds, and every genuine intellectual grasping, or every new discovery,[21] is brought about; it is enough to think of the way in which our free decisions, when they are really free, are made, especially those decisions which commit our entire life—to realize that there exists a deep nonconscious world of activity, for the intellect and the will, from which the acts and fruits of human consciousness and the clear perceptions of the mind emerge, and that the universe of concepts, logical connections, rational discursus and rational deliberation, in which the activity of the intellect takes definite form and shape, is preceded by the hidden workings of an immense and primal preconscious life. Such a life develops in night, but in a night which is translucid and fertile, and resembles that primeval diffused light which was created first, before God made, as the Genesis puts it, "lights in the firmament of heaven to divide the day from the night" so as to be "for signs, and for seasons, and for days and years."

Reason does not only consist of its conscious logical tools and manifestations, nor does the will consist only of its deliberate conscious determinations. Far beneath the sunlit surface thronged with explicit concepts and judgments, words and expressed resolutions or movements of the will, are the sources of knowledge and creativity, of love and suprasensuous desires, hidden in the primordial translucid night of the intimate vitality of the soul. Thus it is that we must recognize the existence of an unconscious or preconscious which pertains to the spiritual powers of the human soul and to the inner abyss of personal freedom, and of the personal thirst and striving for knowing and seeing, grasping and expressing: a spiritual or musical unconscious which is specifically different from the automatic or deaf unconscious.[22]

When man seeking for his own inner universe takes the wrong road, he enters the internal world of the deaf unconscious, while believing he enters the internal world of the spirit, and he thus finds himself wandering in a false kind of self-interiority, where wildness and automatism mimic freedom. Such was the adventure of the Surrealists. I cannot help remembering this passage written long ago by G.-H. von Schubert, at the time of German Romanticism. The poet, he said, in whom does not arise the passionate desire "to rejoin the essential unity, in the contemplation of the external spectacle as well as in the grasping of the obscure data of the innermost world" yields almost necessarily "to another movement, akin to enthusiasm, which carries man along toward the abyss. Like Phaeton, man's freakish egotism wants to seize hold of the chariot of God: he has endeavored to make himself that inner enthusiasm which God alone can create."[23]

The Illuminating Intellect and the Preconscious Activity of the Spirit

8. Before finishing, I should like to propose some philosophical elucidation of a little more technical nature. The notion of the psychological unconscious was made into a self-contradictory enigma by Descartes, who defined the soul by the very act of self-consciousness. Thus we must be grateful to Freud and his predecessors for having obliged philosophers to acknowledge the existence of unconscious thought and unconscious psychological activity.

Before Descartes, the human soul was considered a substantial reality accessible in its nature only to metaphysical analysis, a spiritual entelechy informing the living body, and distinct from its own operations; and this, of course, made a completely different picture. The Schoolmen were not interested in working out any theory about the unconscious life of the soul, yet their doctrines implied its existence. What Thomas Aquinas teaches about the structure of the intellect seems to me especially significant in this regard. The question does not have to do with poetry, but, on the contrary, with abstract knowledge and the birth of abstract ideas. But for that very reason we find there basic views about the spiritual preconscious of the intellect, which can be utilized later on with respect to poetry.

The intellect, as perennial philosophy sees it, is spiritual and, thus, distinct in essence from the senses. Yet, according to the Aristotelian saying, nothing is to be found in the intellect which does not come from the senses. Then it is necessary to explain how a certain spiritual content, which will be seen and expressed in an abstract concept, can be drawn from the senses, that is, the phantasms and images gathered and refined in the internal sensitive powers, and originating in sensation. It is under the pressure of this necessity that Aristotle was obliged to posit the existence of a merely active and perpetually active intellectual energy, *νοῦς ποιητικός* the intellect agent, let us say the Illuminating Intellect, which permeates the images with its pure and purely activating

spiritual light and actuates or awakens the potential intelligibility which is contained in them. Aristotle, moreover, added
few and sometimes ambiguous indications about the Illuminating Intellect, which he only described as superior in nature to everything in man, so that the Arab philosophers
thought that it was *separate,* and consequently one and the
same for all men. The Schoolmen anterior to Thomas
Aquinas also held it to be separate, and identified it with
God's intellect. It was the work of St. Thomas to show and
insist that, because the human person is an ontologically
perfect or fully equipped agent, master of his actions, the
Illuminating Intellect cannot be separate, but must be an
inherent part of each individual's soul and intellectual structure, an inner spiritual light which is a participation in the
uncreated divine light, but which is in every man, through its
pure spirituality ceaselessly in act, the primal quickening
source of all his intellectual activity.

Now the process of formation of intellectual knowledge is
a very complex process of progressive spiritualization. For the
act of intellectual vision can only be accomplished through
the identification of spiritual intelligence with an object
brought itself to a state of spirituality in act. The Illuminating Intellect only activates, it does not know. The intellect, on the other hand, which the ancients called *intellectus
possibilis,* because it is first and of itself a *tabula rasa,* only
in potency with respect to knowing and to the intelligible
forms it will receive—the knowing intellect, in order to
know, must be actuated, and shaped, by what is drawn from
the images, and the images are imbued with materiality.
Thus, at a first step, the intelligible content present in the
images, and which, in the images, was only intelligible in
potency (or capable of *being made capable* of becoming an
object of intellectual vision), is made intelligible in act in a
spiritual form (*specie impressa,* impressed pattern), let us
say, in an intelligible germ, which is received from the images by the intellect, under the activation of the Illuminating Intellect. But still this is not enough to know. It is
necessary that the intelligible content drawn from the im-

ages should be not only intelligible in act, or capable of becoming an object of intellectual vision, but intellected in act, or actually become an object of intellectual vision. Then it is the intellect itself, which, having been impregnated by the impressed pattern or intelligible germ, vitally produces—always under the activation of the Illuminating Intellect—an inner fruit, a final and more fully determined spiritual form (*species expressa*), the concept, in which the content drawn from the images is brought to the very same state of spirituality-in-act in which the intellect-in-act is, and in which this now perfectly spiritualized content is seen, is actually an object of intellectual vision.

9. The reader will excuse me for this brief and rather chill irruption of Scholastic lecturing. For, in the views of Thomas Aquinas I just summarized on the structure of our intellectual activity, some points seem to me to be of basic interest for our purpose. There are two things in this structure of our intellectual activity which play an essential role: the Illuminating Intellect and the intelligible germ or impressed pattern. And philosophical reflection is able to establish, through the logical necessities of reasoning, the fact of their existence, but they totally escape experience and consciousness.

On the one hand, our intellect is fecundated by intelligible germs on which all the formation of ideas depends. And it draws from them, and produces within itself, through the most vital process, its own living fruits, its concepts and ideas. But it knows nothing either of these germs it receives within or of the very process through which it produces its concepts. Only the concepts are known. And even as regards the concepts, they cause the object seen in them to be known, but they themselves are not directly known; they are not known through their essence, they are known only through a reflective return of the intellect upon its own operations; and this kind of reflective grasping can possibly not occur. There can exist unconscious acts of thought and unconscious ideas.

On the other hand, and this is the fundamental point for me, we possess in ourselves the Illuminating Intellect, a spiritual sun[24] ceaselessly radiating, which activates everything in intelligence, and whose light causes all our ideas to arise in us, and whose energy permeates every operation of our mind. And this primal source of light cannot be seen by us; it remains concealed in the unconscious of the spirit.

Furthermore, it illuminates with its spiritual light the images from which our concepts are drawn. And this very process of illumination is unknown to us, it takes place in the unconscious; and often these very images, without which there is no thought, remain also unconscious or scarcely perceived in the process, at least for the most part.

Thus it is that we know (not always, to be sure!) what we are thinking, but we don't know how we are thinking; and that before being formed and expressed in concepts and judgments, intellectual knowledge is at first a beginning of insight, still unformulated, a kind of many-eyed cloud which is born from the impact of the light of the Illuminating Intellect on the world of images, and which is but a humble and trembling inchoation, yet invaluable, tending toward an intelligible content to be grasped.

I have insisted upon these considerations because they deal with the intellect, with reason itself, taken in the full scope of its life within us. They enable us to see how the notion of a spiritual unconscious or preconscious is philosophically grounded. I have suggested calling it, also, musical unconscious, for, being one with the root activity of reason, it contains from the start a germ of melody. In these remarks, on the other hand, we have considered the spiritual unconscious from the general point of view of the structure of the intellect, and with regard to the abstractive function of intelligence and to the birth of ideas. It was not a question of poetry. It was even a question of the origin and formation of the instruments of that conceptual, logical, discursive knowledge with which poetry is on bad terms. Well, if there is in the spiritual unconscious a nonconceptual or preconceptual activity of the intellect even with regard to the birth of the concepts, we can with greater reason assume that such a nonconceptual activity of the intellect, such a nonrational activity of reason, in the spiritual unconscious, plays an essential part in the genesis of poetry and poetic inspiration. Thus a place is prepared in the highest parts of the soul, in the primeval translucid night where intelligence stirs the images under the light of the Illuminating Intellect, for the separate Muse of Plato to descend into man, and dwell within him, and become a part of our spiritual organism.

FOUR

CREATIVE INTUITION AND POETIC KNOWLEDGE

At the Single Root of the Soul's Powers

1. In the last chapter I gave a few indications, general in nature, about the existence in us of a spiritual unconscious or preconscious, specifically distinct from the automatic or Freudian unconscious, though in vital intercommunication and interaction with it. I also suggested that it is in this translucid spiritual night that poetry and poetic inspiration have their primal source. And I referred to the views of Thomas Aquinas on the structure of the intellect and the preconscious intellectual activity on which the birth of ideas depends.

It is once again with some philosophical considerations borrowed from Thomas Aquinas that I shall preface our discussion of creative or poetic intuition. These considerations deal with the manner in which the powers of the soul, through which the various operations of life—biological, sensitive, intellective life—are performed, emanate from the soul. As soon as the human soul exists, the powers with which it is naturally endowed also exist, of course, though with regard to their exercise, the nutritive powers come first (they alone are in activity in the embryo); and then the sensitive powers, and then the intellective powers. But at the very instant of the creation of the soul, there is an order —with respect not to time but to nature—in the way in which they flow or emanate from the essence of the soul. At this point St. Thomas states that with respect to this order of natural priorities, the more perfect powers emanate before the others, and he goes on to say (here is the point in which I am interested) that in this ontological procession one power or faculty proceeds from the essence of the soul *through the medium or instrumentality of another*—which emanates beforehand. For the more perfect powers are the principle or *raison d'être* of others, both as being their end and as being their "active principle," or the efficacious source of their existence. Intelligence does not exist for the senses, but the senses, which are, as he puts it, "a certain defective participation in intelligence," exist for intelligence. Hence it is that in the order of natural origin the senses exist, as it were, from the intellect, in other words, proceed from the essence of the soul through the intellect.

Consequently, we must say that imagination proceeds or flows from the essence of the soul through the intellect, and that the external senses proceed from the essence of the soul through imagination. For they exist in man to serve imagination, and through imagination, intelligence.

2. I am fond of diagrams. I hope that the one I am offering here (*over*), and which represents this order of emanation, will help me to clarify the matter, poor as it may be from the point of view of abstract drawing.

The point at the summit of the diagram represents the essence of the soul. The first—so to speak—cone represents the Intellect, or Reason, emanating first from the soul. The second, which emerges from the first, represents the Imagination, emanating from the soul through the Intellect. The third, which emerges from the second, represents the External Senses, emanating from the soul through the Imagination.

The first circle represents the world of Concepts and Ideas in a state of explicit formation, say, the conceptualized externals of Reason: the world of the workings of conceptual, logical, discursive Reason.

The second circle represents the world of the Images in a state of explicit and definite formation, say, the organized externals of Imagination. This is the world of the achievements of Imagination as stirred by, and centered upon, the actual exercise of External Senses and held in unity by it:

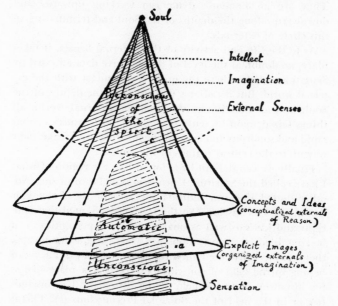

in other words, as engaged in the process of sense perception and used for practical purposes in the current activities of man in the waking state.

The third circle represents the intuitive data afforded by external Sensation (which is, of itself, almost unconscious, and becomes sense perception when it is interpreted and structured through the instrumentality of memory, imagination, and the other "internal senses").

Now our three cones are not empty; each one should be imagined as filled with the life and activity of the power it symbolizes. The life and activity of the Intellect or Reason are not to be viewed only in the circle of the conceptualized externals of Reason. They are an immense dynamism emanating from the very center of the Soul and terminating in this circle of externals.

The life and activity of Imagination are not to be viewed only in the circle of the organized externals of Imagination. They are an immense dynamism working upwards and downwards along the depths of the Soul and terminating in this circle of externals.

As to the life and activity of the External Senses, it takes place, no doubt, at the level of the intuitive data afforded by Sensation—there where the mind is in contact with the external world. But it radiates upwards into the depths of the Soul; and all that it receives from the external world, all things seized upon by sense perception, all treasures of that sapid and sonorous and colorful Egypt, enter and make their way up to the central regions of the soul.[1]

Finally we can delimit by a dotted line the region of what I have called the Spiritual Unconscious or Preconscious. Another dotted line can indicate the area of the Animal or Automatic Unconscious. So the fact is represented that concepts and ideas as well as images and sense perceptions can be contained in these two obscure areas. And as for images, they can be considered in three different states. They can belong in the field of consciousness (say, at a place like *a*, for instance), or in the field of the Automatic Unconscious (*b*), or in the field of the Spiritual Preconscious (*c*). This is a point which can be remembered for some further discussions.

3. So much for the diagram. What matters to us is the fact that there exists a common root of all the powers of the soul, which is hidden in the spiritual unconscious, and that there is in this spiritual unconscious a root activity in which the intellect and the imagination, as well as the powers of desire, love, and emotion, are engaged in common. The powers of the soul envelop one another, the universe of

sense perception is in the universe of imagination, which is in the universe of intelligence. And they are all, within the intellect, stirred and activated by the light of the Illuminating Intellect. And, according to the order of the ends and demands of nature, the first two universes move under the attraction and for the higher good of the universe of the intellect, and, to the extent to which they are not cut off from the intellect by the animal or automatic unconscious, in which they lead a wild life of their own, the imagination and the senses are raised in man to a state genuinely human where they somehow participate in intelligence, and their exercise is, as it were, permeated with intelligence.

But in the spiritual unconscious the life of the intellect is not entirely engrossed by the preparation and engendering of its instruments of rational knowledge and by the process of production of concepts and ideas, which we analyzed at the end of the preceding chapter and which winds up at the level of the conceptualized externals of reason. There is still for the intellect another kind of life, which makes use of other resources and another reserve of vitality, and which is free, I mean free from the engendering of abstract concepts and ideas, free from the workings of rational knowledge and the disciplines of logical thought, free from the human actions to regulate and the human life to guide, and free from the laws of objective reality as to be known and acknowledged by science and discursive reason. But, as it appears, at least in certain privileged or ill-fated people, this freedom is not freedom at random, this free life of the intellect is also cognitive and productive, it obeys an inner law of expansion and generosity, which carries it along toward the manifestation of the creativity of the spirit; and it is shaped and quickened by creative intuition. Here it is, in this free life of the intellect which involves a free life of the imagination, at the single root of the soul's powers, and in the unconscious of the spirit, that poetry, I think, has its source.[2]

Poetry's freedom resembles, thus, as Plato pointed out, the freedom of the child, and the freedom of play, and the freedom of dreams. It is none of these. It is the freedom of the creative spirit.

And because poetry is born in this root life where the powers of the soul are active in common, poetry implies an essential requirement of totality or integrity. Poetry is the fruit neither of the intellect alone, nor of imagination alone. Nay more, it proceeds from the totality of man, sense, imagination, intellect, love, desire, instinct, blood and spirit together. And the first obligation imposed on the poet is to consent to be brought back to the hidden place, near the center of the soul, where this totality exists in the state of a creative source.

Poetic Intuition

4. Thus, when it comes to poetry, we must admit that in the spiritual unconscious of the intellect, at the single root of the soul's powers, there is, apart from the process which tends to knowledge by means of concepts and abstract ideas, something which is preconceptual or nonconceptual and nevertheless in a state of definite intellectual actuation: not, therefore, a mere way to the concept, as was the "impressed pattern" I spoke of in the preceding chapter, but another kind of germ, which does not tend toward a concept to be formed, and which is already an intellective form or act fully determined though enveloped in the night of the spiritual unconscious. In other words, such a thing is knowledge in act, but nonconceptual knowledge.

The problem, then, that I should like to discuss now deals with that kind of knowledge which is involved in poetic activity.

Clearly, what we are considering at this point is not the previous (theoretical) knowledge, in any field whatever of human experience and culture, that is *presupposed* by art and poetry, and which provides them with external materials to be integrated in, and transformed by, the fire of creative virtues.

What we are considering is the kind of inherent knowledge that is immanent in and *consubstantial* with poetry, one with its very essence.

Here our first signpost is, I think—the notion, which I have previously pointed out, of the free creativity of the spirit. In the craftsman the creativity of the spirit is, as it were, bound or tied up to a particular aim, which is the satisfying of a particular need. In the poet it is free creativity, for it only tends to engender in beauty, which is a transcendental, and involves an infinity of possible realizations and possible choices. In this respect the poet is like a god. And in order to discover the first essentials of poetry there is nothing better for us to do than to look to the First Poet.

God's creative Idea, from the very fact that it is creative, does not receive anything from things, since they do not yet exist. It is in no way *formed* by its creatable object, it is only and purely *formative* and *forming*. And that which will be expressed or manifested in the things made is nothing else than their Creator Himself, whose transcendent Essence is enigmatically signified in a diffused, dispersed, or parceled-out manner, by works which are deficient likenesses of and created participations in it. And God's Intellect is determined or specified by nothing else than His own essence. It is by knowing Himself, in an act of intellection which is His very Essence and His very Existence, that He knows His works, which exist in time and have begun in time, but which He eternally is in the free act of creating.

Such is the supreme analogate of poetry. Poetry is engaged in the free creativity of the spirit. And thus it implies an intellective act which is not formed by things but is, by its own essence, formative and forming. Well, it is too clear that the poet is a poor god. He does not know himself. And his creative insight miserably depends on the external world, and on the infinite heap of forms and beauties already made by men, and on the mass of things that generations have learned, and on the code of signs which is used by his fellow men and which he receives from a language he has not made. Yet, for all that he is condemned both to subdue to his own purpose all these extraneous elements and to manifest his own substance in his creation.

At this point we see how essential to poetry is the subjectivity of the poet. I do not mean the inexhaustible flux of superficial feelings in which the sentimental reader recognizes his own cheap longings, and with which the songs to the Darling and Faithless One of generations of poets have desperately fed us. I mean subjectivity in its deepest ontologic sense, that is, the substantial totality of the human person, a universe unto itself, which the spirituality of the soul makes capable of containing itself through its own immanent acts, and which, at the center of all the subjects that it knows as objects, grasps only itself as subject. In a way similar to that in which divine creation presupposes the knowledge God has of His own essence, poetic creation presupposes, as a primary requirement, a grasping, by the poet, of his own subjectivity, in order to create. The poet's aim is not to know himself. He is not a guru. To attain, through the void, an intuitive experience of the existence of the Self, of the Atman, in its pure and full actuality, is the specific aim of natural mysticism. It is not the aim of poetry. The essential need of the poet is to create; but he cannot do so without passing through the door of the knowing, as obscure as it may be, of his own subjectivity. For poetry means first of all an intellective act which by its essence is creative, and forms something into being instead of being formed by things: and what can such an intellective act possibly express and manifest in producing the work if not the very being and substance of the one who creates? Thus it is that works of painting or sculpture or music or poetry the closer they come to the sources of poetry the more they reveal, one way or another, the subjectivity of their author.

5. But the substance of man is obscure to himself. He knows not his soul, except in the fluid multiplicity of passing phenomena which emerge from it and are more or less clearly attained by reflective consciousness, but only increase the enigma, and leave him more ignorant of the essence of

his Self. He knows not his own subjectivity. Or, if he knows it, it is formlessly, by feeling it as a kind of propitious and enveloping night. Melville, I think, was aware of that when he observed that "no man can ever feel his own identity aright except his eyes be closed; as if darkness were indeed the proper element of our essences." Subjectivity *as subjectivity* is inconceptualizable; is an unknowable abyss. How, then, can it be revealed to the poet?

The poet does not know himself in the light of his own essence. Since man perceives himself only through a repercussion of his knowledge of the world of things, and remains empty to himself if he does not fill himself with the universe, the poet knows himself only on the condition that things resound in him, and that in him, at a single wakening, they and he come forth together out of sleep. In other words, the primary requirement of poetry, which is the obscure knowing, by the poet, of his own subjectivity, is inseparable from, is one with another requirement—the grasping, by the poet, of the objective reality of the outer and inner world: not by means of concepts and conceptual knowledge, but by means of an obscure knowledge which I shall describe in a moment as knowledge through affective union.

Hence the perplexities of the poet's condition. If he hears the passwords and the secrets that are stammering in things, if he perceives realities, correspondences, ciphered writings that are at the core of actual existence, if he captures those more things which are in heaven and earth than are dreamt of in our philosophy, he does not do so by knowing all this in the ordinary sense of the word to know, but by receiving all this into the obscure recesses of his passion.[3] All that he discerns and divines in things, he discerns and divines not as something *other* than himself, according to the law of speculative knowledge, but, on the contrary, as inseparable from himself and from his emotion, and in truth as identified with himself.

His intuition, the creative intuition, is an obscure grasping of his own Self and of things in a knowledge through union or through connaturality which is born in the spiritual unconscious, and which fructifies only in the work. So the germ of which I spoke some pages back, and which is contained in the spiritual night of the free life of the intellect, tends from the very start to a kind of revelation—not to the revelation of the *Übermensch* or of the omnipotency of man, as the Surrealists believe, but to the humble revelation, virtually contained in a small lucid cloud of inescapable intuition, both of the Self of the poet and of some particular flash of reality in the God-made universe; a particular flash of reality bursting forth in its unforgettable individuality, but infinite in its meanings and echoing capacity—

> *To see a World in a Grain of Sand,*
> *And a Heaven in a Wild Flower.*

Such is the answer of philosophical analysis to the problem which had imposed itself on our consideration at the end of the merely descriptive or inductive inquiry conducted in the first chapter of this book. At that moment we observed that Oriental art, only intent on Things, nevertheless reveals obscurely, together with Things (and to the very extent to which it truly succeeds in revealing Things), the creative subjectivity of the artist; and that, on the other hand, Occidental art, more and more intent on the artist's Self, nevertheless reveals obscurely, together with this Self (and to the very extent to which it succeeds in revealing it), the transapparent reality and secret significance of Things. And we concluded that at the root of the creative act there must be a quite particular intellectual process, a kind of experience or knowledge without parallel in logical reason, through which Things and the Self are obscurely grasped together.

Now, availing ourselves of the self-awareness which the progress of reflexivity has developed in modern art and poetry, and which causes poets to say with Pierre Reverdy that "the value of a work is proportional to the poignant contact of the poet with his own destiny," we come to perceive in philosophical terms how and why the process in question takes place. A direct inquiry into the inner functioning of the intellect in its preconceptual life makes us realize that poetic intuition and poetic knowledge are both one of the basic manifestations of man's spiritual nature, and a primary requirement of the creativity of the spirit steeped in imagination and emotion.

Nature of Poetic Knowledge

6. I used a moment ago the expression "knowledge through connaturality." It refers to a basic distinction made by Thomas Aquinas, when he explains that there are two different ways to judge of things pertaining to a moral virtue, say fortitude. On the one hand we can possess in our mind moral science, the conceptual and rational knowledge of virtues, which produces in us a merely intellectual conformity with the truths involved. Then, if we are asked a question about fortitude, we will give the right answer by merely looking at and consulting the intelligible objects contained in our concepts. A moral philosopher may possibly not be a virtuous man and know everything about virtues.

On the other hand, we can possess the virtue in question in our own powers of will and desire, have it embodied in ourselves, and thus be in accordance with it or connatured with it in our very being. Then, if we are asked a question about fortitude, we will give the right answer, no longer through science, but through inclination, by looking at and consulting what we are and the inner bents or propensities of our own being. A virtuous man may possibly be utterly ignorant in moral philosophy, and know as well (probably better) everything about virtues—through connaturality.

In this knowledge through union or inclination, connaturality or congeniality, the intellect is at play not alone, but together with affective inclinations and the dispositions of the will, and as guided and shaped by them. It is not rational knowledge, knowledge through the conceptual, logical, and discursive exercise of reason. But it is really and genuinely knowledge, though obscure and perhaps incapable of giving account of itself.

St. Thomas explains in this way the difference between

the knowledge of divine reality acquired by theology and the knowledge of divine reality provided by mystical experience. For the spiritual man, he says,[4] knows divine things through inclination or connaturality: not only because he has learned them, but because he suffers them, as the Pseudo-Dionysius put it.

Knowledge through connaturality plays an immense part in human life. Modern philosophers have thrown it into oblivion, but the ancient Doctors paid careful attention to it and established upon it all their theory of God-given contemplation. I think that we have to restore it, and to recognize its basic role and importance in such domains as moral practical knowledge and natural or supernatural mystical experience—and in the domain of art and poetry. Poetic knowledge, as I see it, is a specific kind of knowledge through inclination or connaturality—let us say a knowledge through affective connaturality which essentially relates to the creativity of the spirit and tends to express itself in a work. So that in such a knowledge it is the object created, the poem, the painting, the symphony, in its own existence as a world of its own, which plays the part played in ordinary knowledge by the concepts and judgments produced within the mind.

Hence it follows that poetic knowledge is fully expressed only in the work. In the mind of the poet, poetic knowledge arises in an unconscious or preconscious manner, and emerges into consciousness in a sometimes almost imperceptible though imperative and irrefragable way, through an impact both emotional and intellectual or through an unpredictable experiential insight, which gives notice of its existence, but does not express it.

7. This particular kind of knowledge through connaturality comes about, I think, by means of emotion. That is why, at first glance, one believes, and often the poet himself believes, that he is like the Ahab of *Moby Dick:* "Here's food for thought, had Ahab time to think; but Ahab never thinks; he only feels, feels, feels; *that's* tingling enough for

mortal man! to think's audacity. God only has that right and privilege." Well, in this people are mistaken. The poet also thinks. And poetic knowledge proceeds from the intellect in its most genuine and essential capacity as intellect, though through the indispensable instrumentality of feeling, feeling, feeling. At this point I would wish to insist that it is in no way a merely emotional or a sentimentalist theory of poetry that I am suggesting. First, I am speaking of a certain kind of knowledge, and emotion does not know: the intellect knows, in this kind of knowledge as in any other. Second, the emotion of which I am speaking is in no way that "brute or merely subjective emotion" to which I alluded in the first chapter, and which is extraneous to art.[5] It is not an emotion expressed or *depicted* by the poet, an emotion as *thing* which serves as a kind of matter or material in the making of the work, nor is it a thrill in the poet which the poem will "send down the spine" of the reader. It is an emotion as *form,* which, being one with the creative intuition, gives form to the poem, and which is *intentional,* as an idea is, or carries within itself infinitely more than itself. (I use the word "intentional" in the Thomistic sense,[6] reintroduced by Brentano and Husserl into modern philosophy, which refers to the purely tendential existence through which a thing—for instance, the object known—is present, in an immaterial or suprasubjective manner, in an "instrument"—an idea for instance, which, in so far as it determines the act of knowing, is a mere immaterial tendency or *intentio* toward the object.) [7]

How can emotion be thus raised to the level of the intellect and, as it were, take the place of the concept in becoming for the intellect a determining means or instrumental vehicle through which reality is grasped?

That's a difficult question, as are all similar questions dealing with the application of the general concept of knowledge through connaturality to the various particular fields in which this kind of knowledge is at play. I think that in all these cases, where the soul "suffers things more than it learns them," and experiences them through resonance in subjectivity, we have to find out a certain specific way in which the great notion developed by John of St. Thomas apropos of mystical knowledge—*amor transit in conditionem objecti,* love passes on to the sphere of the intentional means of objective grasping—has to be used analogically. Here I would say that in poetic knowledge emotion carries the reality which the soul suffers—a world in a grain of sand—into the depth of subjectivity, and of the spiritual unconscious of the intellect, because in the poet, contrary to other men (especially those involved in the business of civilized life), the soul remains, as it were, more available to itself, and keeps a reserve of spirituality which is not absorbed by its activity toward the outside and by the toil of its powers. And this deep unemployed reserve of the spirit, being unemployed, is like a sleep of the soul; but, being spiritual, is in a state of virtual vigilance and vital tension, owing to the virtual reversion of the spirit on itself and on everything in itself. The soul sleeps, but her heart is awake; allow her to sleep . . .

Well, let us suppose that in the density of such a secretly alert sleep and such a spiritual tension, emotion intervenes (whatever this emotion may be; what matters is where it is received). On the one hand it spreads into the entire soul, it imbues its very being, and thus certain particular aspects in things become connatural to the soul affected in this way. On the other hand, emotion, falling into the living springs, is received in the vitality of intelligence, I mean intelligence permeated by the diffuse light of the Illuminating Intellect and virtually turned toward all the harvests of experience and memory preserved in the soul, all the universe of fluid images, recollections, associations, feelings, and desires latent, under pressure, in the subjectivity, and now stirred. And it suffices for emotion disposing or inclining, as I have said, the entire soul in a certain determinate manner to be thus received in the undetermined vitality and productivity of the spirit, where it is permeated by the light of the Illuminating Intellect: then, while remaining emotion, it is made—with respect to the aspects in things which are connatural to, or *like,* the soul it imbues—into an instrument of intelligence judging through connaturality, and plays, in the process of this knowledge through *likeness* between reality and subjectivity, the part of a nonconceptual intrinsic determination of intelligence in its preconscious activity. By this very fact it is transferred into the state of objective intentionality; it is spiritualized, it becomes intentional, that is to say, conveying, in a state of immateriality, things other than itself.[8] It becomes for the intellect a determining means or instrumental vehicle through which the things which have impressed this emotion on the soul, and the deeper, invisible things that are contained in them or connected with them, and which have ineffable correspondence or coaptation with the soul thus affected. and which resound in it, are grasped and known obscurely.

It is by means of such a spiritualized emotion that poetic intuition, which in itself is an intellective flash, is born in the unconscious of the spirit. In one sense it is, as I said a moment ago, a privilege of those souls in which the margin of dreaming activity and introverted natural spirituality, unemployed for the business of human life, is particularly large. In another sense, because it emanates from a most natural capacity of the human mind, we must say that every human being is potentially capable of it: among those who do not know it, many, in point of fact, have repressed it or murdered it within themselves. Hence their instinctive resentment against the poet.

Of itself poetic intuition proceeds from the natural and supremely spontaneous movement of the soul which seeks itself by communicating with things in its capacity as a spirit endowed with senses and passions. And sometimes it is in mature age, when the spirit has been fed with experience and suffering, and turns back toward itself, that it best experiences the sapid sleep in which poetic intuition awakes— and which also exists, in another fashion, and with the acrid taste of greenness, in the child and the primitive. Poetic knowledge is as natural to the spirit of man as the return ~f the bird to his nest; and it is the universe which, together with the spirit, makes its way back to the mysterious nest of the soul. For the content of poetic intuition is both the reality of the things of the world and the subjectivity of the poet, both obscurely conveyed through an intentional or spiritualized emotion. The soul is known in the experience of the world and the world is known in the experience of the soul, through a knowledge which does not know itself. For such knowledge knows, not in order to know, but in order to produce. It is toward creation that it tends.

"Je est un autre," Rimbaud said: "I is another." In poetic intuition objective reality and subjectivity, the world and the whole of the soul, coexist inseparably. At that moment sense and sensation are brought back to the heart, blood to the spirit, passion to intuition. And through the vital though nonconceptual actuation of the intellect all the powers of the soul are also actuated in their roots.[9]

The *Texts without Comment* which follow this chapter contain lines which seem to be significant for my present purpose. I think that by reading those collected under heading II we can see better than through any philosophical arguments how the subjectivity of the poet is revealed (but together with things) in his poem; and by reading the texts collected under heading III, how the *Another,* the things of the world and of the intellect, and their meanings, are also (but together with the Self) revealed in the poem; and how, in this single *and* double revelation, everything derives from a primal creative intuition, born in the soul of the poet, under the impact of a definite emotion.

The direct, intuitive contact with any genuine work of painting, sculpture or architecture, or music, which has spiritual depth and conveys a message of its own, affords us the same evidence.

Poetic Intuition as Cognitive

8. I should like to add a few remarks in an effort to bring out the main aspects or implications involved in the notion of poetic intuition.

It seems to me that the first distinction to be made in this regard deals with the fact that poetic intuition, which is both creative and cognitive, can be considered especially either as creative, and therefore, with respect to the engendering of the work, or as cognitive, and therefore with respect to *what is grasped* by it.

Let us, then, consider first poetic intuition as cognitive. It is cognitive, as we have seen, both of the reality of things and of the subjectivity of the poet. Now is it possible to try to make more precise that "reality of things" of which I just spoke? In other words, what is the *object* of poetic intuition? But the word "object" is equivocal here, for things are objectivized in a concept, and there is no concept, therefore no objectivization, in poetic intuition. Let us say, then, what is the *thing grasped* by poetic intuition?

Our previous consideration of poetic knowledge already contained the answer: poetic intuition is not directed toward essences, for essences are disengaged from concrete reality in a concept, a universal idea, and scrutinized by means of reasoning; they are an object for speculative knowledge, they are not the thing grasped by poetic intuition. Poetic intuition is directed toward concrete existence as connatural to the soul pierced by a given emotion: that is to say, each time toward some singular existent, toward some complex of concrete and individual reality, seized in the violence of its sudden self-assertion and in the total unicity of its passage in time. This transient motion of a beloved hand—it exists an instant, and will disappear forever, and only in the memory of angels will it be preserved, above time. Poetic intuition catches it in passing, in a faint attempt to immortalize it in time. But poetic intuition does not stop at this given existent; it goes beyond, and infinitely beyond. Precisely because it has no conceptualized object, it tends and extends to the infinite, it tends toward all the reality, the infinite reality which is engaged in any singular existing thing, either the secret properties of being involved in its identity and in its existential relations with other things, or the other realities, all the other aspects or fructifications of

being, scattered in the entire world, which have in themselves the wherewithal to found some ideal relation with
this singular existing thing, and which it conveys to the
mind, by the very fact that it is grasped through its union
with, and resonance in, subjectivity spiritually awakened.

Such is, I think, the thing grasped by poetic intuition: the
singular existent which resounds in the subjectivity of the
poet, together with all the other realities which echo in this
existent, and which it conveys in the manner of a sign.

So it is true that poetry, as Aristotle said, is more philo-
sophic than history. Not, surely, with respect to its mode or
manner of knowing, for this mode is altogether existential,
and the thing grasped is grasped as nonconceptualizable.
But with respect to the very thing grasped, which is not a
contingent thing in the mere fact of its existence, but in
its infinite openness to the riches of being, and as a sign of
it. For poetic intuition makes things which it grasps diaph-
anous and alive, and populated with infinite horizons. As
grasped by poetic knowledge, things abound in significance,
and swarm with meanings.

Things are not only what they are. They ceaselessly pass
beyond themselves, and give more than they have, because
from all sides they are permeated by the activating influx of
the Prime Cause. They are better and worse than themselves, because being superabounds, and because nothingness
attracts what comes from nothingness. Thus it is that they
communicate with each other in an infinity of fashions and
through an infinity of actions and contacts, sympathies and
ruptures. I would think that this mutual communication in
existence and in the spiritual flux from which existence proceeds, which is in things, as it were, the secret of creative
sources, is perhaps in the last analysis what the poet receives
and suffers, and grasps in the night of his own Self, or knows
as unknown.

9. Coming now to the other cognitive function of poetic
intuition, I mean poetic intuition as obscurely revealing the
subjectivity of the poet, I need not dwell long on this sub-

ject. It is clear that poetic intuition is filled with the subjectivity of the poet as well as with the thing grasped, since the
thing grasped and the subjectivity are known together in the
same obscure experience, and since the thing grasped is
grasped only through its affective resonance in and union
with the subjectivity. Nay more, as we have seen, it is in
order to express the subjectivity of the poet in the work
which proceeds from the creativity of the spirit that the
grasping of things comes about, together with the awakening of subjectivity to itself. As a result, we may say, it seems
to me, that in the attainments of poetic intuition what is
most immediate is the experience of the things of the world,
because it is natural to the human soul to know things
before knowing itself; but what is *most principal* is the experience of the Self—because it is in the awakening of subjectivity to itself that emotion received in the translucid
night of the free life of the intellect is made intentional and
intuitive, or the determining means of a knowledge through
congeniality.

10. As concerns finally the work, it also will be, in indissoluble unity—as the poetic intuition from which it proceeds—both a revelation of the subjectivity of the poet and
of the reality that poetic knowledge has caused him to perceive.

Be it a painting or a poem, this work is a made object—
in it alone does poetic intuition come to objectivization.
And it must always preserve its own consistence and value
as an *object*. But at the same time it is a sign—both a *direct*
sign of the secrets perceived in things, of some irrecusable
truth of nature or adventure caught in the great universe,
and a *reversed sign* of the subjective universe of the poet,
of his substantial Self obscurely revealed. Just as things
grasped by poetic intuition abound in significance, just as
being swarms with signs, so the work also will swarm with
meanings, and will say more than it is, and will deliver to
the mind, at one stroke, the universe in a human countenance.

Il fallait bien qu'un visage
Réponde à tous les noms du monde.[10]

The work will make present to our eyes, together with itself, something else, and still something else, and still something else indefinitely, in the infinite mirrors of analogy. Through a kind of poetic ampliation, Beatrice, while remaining the woman whom Dante loved, is also, through the power of the sign, the light which illuminates him. Sophie von Kühn, while remaining the dead fiancée of Novalis, is also the call of God that seduces him.

Thus it is that poetry captures the secret senses of things, and the all-embracing sense, still more secret, of subjectivity obscurely revealed: in order to throw both into a matter to be formed. And both, the senses perceived in things and the deeper and more vital, unifying sense of the avowal of creative subjectivity, compose together one single complete and complex sense, through which the work *exists,* and which is what we called in a previous chapter the poetic sense of the work.

11. Are there some particular observations to be made regarding poetic intuition in the painter, as contradistinguished to poetic intuition in the poet? I would say that in both of them poetic intuition has the same fundamental characteristics, but with further differences which seem to me to have essential significance. The reason for this is the fact that the reality with which the poet is confronted is the very object of intelligence, that is, the ocean of Being, in its absolute universality; whereas the reality with which the painter is confronted is the universe of visible matter, of Corporal Being, through which alone the ocean of Being in its infinity comes to show through for him. The world of the painter is the world of the eye before being and while being the world of the intellect.

As a result, in order to describe the painter's poetic intuition, we must first remember that he is a captive of Nature, he is bound to her, he cannot escape her—"one cannot go against nature," as Picasso himself put it: and all painters

feel the same way. But, as I pointed out in previous remarks (that I should like to resume in giving them now full
philosophical bearing), the painter does not look at nature
as at a separate thing-in-itself, to be copied or imitated in its
external appearances. He looks at nature as at a creative
mystery which he tries to imitate in its secret workings
and inner ways of operation, and which, by means of poetic
intuition, comes through his eyes to the recesses of his own
creative subjectivity as a germ or a key of that object which
is the work to be produced into existence. What the intellect of the painter grasps in the dark of Things and his own
Self together, is an aspect of the infinite depths of Visible
Corporeal Being in so far as constructible or feasible in
colors and lines, an aspect or element of the mystery of the
universe of visible matter or corporeal existence in so far as
this aspect or element is meant to fructify into a work—
which itself is an object for the eye before being and while
being an object for the intellect.

But this very process cannot come about without going at
the same time beyond the universe of visible corporeal existence and attaining enigmatically the infinity of the universe
of Being and existence. Since in poetic intuition subjectivity
is the very vehicle to penetrate into the objective world,
what is looked for by the painter in visible things must possess the same kind of inner depth and inexhaustible reserves
for possible revelation as his own Self. While grasping some
aspect of visible corporeal existence as a reality, he grasps it
also as a sign, through which are brought to him, in a kind
of indeterminable fluidity, the same secret meanings, correspondences, echoes, and intercommunications which the poet
obscurely catches in the universe of Being and the human
universe. Yet the painter catches them still more obscurely,
and only in the manner of resonances or overtones. The
painter's poetic intuition conveys to him—as a "seminal
principle" or key to operation—some of the inexhaustible
inside aspects of visible matter, and, by the same stroke, some
of the more inexhaustible meanings which make the invisible universe of Being show through—and all this is caught

by way of knowledge through connaturality, according to any direction whatever in which an act of spiritual communication with the things of the world can be brought about, and all this can be expressed only be recasting these things into a new visible fabric.

Thus it is that genuine painting, while remaining strictly painting, attains—especially after the "liberation" accomplished in modern times—to a kind of metaphysical vastness and a degree of intellectuality which resemble those peculiar to poetry. It does so through its obscure grasping, by means of creative intuition, both of the workable secrets of the world of visible matter and the implied or suggested inner realities of the world of Being.

Modern painting longs, like modern poetry, for a superior degree of intellectuality, and is intent on the impact of Things on intuitive reason—to the very extent to which it is true to poetic knowledge. But at the same time modern painting (like modern poetry) is tempted to go in the opposite direction, and runs the risk of dispersing in mere sensationalism or in a merely taste-guided and superficial release of imagination, to the very extent to which it mistakes the nonlogical character of poetic knowledge, or the liberation from conceptual reason, for a total break with and liberation from reason itself and the intellect itself, thus losing any spiritual or emotional gravity, and neglecting those "mysterious centers of thought" of which Gauguin spoke. This ambivalence of modern painting seems to me singularly striking, and singularly instructive for the philosopher.

I should like to observe, in addition, that it is not surprising—precisely because of the particular conditions I just tried to point out—that the utterances of painters about the peculiar poetic intuition of their own are poorer than those of the poets. They confess themselves in their canvas, not in their words. And they use as a rule, in point of introspection, a humble vocabulary, in which they choose quite modest (sometimes all the more moving) words that convey in reality a deeper meaning for which they have no expression. They speak in this way of their "little sensation," as Cézanne put it, of their "impressions," their "feelings," their "interior promptings," their "vision"—this word "vision" is probably for them a very close equivalent of what in a philosophical perspective we call poetic intuition.

Yet some more significant evidences are not lacking, not to speak of the great testimony of Chinese painters. It is in the full force of the sense with which they are laden that we must understand the words of a painter or a sculptor when he tells us that for him "everything he sees has an inexhaustible fullness and value," (Hans von Marées) that he has put "as far as possible . . . the logic of the visible at the service of the invisible," (Odilon Redon) or that "the artist . . . sees; that is to say, his eye, grafted on his heart, reads deeply into the bosom of nature"; (Rodin) or that to express the "big forms" in which all the richness of nature is concealed "you have to love these, to be a part of these in sympathy"; (John Marin) or the words of van Gogh, when he writes: "Instead of trying to reproduce exactly what I have before my eyes, I use color more arbitrarily so as to express myself forcibly," "I want to paint men and women with that something of the eternal which the halo used to symbolize, and which we seek to give by the actual radiance and vibration of our colorings"; and the words of Poussin when he says that "painting is nothing but an image of incorporeal things despite the fact that it exhibits bodies," and that there are, in the components of the work, "parts" which "are of the painter himself and cannot be learned. That is the golden bough of Vergil, which no one can find nor gather if he is not led by destiny."

On the other hand, if the observations I have submitted are true, we may realize that friendship and community of efforts and theories between painters and poets, as developed especially since the time of German Romanticism and of Baudelaire and Delacroix, are of course a blessing, but that they can also be detrimental to both sides. The groups in which they exchange ideas, claims, mutual admiration, and mutual jealousy, serve to stimulate and enlarge the creative instinct in an invaluable manner. But they also may result in having either painters or poets disregard what is most specific in their own particular approach to the work. Poets instructed by painters may see in the poem a mere construction of images. Painters instructed by poets may try to get clear of that concentration on the world of visible corporeal existence which a Cézanne went in for with such heroic tenacity, and thus forget the primary requirement of painting's peculiar poetic intuition. Then, in quest of a direct attainment of the world of Being in its absolute universality, they will endeavor to go out of painting—only to slip into some kind of other of expressionist literature; or else, disappointed and discouraged, they will fall back on any new sort of academicism, covered by a pretense of freedom and a display of ideological tenets.

Poetic Intuition as Creative

12. My last remarks will deal with the second of the two aspects that can be distinguished in poetic intuition, namely poetic intuition as creative.

From the very start poetic intuition is turned toward operation. As soon as it exists, the instant it awakens the substance of the poet to itself and to an echoing secret of the reality, it is, in the depth of the nonconceptual life of the intellect, an incitation to create. This incitation can remain virtual. The poet, because poetic intuition is his ordinary frame of mind, is constantly open to such hidden incitations,

> *Tu lis les prospectus, les catalogues, les affiches*
> *qui chantent tout haut,*
> *Voilà la poésie ce matin . . .*[11]

and not all of them can pass to the act. Nay more, a poetic intuition can be kept in the soul a long time, latent (though never forgotten), till some day it will come out of sleep, and compel to creation. But at that moment there is no need of any additional element, it is only a question of application to actual exercise. Everything was already there, contained in poetic intuition, everything was given, all the vitality, all the insight, all the strength of creativity which is now in act, like a dart empowered with a power of intellectual direction; and in a certain sense (intensively—whatever part adventitious chance may have in the development) the totality of the work to be engendered was already present in advance, whether this totality is now virtually given in the first line of a poem, as a gift from the preconscious life of the soul, or virtually concentrated in the spiritual germ of a novel or a drama.

With respect to the work made, it might be said, it seems to me, that that element in beauty which is *integrity* has principally to do with poetic intuition as objectivizing itself into the action or the theme, whereas that element which is *radiance* has principally to do with poetic intuition in its native and original state. Hence it is that poetic intuition may happen to appear with striking radiance even in a poem lacking in integrity; and such splintered fragments, transparent to the rays of being, may be enough to reveal the pure essence of poetry. For nothing is more precious than a capture on the high seas of poetry, be it offered in a single line—

L'espoir luit comme un brin de paille dans l'étable . . .[12]

O Thou steeled Cognizance whose leap commits
The agile precincts of the lark's return . . .[13]

Odour of blood when Christ was slain
Made all Platonic tolerance vain.[14]

And I shall always prefer a haikai, if it has this kind of transparency, to a big noisy machine deafening me with ideas. Yet the fact remains that from the very start poetic intuition virtually contains and encompasses the poem as a whole, and demands to pass through it as a whole; when it does not succeed in appearing save in a fragmentary way, it is because it has been betrayed by the art of the poet.

13. Now a further issue must be examined. If we turn to the useful arts we observe that poetic knowledge or intu-

itive emotion is not in them the spiritual germ of the work to be made. Poetic intuition can play a part in them—then a concern for beauty will creep into them; but poetic intuition is not the determinative focus of their creativity. This determinative focus is what the Schoolmen called the *idea factiva,* say the "creative idea." They took care, moreover, to warn us that the craftsman's creative *idea* is in no way a *concept,* for it is neither cognitive nor representative, it is only generative; it does not tend to make our mind conformed to things, but to make a thing conformed to our mind. They never even used the word "idea" in the sense of "concept," as we have done since the time of Descartes. And so, if we may continue to speak of the craftsman's creative idea, it is on the condition that we be aware of the fact that this word idea is merely analogous when applied to that creative idea and to what we usually call ideas. The craftsman's creative idea is an intellectual form, or a spiritual matrix, containing implicitly, in its complex unity, the thing which, perhaps for the first time, will be brought into actual existence. And this creative idea pertains to the virtue of art, is involved in the virtue of art, is the initial determinative focus in the exercise of this virtue.

Well, by a most unfortunate occurrence, it happened that this same expression, creative idea, was transferred from the realm of the useful arts to the realm of the fine arts, better to say, of those arts which depend on the Platonic *mousikè,* or on poetry. As a result, the worst confusions came about. Theoreticians of art, mistaking this "idea" for a concept, fancied that the so-called creative idea was an ideal model sitting for the artist in his own brain, the work supposedly being a *copy* or portrait of it. This would make of art a cemetery of imitations. The work is an original, not a copy, and never has such a thing as this idea as model existed except in the mind of some aestheticians imbued with spurious Platonism, or some philosophers misreading the theological notion of the divine Ideas.

At the same time the expression "creative idea," which makes sense only as the craftsman's creative idea, was used to designate the poetic intuition itself in its creative aspect, the poetic intuition born in emotion, in the primeval sources of the preconscious life of the intellect. And poor Eckermann was to ask his wonderful Goethe what was the *idea* he had endeavored to embody in *Faust.* "As if I knew," Goethe answered, "as if I myself could tell! *From Heaven, through Earth, down to Hell,* there's an explanation, if you want one: but that is not the idea, that's the development of the action. . . ."

That was not the idea, for there was no idea, but only poetic intuition, which is in no way an idea. In reality—this is a point I shall emphasize again in the next chapter—poetic intuition transcends the virtue of art. And poetic intuition involves and contains within itself, in a superior state and eminent manner, *formaliter-eminenter,* as a scholastic would say, all that exists—and infinitely more (for it is both cognitive and creative)—in the craftsman's creative idea. It is enough for poetic intuition to pass to actual operative exercise; by the same stroke it will enter the sphere and dynamism of the virtue of art, whose more or less adequate means it will bring into play.[15]

14. Such is the case, indeed, with every genuine poet. Now not all artists and poets are genuine poets. What I mean is that, at the initial moment of the operative exercise, another process can take place. Then, the poetic intuition becomes a craftsman's creative idea, losing its inherent transcendence and descending, as it were, into the mechanical noise and the merely intellectual concerns for manufacturing with which the craftsman's creative idea is pregnant; and to the extent to which it becomes a craftsman's creative idea, the poetic intuition leaves behind many of its essentials, especially the creative power inherent in the superior unity of the grasping effected by poetic knowledge and intuitive emotion. This phenomenon comes about, it seems to me, when man, in a hurry to display his own energy and to produce something great, or because poetic intuition is weak in him, goes *beyond* poetic intuition, and, instead of listening to it,

endeavors to supplement it in his own way—not to speak of those in whom poetic intuition is simply lacking. Thus it is that we meet in bookstores, concerts, and exhibitions so many works which have nothing or little to say; and that in so many dramas there is plot but no action; and that in so many novels the characters are either creatures deprived of freedom which only execute the pre-established plan of a watchmaker god, or creatures wandering on the loose which ceaselessly escape the weak purposes of an impotent god. Only, I think, an exceptionally powerful poetic intuition can cause the relationship between the novelist and his characters to be what it must be—an image, I mean, of the relationship between the transcendent creative eternity of God and the free creatures who are both acting in liberty and firmly embraced by His purpose.

The remarks I just put forward give account, I believe, of a distinction which, like all essential distinctions, can be difficult of application of particular cases, but of which literary and art criticism has always been basically aware: on the one hand, the sons of *Mousikè*, the poets and creators (who can also be perfect craftsmen), and on the other hand the sons of *Technè*, the men of letters, or the professionals (who can also be bad craftsmen).

15. We may observe, in closing, that the craftsman's creative idea, which is part of the virtue of art, improves from the very fact that this virtue itself improves, both by exercise and by discipline.

On the other hand, poetic intuition can neither be learned nor improved by exercise and discipline, for it depends on a certain natural freedom of the soul and the imaginative faculties and on the natural strength of the intellect. It cannot be improved in itself, it demands only to be listened to. But the poet can make himself better prepared for or available to it by removing obstacles and noise. He can guard and protect it, and thus foster the spontaneous progress of its strength and purity in him. He can educate himself to it, by never betraying it (this is a serious school in discipline) and by making everything second to it (this is a serious school in sacrifice).

As to the operative exercise of poetic intuition, moreover, it can be improved by a certain humility, I don't mean with regard to men, but with regard to this intuition itself—and also by the work of intelligence and of the virtue of art dealing with the ways and means of execution. For poetic intuition, as concerns its operative exercise, perfects itself in the course of the artistic process. I do not mean that at the beginning poetic intuition is something either formless or fragmentary, as Claudel says—too harshly—of the results of inspiration (because he thinks only of what emerges as conceptually seizable into the field of consciousness); I mean that poetic intuition, though full and complete from the very start, involves, at the beginning, a great part of virtuality. It is with the steady labor of intelligence intent on the elaboration of the form that this virtuality contained in poetic intuition actualizes and unfolds itself all along the process of production. And then the very exercise of artistic science and intellectual perspicacity, choosing, judging, cutting out all the nonsignificant, the fat, the superfluous, causes—precisely because it is always listening to creative emotion and appealing to it—new partial flashes of poetic intuition to be released at each step of the work. Without this steady labor poetic intuition would not, as a rule, disclose its entire virtue.

But let us return to the intrinsic quality of poetic intuition itself in the poet, and to the question of its higher or lesser degree. What matters most in this connection is inner experience and its deepening into further and further recesses of subjectivity. Since poetic intuition is born in these recesses, where the intellect, the imagination, all the powers of the soul suffer in unity some reality of existence brought to them by intentional emotion, it involves first of all a certain alert receptivity. As the mystic suffers divine things, the poet is here to suffer the things of this world, and to suffer them so much that he is enabled to speak them and himself out. And when he is most engaged in the act of spiritual communication, it is because then he still suffers attentively an inexorable hand stronger than he, that passes and does not return. The degree of creative strength of poetic intuition is proportional to the degree of depth of such attentive passivity.

I should like to repeat at this point what I have tried to say in another essay.[16] "In order that there should grow unceasingly, conforming to its law, the life of the creative spirit, it is necessary that the center of subjectivity where this creative spirit awakens to itself in suffering the things of the world and those of the soul should unceasingly be deepened. In following this line of reflection one would probably be led to ask oneself whether, beyond a certain degree of depth, this progress in spirituality can continue unless, under one form or another, a religious experience properly so called helps the soul of the poet to quit the surface levels. Continuing at any price, refusing heroically to renounce the growth of the creative spirit, when one has nevertheless made impossible such an experience postulated by the whole being, wasn't this perhaps the secret of Nietzsche's disaster? In any case, what I want to keep in mind here, is that creation takes form at different levels within the spiritual fabric of the soul—everyone by this very fact confesses what he is. The more the poet grows, the deeper the level of creative intuition descends into the density of his soul. Where formerly he could be moved to song, he can do nothing now, he must dig down deeper. One would say that the shock of suffering and vision breaks down, one after another, the living sensitive partitions behind which his identity is hiding. He is harassed, he is tracked down, he is destroyed. Woe to him if in retiring into himself he finds a heaven devastated, inaccessible; he can do nothing then but sink into his hell. But if at the end of the ends the poet turns silent, it is not that the growth of which I speak may ever come to an end, it is not that of itself the song does not still ask to be more deeply born in him, less distant from the creative uncreated spirituality, archetype of all creative life: it is that the last partition of the heart has been attained, and the human substance consumed."

These lines, which deal with poetic intuition in general, were written in relation to music, and to Arthur Lourié, who to my mind provides us with the greatest example, in contemporary music, of that depth in creative inspiration of which I spoke.[17] The composer offers indeed a privileged experience to the speculations of the philosopher. Less bound to the universe of human ideas and human values than he who creates with the vocables of the language of men, less bound than the painter or the sculptor to the forms and images of things, less bound than the architect to the conditions for the use of the thing created, it is in the composer that are verified in the most limpid fashion the metaphysical exigencies of poetry. It is in him, when he falls short of them, that the gap is most apparent. None other than a maker of operas could instruct a Nietzsche by so perfectly decisive a disappointment.

The Creative Self and the Self-centered Ego

16. All the preceding considerations on poetic knowledge help us to understand the essential disinterestedness of poetic activity. They also oblige us to realize that a crucial distinction must be made between the creative Self and the self-centered ego.

This distinction has something to do with the metaphysical distinction between the human person *as person* and the human person *as individual*. Matter (in the Aristotelian sense of *materia prima*) is the primary root of individuality, and matter both longs for being (as a pure potency which has no determination of itself) and narrows being (which it limits to its own capacity or receptivity under given conditions). In each of us, individuality, being that which excludes from ourselves that which other men are, might be described as the narrowness of the ego, always threatened and always eager to grasp for itself. Personality, on the other hand, is rooted in the spirit inasmuch as the spirit holds itself in existence and superabounds in existence. It is the subsistence of the spiritual soul communicated to the whole fabric of the human being and holding it in unity, and it testifies to the generosity or expansiveness in being which pertains to its spiritual principle. Personality means interiority to oneself and requires at the same time the communications of knowledge and love. By the very fact that each of us is a person and has spiritual inwardness, each of us requires communication with *other* and *the others* in the order of knowledge and love; and the supreme act of the person as such as that giving of oneself which is one with love. The new and eternal name, inscribed on the white stone, which will be given us one day, and "which no one knoweth but he that receiveth it," reveals our personality. The name by which men know us, and which is inscribed on our passports, is but one of the designations of our individuality. "Thou art thyself though," Juliet said, "not a Montague. . . . Romeo, doff thy name; And for that name, which is no part of thee, Take all myself."

The creative Self of the artist is his person as *person*, in the act of spiritual communication, not his person as material individual or as self-centered ego.

Lionel de Fonseka asserts that "vulgarity always says *I*." Let us add that vulgarity says *one* also, and this is the same thing, for vulgarity's *I* is nothing but the self-centered ego, a neuter subject of predicates and phenomena, a subject as *matter*, marked with the opacity and voracity of matter, like the *I* of the egoist.

But in an entirely different manner poetry likewise always says *I*. "*My* heart hath uttered a good word," David sang, "Vivify *me* and *I* will keep Thy commandments." Poetry's *I* is the substantial depth of living and loving subjectivity, it is the creative Self, a subject as *act*, marked with the diaphaneity and expansiveness proper to the operations of the spirit. Poetry's *I* resembles in this respect the *I* of the saint, and likewise, although to quite other ends, it is a subject which gives.[18]

Thus, by necessity of nature, poetic activity is, of itself, disinterested. It engages the human Self in its deepest recesses, but in no way for the sake of the ego. The very engagement of the artists's Self in poetic activity, and the very revelation of the artist's Self in his work, together with the revelation of some particular meaning he has obscurely grasped in things, are for the sake of the work. The creative Self is both revealing itself and sacrificing itself, because it is *given;* it is drawn out of itself in that sort of ecstasy which is creation, it dies to itself in order to live in the work (how humbly and defenselessly).

This essential disinterestedness of the poetic act means that egoism is the natural enemy of poetic activity.

The artist as a man can be busy only with his craving for creation. He can say, like Baudelaire: "I don't give a damn for the human race," he can be concerned only with his work, like Proust, he can be an out-and-out egoist, as Goethe was: in his process of creation, inasmuch as he is an artist, he is not an egoist, he is disinterested in his ego.

But the artist as a man can have his craving for creation involved in the movement of expansion and generosity of a soul whose passions and ambitions are not those of an egoist. And such internal abundance and magnanimity is the normal and connatural climate of the virtue of art. Narrowness and avarice in human desires make it live in cold and sleet. After all Shelley was right in writing that the "state of mind" naturally linked with poetic inspiration "is at war with every base desire."

17. It is, I think, an effect of the essential disinterestedness of the poet in the very act of poetry, and an effect of his natural orientation toward creation, that the poets and artists of the past gave us such poor indications of their own inner creative experience. They spoke in the most conventional and shallow rhetoric and the most commonplace stock phrases—*nascuntur poetae,* the Muses, Caelestial Patroness, the Genius, the Poetic Faculty, the divine spark, later on the goddess Imagination—of this experience, which at least the

greatest among them lived in fact, to be sure, but which their conscious intellect did not seek to grasp. They were not interested in reflexive self-awareness. The *reflex age,* the age of *prise de conscience,* which roughly speaking began for mysticism at the time of St. Teresa of Ávila and St. John of the Cross, came later for poetry. When it began for it, at the time of Romanticism, it brought to completion the slow process of "revelation of the Self" which had developed in the course of modern centuries.

This revelation of the Self is a blessing inasmuch as it takes place in the genuine line of poetry. It becomes a curse when it shifts from the line of poetry, and of the creative Self in the fire of spiritual communication, to the line of man's material individuality, and of the self-centered ego, busy with self-interest and power. Then the egoism of man enters the sphere of the poetic act, and feeds on this very act. And being there in an unnatural state, it grows boundlessly. The poetic act itself, on the other hand, is insidiously wounded, even in great poets, as some points taken up in the next chapter will permit us to see.

The shift in question came about, in fact, simultaneously with the incomparable progress that poetry owes to the definitive revelation of the creative Self. That is one of the usual predicaments of human history. And nevertheless the essential disinterestedness of the poetic act is so ineradicable that the final result of this invasion by the human ego in the universe of art could not possibly be to make the artist into a *creative usurer* (that is a contradiction in terms); it was —I shall return to this point—to make him into a hero, a priest, or a savior, offering himself in sacrifice no longer to his work but both to the world and to his own glory.

TEXTS WITHOUT COMMENT
(for Chapter Four)

I

1. SHELLEY, in *A Defence of Poetry:*

Poetry defeats the curse which binds us to be subjected to the accident of surrounding impressions. And whether it spreads its own figured curtain, or withdraws life's dark veil from before the scene of things, it equally creates for us a being within our being. . . . It creates anew the universe, after it has been annihilated in our minds by the recurrence of impressions blunted by reiteration.

2. THOMAS DE QUINCEY, in *The Poetry of Pope:*

The Scriptures themselves never condescended to deal by suggestion or co-operation with the mere discursive understanding; when speaking of man in his intellectual capacity, the Scriptures speak not of the understanding, but of *"the understanding heart"*—making the heart, i.e., the great *intuitive* (or non-discursive) organ, to be the interchangeable formula for man in his highest state of capacity for the infinite.

3. EMERSON, in *The Poet:*

The poet has a new thought; he has a whole new experience to unfold; he will tell us how it was with him, and all men will be the richer in his fortune. For the experience of each new age requires a new confession, and the world seems always waiting for its poet. . . .

We are symbols and inhabit symbols; workmen, work, and tools, words and things, birth and death, all are emblems; but we sympathize with the symbols, and being infatuated with the economical use of things, we do not know that they are thoughts. The poet, by an ulterior intellectual perception, gives them a power which makes their old use forgotten, and puts eyes and a tongue into every dumb and inanimate object. . . . As the eyes of Lyncaeus were said to see through the earth, so the poet turns the world to glass, and shows us all things in their right series and procession. For through that better perception he stands one step nearer to things, and sees the flowing or metamorphosis. . . .

4. PAUL CLAUDEL, in *La Muse qui est la Grâce:*

Et cependant quand tu m'appelles ce n'est pas avec moi seulement qu'il faut répondre, mais avec tous les êtres qui m'entourent,

Un poème tout entier comme un seul mot tel qu'une cité dans son enceinte pareille au rond de la bouche.

Comme jadis le magistrat accomplissait le sacrifice du bœuf, du porc et du mouton,

Et moi c'est le monde tout entier qu'il me faut conduire à sa fin avec une hécatombe de paroles!

Je ne trouve ma nécessité qu'en toi que je ne vois point et toutes choses me sont nécessaires en toi que je ne vois point,

Elles ne sont pas faites pour moi, leur ordre n'est pas avec moi, mais avec la parole qui les a créées.

Tu le veux! il faut me donner enfin! et pour cela il faut me retrouver

En tout, qui de toutes choses latent suis le signe et la parcelle et l'hostie.

Qu'exiges-tu de moi? est-ce qu'il me faut créer le monde
pour le comprendre? Est-ce qu'il me faut engendrer le
monde et le faire sortir de mes entrailles?

. . . .

Ainsi je travaille et ne saurai point ce que j'ai fait, ainsi
l'esprit avec un spasme mortel

Jette la parole hors de lui comme une source qui ne con-
naît point

Autre chose que sa pression et le poids du ciel.[1]

5. ST. JOHN OF THE CROSS, in *Canciones entre el Alma y el
Esposo (Cantico Espiritual)*:

VII   Y todos cuantos vagan,
       De ti me van mil gracias refiriendo,
       Y todos más me llagan,
       Y déjame muriendo
       Un no sé qué quedan balbuciendo.

. . . .

XXXVI   Gocémonos, Amado,
       Y vámonos a ver en tu hermosura
       Al monte o al collado,
       Do mana el agua pura,
       Entremos más adentro en la espesura.

XXXVII   Y luego a las subidas
       Cavernas de la piedra nos iremos,
       Que están bien escondidas,
       Y allí nos entraremos,
       Y el mosto de granadas gustaremos.

XXXVIII   Allí me mostrarías
       Aquello que mi alma pretendía
       Y luego me darías
       Allí tú, vida mía,
       Aquello que me diste el otro día.

XXXIX   El aspirar del aire,
       El canto de la dulce filomena,

   El soto y su donaire,
   En la noche serena
   Con llama que consume y no da pena.

XL Que nadie lo miraba,
   Aminadab tampoco parecía,
   Y el cerco sosegaba,
   Y la caballería
   A vista de las aguas descendía.

———

VII All those that haunt the spot
   Recount your charm, and wound me worst of all
   Babbling I know not what
   Strange rapture, they recall,
   Which leaves me stretched and dying where I fall.

XXXVI Rejoice, my love, with me
   And in your beauty see us both reflected:
   By mountain-slope and lea,
   Where purest rills run free,
   We'll pass into the forest undetected:

XXXVII Then climb to lofty places
   Among the caves and boulders of the granite,
   Where every track effaces,
   And, entering, leave no traces,
   And revel in the wine of the pomegranate.

XXXVIII Up there, to me you'll show
   What my soul has longed for all the way:
   And there, my love, bestow
   The secret which you know
   And only spoke about the other day.

XXXIX The breathing air so keen;
   The song of Philomel: the waving charm
   Of groves in beauty seen:

The evening so serene,
With fire that can consume yet do no harm.

XL With none our peace offending,
Aminadab has vanished with his slaughters:
And now the siege had ending,
The cavalcades descending
Were seen within the precinct of the waters.[2]

6. GERARD MANLEY HOPKINS, *Carrion Comfort*:

Not, I'll not, carrion comfort, Despair, not feast on thee;
Not untwist—slack they may be—these last strands of man
In me ór, most weary, cry *I can no more*. I can;
Can something, hope, wish day come, not choose not to be.
But ah, but O thou terrible, why wouldst thou rude on me
Thy wring-world right foot rock? lay a lionlimb against me?
    scan
With darksome devouring eyes my bruisèd bones? and fan,
O in turns of tempest, me heaped there; me frantic to avoid
    thee and flee?

Why? That my chaff might fly; my grain lie, sheer and clear.
Nay in all that toil, that coil, since (seems) I kissed the rod,
Hand rather, my heart lo! lapped strength, stole joy, would
    laugh, chéer.
Cheer whom though? the hero whose heaven-handling flung
    me, fóot tród
Me? or me that fought him? O which one? is it each one?
    That night, that year
Of now done darkness I wretch lay wrestling with (my God!)
    my God.[3]

7. JULES SUPERVIELLE, *Les chevaux du temps*:

Quand les chevaux du Temps s'arrêtent à ma porte
J'hésite un peu toujours à les regarder boire
Puisque c'est de mon sang qu'ils étanchent leur soif.
Ils tournent vers ma face un œil reconnaissant

Pendant que leurs longs traits m'emplissent de faiblesse
Et me laissent si las, si seul et décevant
Qu'une nuit passagère envahit mes paupières
Et qu'il me faut soudain refaire en moi des forces
Pour qu'un jour où viendrait l'attelage assoiffé
Je puisse encore vivre et les désaltérer.[4]

8. EMILY DICKINSON, *The Chariot:*

> Because I could not stop for Death
> He kindly stopped for me;
> The carriage held but just ourselves
> And Immortality.
>
> We slowly drove, he knew no haste,
> And I had put away
> My labor, and my leisure too,
> For his civility.
>
> We passed the school where children played,
> Their lessons scarcely done;
> We passed the fields of gazing grain,
> We passed the setting sun.
>
> We paused before a house that seemed
> A swelling of the ground;
> The roof was scarcely visible,
> The cornice but a mound.
>
> Since then 'tis centuries; but each
> Feels shorter than the day
> I first surmised the horses' heads
> Were toward eternity.[5]

9. PIERRE REVERDY, *Le Cœur écartelé:*

> Il se ménage tellement
> Il a si peur des couvertures
> Les couvertures bleues du ciel
> Et les oreillers de nuages

Il est mal couvert par sa foi
Il craint tant les pas de travers
Et les rues taillées dans la glace
Il est trop petit pour l'hiver
Il a tellement peur du froid
Il est transparent dans sa glace
Il est si vague qu'il se perd
Le temps le roule sous ses vagues
Parfois son sang coule à l'envers
Et ses larmes tachent le linge
Sa main cueille les arbres verts
Et les bouquets d'algues des plages
Sa foi est un buisson d'épines
Ses mains saignent contre son cœur
Ses yeux ont perdu la lumière
Et ses pieds traînent sur la mer
Comme las bras morts des pieuvres
Il est perdu dans l'univers
Il se heurte contre les villes
Contre lui-même et ses travers
Priez donc pour que le Seigneur
Efface jusqu'au souvenir
De lui-même dans sa mémoire.[6]

10. RAÏSSA MARITAIN, *De Profundis:*

Dieu mon Dieu la distance entre nous n'est
    pas tolérable
Montrez-moi le chemin droit et nu et totalement
    véritable
Le chemin de mon âme à votre esprit sans
    aucun intermédiaire
De ce que les hommes ont construit entre
    le ciel et la terre
Je suis pauvre et dépouillée et tout me
    blesse
Tout est trop dur de ce qui se dit et trop
    humain pour ma détresse
La douleur m'a ravi mon enfance

Je ne suis plus qu'une âme en deuil de
 sa joie
Dans la terrible et stricte voie
Où vit à peine l'espérance
Tout juste de quoi lever les yeux vers vous
 et ma solitude est totale
Et ces ténèbres sont sur moi comme une pierre
 sacrificielle et tombale
Comment avoir accès auprès de vous par
 delà les symboles
Et connaître sans nulle erreur la vérité
 de votre Parole
Tout ce qui se dit de vous est sacrilège
Et ce que vous-même avez prononcé par nos
 mots un mystère infini le protège
Et pendant que vous vous enveloppez
 de toutes ces ombres
Le monde que vous avez fait resplendit de
 ses étoiles sans nombre
Et le vertige de l'abîme saisit mon âme
Et je crie vers vous mon Dieu
Du fond de l'abîme.[7]

III

11. WILLIAM BLAKE, *Auguries of Innocence:*

To see a World in a Grain of Sand,
And a Heaven in a Wild Flower,
Hold Infinity in the palm of your hand,
And Eternity in an hour.
A Robin Redbreast in a Cage
Puts all Heaven in a Rage.

. . . .

A Skylark wounded in the wing,
A Cherubim does cease to sing.

. . . .

Joy and Woe are woven fine,
A Clothing for the soul divine;

Under every grief and pine
Runs a joy with silken twine.

. . . .

Every Morn and every Night
Some are Born to Sweet Delight.
Some are Born to Sweet Delight,
Some are Born to Endless Night.

12. VAN GOGH, in a *Letter to Theo* (Arles, 1888):

'To express hope by some star, the eagerness of a soul by a sunset radiance.[8]

13. KEATS, in the *Ode to a Nightingale:*

Darkling I listen; and, for many a time
    I have been half in love with easeful Death,
Call'd him soft names in many a mused rhyme,
    To take into the air my quiet breath;
Now more than ever seems it rich to die,
    To cease upon the midnight with no pain,
        While thou art pouring forth thy soul abroad
            In such an ecstasy!
    Still wouldst thou sing, and I have ears in vain—
        To thy high requiem become a sod.

. . . .

Forlorn! the very word is like a bell
    To toll me back from thee to my sole self!
Adieu! the fancy cannot cheat so well
    As she is fam'd to do, deceiving elf.
Adieu! adieu! thy plaintive anthem fades
    Past the near meadows, over the still stream,
        Up the hill-side; and now 'tis buried deep
            In the next valley-glades:
    Was it a vision, or a waking dream?
        Fled is that music:—Do I wake or sleep?

14. JULES SUPERVIELLE, *Un Poète:*

Je ne vais pas toujours seul au fond de moi-même
Et j'entraîne avec moi plus d'un être vivant.

Ceux qui seront entrés dans mes froides cavernes
Sont-ils sûrs d'en sortir même pour un moment?
J'entasse dans ma nuit, comme un vaisseau qui sombre,
Pêle-mêle, les passagers et les marins.
Et j'éteins la lumière aux yeux, dans les cabines,
Je me fais des amis des grandes profondeurs.[9]

15. MAX JACOB, in *Devant une colonne blanche d'église:*

Je suis mourant d'avoir compris
Que notre terre n'est d'aucun prix.[10]

16. GEORGE MEREDITH, *Dirge in Woods:*

A wind sways the pines,
   And below
Not a breath of wild air;
Still as the mosses that glow
On the flooring and over the lines
Of the roots here and there.
The pine-tree drops its dead;
They are quiet, as under the sea.
Overhead, overhead
Rushes life in a race,
As the clouds the clouds chase;
   And we go,
And we drop like the fruits of the tree,
   Even we,
   Even so.[11]

17. RAÏSSA MARITAIN, *Le Quatrième Jour:*

J'ai vu la terre en sa beauté native
Elle émergeait de l'océan fleuri
Partout des arbres aux verdures vives
Composaient de clairs paradis

(Ainsi le songe nous emporte
Bien loin de tous les temps connus

Il ouvre ses portes dorées
Sur des spectacles abolis)

Je traversais des espaces immenses
Sans nul effort emportée et ravie
En moi naissaient les rythmes de la danse
Et les voix de la mélodie

Vers moi venaient les bois et les prairies
Et les gazons nommés dans la Genèse
Et les fleuves roulant sans bruit
Et les monts colorés de neige

Un air pensif flottait dans la lumière
Comme un gai visage rêveur
Des chants élevaient leurs vagues légères
Mais invisibles étaient les chanteurs

Sans nul désir et toute amour donnée
Je reposais dans la pleine envolée
De toutes choses vers le Créateur
Dans l'unité se tenait le bonheur

La joie montait—ivresse transparente
Rose de feu dans le souffle du vent
Seul mon cœur était lourd de connaissance
Et du poids de notre sang

Des mots nouveaux jaillissaient de mes lèvres
De saveur infinie et de sens éternel
Un hymne intelligible émanait de la terre
Langage d'avant la brisure de Babel

Mais les ondes de la connaissance
Sont venues me frapper en retour
Entre la science et la nescience
L'âme désaccordée
Je m'éveillai au sixième jour.[12]

18. JOHN CROWE RANSOM, in *The Equilibrists*:

In Heaven you have heard no marriage is,
No white flesh tinder to your lecheries,
Your male and female tissue sweetly shaped
Sublimed away, and furious blood escaped.

Great lovers lie in Hell, the stubborn ones
Infatuate of the flesh upon the bones;
Stuprate, they rend each other when they kiss,
The pieces kiss again, no end to this.

But still I watched them spinning, orbited nice.
Their flames were not more radiant than their ice.
I dug in the quiet earth and wrought the tomb
And made these lines to memorize their doom:—[13]

EPITAPH

Equilibrists lie here; stranger, tread light;
Close, but untouching in each other's sight;
Mouldered the lips and ashy the tall skull,
Let them lie perilous and beautiful.

19. LÉON-PAUL FARGUE, *Postface*:

Un long bras timbré d'or glisse du haut des arbres
Et commence à descendre et tinte dans les branches.
Les fleurs et les feuilles se pressent et s'entendent.
J'ai vu l'orvet glisser dans la douceur du soir.
Diane sur l'étang se penche et met son masque.
Un soulier de satin court dans la clairière
Comme un rappel du ciel qui rejoint l'horizon.
Les barques de la nuit sont prêtes à partir.
D'autres viendront s'asseoir sur la chaise de fer.
D'autres verront cela quand je ne serai plus.
La lumière oubliera ceux qui l'ont tant aimée.
Nul appel ne viendra rallumer nos visages.
Nul sanglot ne fera retentir notre amour.
Nos fenêtres seront éteintes.

Un couple d'étrangers longera la rue grise.
Les voix
D'autres voix chanteront, d'autres yéux pleureront
Dans une maison neuve.
Tout sera consommé, tout sera pardonné,
La peine sera fraîche et la forêt nouvelle,
Et peut-être qu'un jour, pour de nouveax amis,
Dieu tiendra ce bonheur qu'il nous avait promis.[14]

FIVE

POETRY AND BEAUTY

The Philosophical Concept of Beauty

1. I am aware that it is old-fashioned to hold forth on beauty apropos of art, almost as much so as to speak of truth apropos of philosophy. The discussion attempted in this chapter has perhaps a chance to elucidate this fact a little.

"Without beauty," Plotinus said, "what would become of being? Without being what would become of beauty?" And Plato: "Love of beauty set in order the empire of the gods—as is evident, for of deformity there is no love." Before Plato Greek thinkers seemed hardly concerned with beauty. It is through Plato that beauty irrupted into metaphysics. Our Western tradition has long been nourished by a theory of beauty which originates in him, and has been elaborated by the architects of perennial philosophy. In order to clarify the concepts we are using, I shall refer to that theory as summed up and formulated in Thomas Aquinas' teachings.

The beautiful, he said, is *"id quod visum placet,"* that which, being seen, pleases: a statement which encompasses the essentials of Beauty—as well as the misfortunes it entails, since as far back as the Trojan War, and before.[1] Beauty consists of intuitive knowledge, and delight. Beauty makes us delighted in the very act of knowing—a delight which overflows from the thing this act attains.

Now, that which knows, in the full sense of this word, is intelligence. Intelligence, then, is the proper perceiving power, the sense, as it were, of the beautiful. If beauty delights the intellect, it is because it essentially means a certain excellence in the proportion of things to the intellect. Hence the three essential characteristics or integral elements traditionally recognized in beauty: *integrity,* because the intellect is pleased in fullness of Being; *proportion or consonance,* because the intellect is pleased in order and unity; and *radiance or clarity,* because the intellect is pleased in light, or in that which, emanating from things, causes intelligence to see.[2]

This element of radiance or clarity, which relates to the most essential yearning of the intellect, and is, therefore, the most important, is also the most difficult to explain. If we were able fully to realize the implications of the Aristotelian notion of *form*—which does not mean external form but, on the contrary, the inner ontological principle which determines things in their essences and qualities, and through which they are, and exist, and act—we would also understand the full meaning intended by the great Schoolmen when they described the radiance or clarity inherent in beauty as *splendor formae,*[3] the splendor of the form, say the splendor of the secrets of being radiating into intelligence. Thus the very words we are obliged to use—the clarity, radiance, light, splendor—could be terribly misleading, if we came to forget that being is intelligible *in itself,* but not necessarily *for us,* and remains most often obscure to us, either because its intelligibility in itself is obscured in matter or because it is too high and too pure for our intellect. Descartes, with his clear ideas, divorced intelligence from mystery. Modern science is making us aware of his mistake. The Schoolmen, when they defined beauty by the radiance of the form, in reality defined it by the radiance of a mystery.

2. Obviously, the three characteristics in question must be understood in their largest significance, and not in any

narrowly delimited specification. Each one of them is realized in an infinity of various manners, as well as beauty itself. In other words, these notions are not univocal, but analogous notions. The beauty of a bunch of flowers or of a landscape is not the same as the beauty of a mathematical demonstration or the beauty of an act of generosity, or the beauty of a human being. They all are beauty, but kinds of beauty typically or basically different from one another, which imply no univocal community in species, genus, or category. (And yet, because of the analogical community involved in beauty, they may happen surreptitiously to evoke one another in our mind: hence an ambiguity by which the poet will profit.)

The reason for this analogous character of beauty lies in the fact that beauty belongs in the realm of transcendentals,[4] of those "passions or properties of being," as the Schoolmen said—Unity, Truth, Goodness—which are but various aspects of Being—Being as undivided, Being as confronting the power of knowledge, Being as confronting the power of desire—and which are, in actual fact, one with Being, and as infinite as Being itself, in so far as they are considered in their metaphysical reality. It may be said that Beauty is the radiance of all transcendentals united.

Now the essential characteristic of transcendentals is the fact that they cannot be enclosed in any class; they transcend or go beyond any genus or category, because they permeate or imbue everything, and are present in any thing whatsoever. Thus, just as everything *is* in its own way, and is *good* in its own way, so everything is beautiful in its own way. And just as being is present everywhere, and everywhere diversified, so beauty spills over or spreads everywhere, and is everywhere diversified.

From this transcendental nature of beauty the ancients concluded that the attribute of beauty can and must belong to the Prime Cause, the Pure Act, who is the *supreme analogate* of all transcendental perfections; and that beauty is one of the Divine Names. It is in his treatise on the Trinity, and in order to show that beauty is not only a perfection of Divine Nature, but is also to be ascribed, in a more appropriate manner, to the Person of the Son, that Thomas Aquinas has enumerated the three essential components of beauty. It was obvious to him, as to Dante, that, as he put it, the "beauty of anything created is nothing else than a similarity of divine beauty participated in by things," so that, in the last analysis, "the existence of all things derives from divine beauty." [5]

3. At this point it may be added that in the eyes of God all that exists is beautiful, to the very extent to which it participates in being. For the beauty that God beholds is transcendental beauty, which permeates every existent, to one degree or another.

This is not the beauty that our senses perceive, and here we are obliged to introduce a new idea, the idea of aesthetic beauty, as contradistinguished to transcendental beauty. For when it comes to aesthetic beauty, we have to do with a province of beauty in which senses and sense perception play an essential part, and in which, as a result, not all things are beautiful. The presence of the senses, which depends on our fleshly constitution, is inherently involved in the notion of aesthetic beauty. I would say that aesthetic beauty, which is not all beauty for man but which is the beauty most naturally proportioned to the human mind, is a particular determination of transcendental beauty: it is transcendental beauty as confronting not simply the intellect, but the intellect and the sense acting together in one single act; say, it is transcendental beauty confronting the sense as imbued with intelligence, or intellection as engaged in sense perception. As a result, in the realm of aesthetic beauty, that is, with respect to the requirements of the intelligence-permeated sense, or with respect to what does or does not fit human senses, things divide into beautiful and ugly. It is with respect to man, or to the intelligence-permeated sense, that things divide into these two categories.

Here we meet with the category of the Ugly, the Foul, the Disgusting, the Nasty, the Filthy, the Gluey, the Viscous, and the Nauseous. Jean-Paul Sartre is quite right in recognizing it as a category in existence. But the fact is that this category of the Ugly has no sense for a pure spirit, and no sense for God. Because a pure spirit sees everything in a merely intellectual, not sensitive manner. Ugly is what, being seen, displeases: where there are no senses, there is no category of ugliness. There are things deprived in some respect of due proportion, radiance, or integrity, but in which Being still abounds, and which keep on pleasing the sight to that very extent. For a pure intellect, everything is a kind of spatial-temporal number, as Pythagoras saw it. Number, measure, position in space-time, physical energies and qualities, it is in these terms that a pure intellect knows material things. Being this, all are beautiful, and there is nothing ugly in nature. In the eyes of God all things are more or less beautiful, none is ugly.[6]

But *we* know through our senses. And no doubt many ugly or disgusting things are noxious to man. But not all of them are, and if they are ugly, disgusting, or nauseous, it is not because they are noxious, it is essentially because they are repugnant to the inner proportion or harmony of the sense itself; for the sense, as St. Thomas puts it, is a sort of logos or ratio. We may observe at this point that art endeavors to imitate in its own way the condition peculiar to the pure spirits: it draws beauty from ugly things and monsters, it tries to overcome the division between beautiful and ugly by absorbing ugliness in a superior species of beauty, and by transferring us *beyond* the (aesthetic) beautiful and ugly. In other words, art struggles to surmount the distinction between aesthetic beauty and transcendental beauty and to absorb aesthetic beauty in transcendental beauty.

This is a token both of its own spirituality, and of the indestructible relationship of beauty, even aesthetic beauty, to the kingdom of intelligence, to which it belongs and in which it is rooted. For the beauty of sensible things is not perceived by senses only but, as I noted a moment ago, by the sense as a sharp point of the intellect intent on the world of experience—by the sense as permeated by intelligence and intellection. Hence it is that beauty keeps its transcendental essence, as well as its essentially analogous character, even when encompassed within the limits of aesthetic beauty. This transcendental and analogous character even appears to man in the most striking manner in artistic beauty because, there, beauty, in order to exist in a thing, was previously conceived and nurtured in a human intellect. Then, the intellect, confronting a work born out of man, finds itself in the most appropriate condition to experience, through the intuition of the sense, a delectation both of the sense and intelligence —that delectation which, according to Poussin, is the aim of art; and the more it becomes acquainted with the works of human art, the more it becomes aware of the transcendental and analogous nature of beauty.

It is by virtue of this essential analogousness that art is striving ceaselessly to discover new analogates of beauty, and that a canvas of Goya has integrity, consonance, and radiance as well as—though quite differently from—a Chinese drawing or a Rembrandt painting. And it is by virtue of this transcendental nature of beauty, even aesthetic beauty, that all great poetry awakes in us, one way or another, the sense of our mysterious identity, and draws us toward the sources of being. One remembers the page where Baudelaire, to whom modern art owes its having become aware of the theological quality and tyrannical spirituality of beauty, translated into his own language a passage from Poe's "The Poetic Principle." It is the instinct for beauty, he said, "which makes us consider the world and its pageants as a glimpse of, a *correspondence* with, Heaven. . . . It is at once by poetry and *through* poetry, by music and *through* music, that the soul divines what splendors shine behind the tomb; and when an exquisite poem brings tears to the eyes, such tears are not the sign of an excess of joy, they are rather a witness to an irritated melancholy, an exigency of nerves, a nature exiled in the imperfect which would possess immediately, on this very earth, a paradise revealed." [7]

Here perhaps we can best realize why beauty does not mean simply perfection. For anything perfect in every respect in its own genus—anything "totally perfect" on earth —is both totally terminated and without any lack, therefore *leaves nothing to be desired*—and therefore lacks that longing and "irritated melancholy" of which Baudelaire spoke, and which is essential to beauty here below. It is lacking a lack. A lack is lacking in any totally perfect performance (with all due respect to Toscanini). A totally perfect finite thing is untrue to the transcendental nature of beauty. And nothing is more precious than a certain sacred weakness, and *that kind* of imperfection through which infinity wounds the finite.

Thus it is that if grace is beauty in motion, grace, as Plotinus put it, is better than beauty, that is, Greek totally perfect or immobile beauty. Beauty moves, and "Beauty limps." [8] And does not, in quite another order, contemplation also limp? Just as Jacob limped after his struggle with the Angel, St. Thomas says, the contemplative limps in one foot, for having known God's sweetness he remains weak on the side that leans on the world.

Beauty Is Not the Object, but the "End Beyond the End" of Poetry

4. We are now in a position, I hope, to tackle a particularly delicate issue, namely the relation between poetry and beauty. I have a notion that something can be said on the matter, but the region is perilous and the vocabulary inadequate.

In a previous chapter we related poetry to the free (nonconceptual) life of the intellect and the free creativity of the spirit. I think that, therefore, the starting point for our considerations must be the notion of the creativity of the spirit, or of the urge and tendency to express, manifest, and create which is one with the nature of the intellect.

I do not forget that another urge and tendency is one, also, with the nature of the intellect: the urge and tendency to know. Cognitivity and creativity are the two essential aspects of the intellectual nature.

Now let us consider these two aspects of the intellect in three significant instances: Science, Art, and Poetry (poetry as distinct from art, and quickening all the arts).

In the case of science, the creative function deals with the production, within the mind, of concepts, judgments, and reasonings by means of which things are known, or intellectually seen. The intellect knows by producing the "mental word" or concept, and it produces the "mental word" or concept by knowing—that is a single and indivisible operation:[9] the creative function of the intellect is entirely subordinate to its cognitive function. It is for the sake of knowledge to be engendered and expressed within the mind that the concepts are produced. And these fruits of the creativity of the spirit, as well as the immanent activity of knowing, in which they are involved, are formed and perfected inside the soul.

In the case of art, on the contrary, the cognitive function of the intellect is entirely subordinate to its creative function. The intellect knows in order to create. It is for the sake of the work to be made that both previously acquired knowledge and artistic knowledge come into play, and that the rules of making are discovered and applied. And the fruit of the creativity of the spirit is the work, which is caused to exist outside the soul.

In the case of poetry, the cognitive function of the intellect comes into play in *poetic intuition;* and the creativity of the spirit is *free* creativity.

5. It is with this free creativity of the spirit, essential to poetry, that I am concerned. What is its significance, what are its implications, in so far as it is contradistinguished, or opposed, to the creativity of the spirit in science and in art?

My contention is that in science and in art the creativity of the spirit is not free—I don't mean, of course, in the sense that it does not enjoy the spontaneity of the most autonomous life of which man is capable—I mean in the quite precise sense that in science and in art the creativity of the spirit is *subordinate* to an *object,* which holds command and mastery.

Science has an object, which is infinite: Being to conquer. And the creativity of the intellect is, there, entirely subordinate to its cognitivity, and both creativity and cognitivity are entirely subordinate to this object, which is independent of them, and with which they must make themselves consonant and commensurate.

Art, also, has an object, which is finite and enclosed in a genus: the work to be made. Then, the creativity of the intellect, to which its cognitivity is subordinate, is itself subordinate to this object, which must be good, and on the good of which this creativity is all intent. All the activity of art is specified and formed by the rules intended for the object to be made to exist. Here again the object is master.

But poetry has no object. And that's why, in poetry, the creativity of the spirit is *free* creativity.

Poetry, as distinct from art, has no object. I mean to say that in the case of poetry, there is nothing to which the creativity of the spirit tends so as to be *specified* and *formed,* nothing which originally plays with regard to this creativity a specifying or formally determining part; nothing, then, which may exercise command or mastery over it. In poetry, there is only the urge to give expression to that knowledge which is poetic intuition, and in which both the subjectivity of the poet and the realities of the world awake obscurely in a single awakening.

Well, poetry has no object. But the free creativity of the intellect, as soon as it comes into play, cannot help tending, by virtue of an implied necessity, toward that in which the intellect has its ultimate exultation, in other words, that which causes the pleasure or delight of the intellect. Thus beauty is not the *object* of poetry, it is—here I am groping for an appropriate word; I shall say that beauty is—the transcendental *correlative* of poetry. Beauty is not an object, even infinite (as Being is for science), which specifies poetry, and to which poetry is subordinate. But beauty is a necessary correlative for poetry. It is like its native climate and the air it naturally breathes in, nay more, it is as life and existence are for a runner running toward the goal—an end beyond the end. For poetry there is no goal, no specifying end.[10] But there is an *end beyond*. Beauty is the necessary *correlative* and *end beyond any end* of poetry.

On the other hand, if in poetry the creativity of the spirit has no object, this means that by that very fact poetry has to make or create an object for itself.[11] For no power can proceed to act without an object. Poetry must, by reason of abundance, make or create an object for itself. Thus poetry is engaged, by necessity of nature, in a dynamic trend which is the trend of art: the expression it yearns to give to poetic intuition will necessarily be something *made,* and passing outside. Poetry is committed to the productive activity of art; it cannot escape its role as motive spirit which is destined to quicken art and, therefore, which knows in order to terminate in utterance and production.

My first conclusion, then, is that poetry, in the tendential movement which is inherent in every thing created, tends to beauty as to its natural correlative, and to an end beyond any end; and that poetry is engaged by nature in the movement of art striving toward production.

6. Yet there is an opposite side. On the one hand poetry, though engaged in the movement of art, transcends art, and so is attached to it not as a soul animating a body but rather as those separate spirits which in old astronomy moved the celestial bodies. For the activity of art is specified by an object, which is a work enclosed in a genus and which dominates as a master; and the activity of art is engrossed in the making of this object, and needs to use in the process the rules of making. But, as we have seen, poetry in its pure essence, or as the prime actuation of the free creativity of the spirit, has neither object nor master, is not at the service of any work to be made, and knows no rule, except poetic intuition,[12] which is poetry itself. Thus, though it is committed to the productive activity of art, poetry remains essentially superior to this productive activity, and remains

always free with respect to it, in the sense that it moves and directs and masters it at its own sweet will.

On the other hand, if it is true that poetry in its pure essense, or as the prime actuation of the free creativity of the spirit, has no object; if it is true that poetry does not tend toward beauty as toward an object which specifies it and which exercises command and mastery over it—how, then, can we characterize the relationship between beauty and poetry? Here again, I don't feel at ease with the vocabulary. Poetry is not *subordinate* to beauty: I would say, therefore, that poetry is on terms of *coequality* or *connaturality* with beauty: they love one another without any subordination, and without any definite purpose. Poetry tends toward beauty, not as toward an object to be known or to be made, or a definite end to be attained in knowledge or realized in existence, but as toward that very life of yours which is in the one whom love has transformed into another yourself. That is the end beyond any end of which I spoke.[13] To transform it into a definite end possible of direct attainment would be spoiling the relationship I have tried to bring out, and would be deficient in respect both to Poetry and to Beauty. For Beauty cannot be attained except as in a mirror, and is still escaping our grasp, and Poetry is not directed to any definite end. Poetic intuition is not ordained to beauty as to a specifying end or object, it only wants to manifest the inwardness of the poet together with the things which resound in it—and if poetic intuition is *really* expressed it will inevitably be expressed in beauty, even without meaning it, for any real expression of poetic intuition derives from it integrity, consonance, and radiance.

Thus my second conclusion is that poetry transcends art while being committed to it, like an imaginary separate intellect committed to create a world; and that poetry is with beauty on terms of coequality and connaturality, and therefore cannot live except in beauty. Poetry cannot do without beauty, not because it is submitted to beauty as an object, but because poetry is in love with beauty, and beauty in love with poetry.[14]

7. The previous considerations help us, probably, to realize how philosophy succeeds in making difficult issues a little more obscure. Yet it seems to me that they help me to understand more clearly the following facts.

First. If the fine arts are able to behave in accordance with their name, and to engender in beauty, this is, in the last analysis, because the virtue of art, at its very origin, in the soul, is moved by the grace of poetry.

Second. But the fine arts, like every kind of art, intend more immediately (though less profoundly) to produce a *good* work than to produce a beautiful work: not, I mean, by reason of any disregard for beauty, rather by reason of fear and trembling.

Third. As a matter of fact, to the very extent to which the fine arts make beauty an object, *their* object, and in tending toward beauty forget that beauty is *more* than their operational end—being the end beyond the end—they recede from beauty, and deviate toward academicism; that is to say, they tend to "produce beauty," which is a transcendental, in the manner in which a workman produces a bicycle or a watch, which is a work enclosed in a genus. Academicism is thus the proper perversion of the fine arts. Art engenders in beauty, it does not produce beauty as an object of making or as a thing contained in a genus.[15] A village ironsmith, if he has sensitivity in his soul and his hands, creates, because he obeys an instinct of poetry, something more beautiful than most of the products of which, as a rule, the studious students of our modern schools of fine arts are capable.

Fourth. Furthermore, just as the grace of poetry can and demands to quicken any kind of art, so any kind of art can, and aspires to, engender in beauty. As a result, to engender in beauty is not a special property of the fine arts, and it seems that the fine arts have no domain of their own. Conversely, the part played by utility—as is obvious in architecture—or by any sort of human concerns and interests is or can be as great in the fine arts as in the useful arts, so that it seems that the useful arts have no domain of their own either.

Fifth. The trouble started from an insufficiently precise vocabulary. The fine arts, to be sure, have essentially to do with beauty. But no transcendental, even aesthetic beauty,[16] can be used to define a genus, since transcendentals permeate all genera. Thus in a rigorous use of terms it would be better to define the fine arts with respect to some particular difference in that generic quality, the good of the work, which pertains to the artifact as artifact, or as object of making, and direct terminus of the process of production. I would say that the good of the work, which is the aim of every art, depends *more,* in certain arts, on its relations to the needs of human life, and on the fact of the work being *good for something else;* and that, in certain other arts, the good of the work succeeds *more* in being a *good in itself and for itself,* a world of its own—whatever the relations it can and must continue to have with the concerns of human life may be. When the good of the work reaches such self-interiority, the art involved is not subservient, but free, as is the case with architecture and still more with painting and sculpture (which are happier, moreover, in serving the purposes of architecture than in enjoying the false freedom of museums), and still more in music and poetry.

As regards the names to be used, I would prefer to call the first category *subservient arts,* and the second *free* or *self-sufficient arts.* (This second category is part of the "liberal arts"; it is this group of liberal arts which are concerned with producing an external work.) Poetry and beauty walk everywhere in the realm of art. But in those self-sufficient arts poetry is freer, and more prepared to master everything. And beauty demands more despotically, not to be "produced as an object of making, but to be loved, and mirrored in the work.

Sixth—and last. During long periods in human history, it was by men who did not claim to be artists creating in beauty, and who had no awareness that they were at the service of the beautiful, that masterworks in beauty were produced. As I noted in the first chapter, in an attempt at general characterization, one might say, no doubt a little too systematically, that in India the virtue of art itself did not strive toward beauty except by stealth, or in so far as a root tendency broke its way through its inner self-imposed discipline. In this sense neither Indian *art* nor the Indian *artist* were seeking after beauty. And if both Chinese *art* and Medieval *art* were seeking after beauty in an unconscious manner—in other words, if the virtue of art, more freed than in India from total subservience to a spiritual practical result to be achieved in the beholders' souls, tended then more freely, in its own inner dynamism, to the end beyond the end— nevertheless neither the Chinese *artist* nor the Medieval *artist* were consciously seeking after beauty; they considered themselves craftsmen, and they consciously sought only to do a good work.

It is only in Greece, and in modern times since the Renaissance, that the process of *prise de conscience* developed in this regard, and that both art and the artist set about consciously seeking after beauty. In perverted (academicist) periods, they sought after beauty as a thing to be produced. In genuine epochs, they with full purpose and awareness sought after beauty as an infinite to be mirrored in the work, or participated in by it. And this was of itself progress of invaluable significance, a kind of epiphany of the natural spirituality of art. Yet it was paid for by no fewer risks. Once the artist became a priest performing the rites of beauty, it was difficult for him not to adore beauty. And once beauty was made into a goddess, it was difficult for the artist, when later on he continued advancing in self-awareness and in the discovery of his own spiritual powers, not to quarrel with the goddess, and sometimes to be fed up with her, and sometimes to break with beauty, or keep house with beauty only grudgingly and spitefully, because he had fallen in love with some foreign seducer, closer to man than to art.

The Spiritual Experience of Modern Poetry

8. Baudelaire was aware, too aware, of the kind of transcendental indifference which beauty, as the end beyond the end of poetry, enjoys with regard to human things:

> *Tu marches sur des morts, Beauté, dont tu te moques;*
> *De tes bijoux l'Horreur n'est pas le moins charmant,*
> *Et le Meurtre, parmi tes plus chères breloques,*
> *Sur ton ventre orgueilleux danse amoureusement.*

He knew that beauty is one of the Divine Names. But the fact with which his own experience was obsessed and which his extraordinary power of perception made clear—and this event has a crucial significance for poetry in modern times—is that now this Divine Name is detached from God, and reigns *separate* in our human heaven. Where Thomas Aquinas had said: "The existence of all things derives from God's beauty," Baudelaire says: *"Que tu viennes du ciel ou de l'enfer, qu'importe,"*—whether beauty comes from heaven or hell, what do we care?—it is always beauty; and the devil is still beautiful. Beauty thus became the all-exacting idol of art. Yet when a Divine Name detached from God falls on earth, it shows a strange, ambiguous face to men, and faces itself a strange, ambiguous destiny.

I need not insist on the historic importance of the process of self-awareness which poetry has experienced in modern times. This process had begun before Baudelaire, with the German Romantics, Novalis, Tieck, Hölderlin, on whom Albert Béguin's book[17] brings us significant data. Edgar Allan Poe and Nerval played their part in it. But it is after Baudelaire that it took on its full dimensions. As a result, poetry entered a state of spiritual ambivalence which is extraordinarily significant. Because its own spirituality was revealed to it, poetry was engaged more and more deeply, more and more irremediably, in a spiritual experience of its own. But while descending into spiritual experience, one inevitably meets with the enigma of destiny, and with the prime questions and choices which hold sway over existence. By virtue of the option made in these depths, the spiritual experience of modern poetry has been ambivalent, and this basic ambivalence has been inevitably revealed by the two directions, more and more definite, in which poetry has simultaneously moved forward, in proportion as the poets were more and more aware of their fundamental options and committed themselves more profoundly to them. Hence it is that finally the spiritual experience of modern poetry is double-faced and self-divided; while determining itself, and this is its grandeur, with respect to the Prime Being, it has here the countenance of the ardor in refusal, there the countenance of the ardor in acceptance.

Modern poetry cannot be judged and understood in the perspective of classical aesthetics and mere literature. We might as well ask a butterfly hunter to catch an octopus or a whale. In the seemingly purely verbal researches of a Mallarmé or a Valéry, a crucial spiritual experience and the consciousness of a tragic struggle were involved. Nothing is more significant in this regard than the letter in which Mallarmé tells his friend Cazalis of his struggle with God: *ma lutte terrible avec ce vieux et méchant plumage, terrassé heureusement, Dieu!"* [18] "I fell, victorious," he goes on to say. "I am now impersonal, and no longer Stephan, whom you knew—but an aptitude which the spiritual universe possesses to see itself and to develop, through that which was me"—*"à travers ce qui fut moi."* As a result he is perfectly dead, *"je suis parfaitement mort."* And he will give expression to the Universe in three poems in verse "of purity that man has not reached," and in "four poems in prose, on the spiritual conception of Nothingness." His *Hérodiade* was to say:

> *Mais avant, si tu veux, clos les volets, l'azur*
> *Séraphique sourit dans les vitres profondes,*
> *Et je déteste, moi, le bel azur!*

He also took his stand against "the beautiful azure." And as for Paul Valéry, it is enough to read his last book, *Mon Faust,* to realize the seriousness of the spiritual struggle of a man who all his life endeavored to be more intelligent than both Faust and Mephistopheles.

With Mallarmé and Valéry, the option for the rejection of transcendence taught modern poetry the experience of the void (and also, as concerns Mallarmé, a faint hope in magic). I wonder whether the Olympus of words to whose mysterious rites the great mind of Joyce dedicated itself did not emerge from some similar experience of the void— and a haunting memory of a lost paradise guarded by the sword of a fiery Irish angel.

With D. H. Lawrence the option of which I am speaking taught poetry the experience of an intolerable solitude craving for mystical fusion with the demonism of Nature. With Lautréamont it had taught poetry the experience of revolt, and of a letting loose of hate and blasphemy which proves that the reality of God has always haunted this horrified poet, who could not accept being the son of Man and Woman: *"Je suis le fils de l'homme et de la femme, d'après ce qu'on m'a dit; ça m'étonne. Je croyais être davantage,"* and who told us, as Léon Bloy put it, "the good tidings of damnation." The appeal of the spiritual experience of atheism had been felt by modern poetry long before these poets—did not Jean Paul Richter, in his famous dream, hear Jesus bathed in tears answering mankind, from the summit of the world: "We are all orphans, you and I, we are without a father"? And this appeal continued after them, and is still continuing. I am not sure that in this very appeal an obscure, or reversed, longing for faith is not sometimes commingled. But if it ever exists, such longing is repressed as a temptation of weakness—with the eagerness of a soul pledged to some unbending inner exigency.[19]

In the other direction, it was another appeal, no less definite, no less imperious, to another spiritual experience, that modern poetry felt. The option for the reality of the Absolute taught it either its own evangelic affinities, or the experience of the presence of God and the wounds of the Redeemer, or that of a contemplative knowledge of the soul and the world. The inner struggles and ventures of

Francis Thompson and Hopkins, Verlaine and Max Jacob, Milosz and Léon Bloy, Eliot, Claudel, and Péguy, are also an essential part of the spiritual experience of modern poetry.

And even if there were no definite or no lasting option, we know that many poets in our times, by seeking poetic purity, were prepared unawares to be seduced one day by the promise of another purity, which is no less exacting. "Because Poetry, my God, it is you," as Cocteau put it at the end of *Orpheus*. And he also wrote, many years ago: "Literature is impossible. We must get out of it. No use trying to get out through more literature; only love and faith allow us to get out of ourselves." If among the promises of a recent past many failed to materialize, at least suffering and nostalgia never fail poets. The nostalgia that appears in a Unamuno, still more in an Alexander Blok or a Michaux, or a Reverdy, witnesses to the abiding élan of their spiritual experience. The sad world itself of our day may stir in poets an instinct from the beyond.

> *A King of speechless clods and infants. Still*
> *The world out-Herods Herod; and the year*
> *The nineteen-hundred-forty-fifth of grace,*
> *Lumbers with losses up the clinkered hill*
> *Of our purgation; and the oxen near*
> *The worn foundations of their dwelling-place,*
> *The holy manger where their bed is corn*
> *And holly torn for Christmas. If they die,*
> *As Jesus, in the harness, who will mourn?*
> *Lamb of the shepherds, Child, how still you lie.*[20]

"*Tu es en nous, Seigneur,*" a French poet writes "*et dans ce moment où l'absurdité nous paraît si totale que nous n'attendons plus rien de rien fût-ce de la mort, où nous sommes au-delà du dernier gémissement de la bête, vivant d'une inexistence vitreuse infiniment docile à n'importe quoi voici qu'à la surface de cette vase que nous formons crèvent déjà des bulles de parole tout irisées des couleurs du ciel. . . .*"[21] And the ancient longing of the soul *in terra aliena* is still alive:

May my bones burn and ravens eat my flesh
If I forget thee, contemplation!
May language perish from my tongue
If I do not remember thee, O Sion, city of vision,
Whose heights have windows finer than the firmament
When night pours down her canticles
And peace sings on thy watchtowers like the stars of Job.[22]

Thus appears, through the two lineages I just mentioned, the ambivalence of modern poetry's spiritual experience. The most striking sign of it is the fact that Rimbaud, the same Rimbaud, was a revealing light both for Claudel and André Breton.

Now my point is that modern poetry has shown a similar ambivalence with regard to Beauty. Feeling more and more deeply the fact, which I have tried to stress, of beauty's being an end beyond any end, modern poetry has either adored beauty, and striven after it with desperate effort—through spiritual experience—(think of Baudelaire or Mallarmé)—or modern poetry has concentrated exclusively on spiritual experience, and left everything for it, and so was diverted from the end beyond any end, disregarding as far as possible and ignoring beauty, or pretending to despise it—think for instance of Dadaist poetry, or of one of the most remarkable contemporary poets, Henri Michaux, intent only on digging for the roots of the poetic state, tearing the veil of Hermes, rummaging in his own heart and exorcizing its monsters. *"L'exorcisme, réaction en force, en attaque de bélier, est le véritable poème du prisonnier. Dans le lieu même de la souffrance et de l'idée fixe, on introduit une exaltation telle, une si magnifique violence, unies au martèlement des mots, que le mal progressivement dissou est remplacé par une boule aérienne et démoniaque—état merveilleux!"* [23]

I do not disregard the fact that by virtue of the tendency of our human language spontaneously to depreciate, the word beauty has not uncommonly lost its genuine transcendental sense, coming to designate only a particular sort of beauty, the most obvious one, that special kind of regularity, soundness and freshness which distinguishes in Nature a beautiful thing from an ugly one, and which pleases even the most uneducated eye; hence we have the "shapely," the "handsome," or the "pretty," or still worse the "charming," which are hardly artistic categories.

But the phenomenon I am speaking of is much deeper and incomparably more important. It is with beauty in its genuine transcendental sense that certain of the most significant elements of modern art have fallen out, because other constellations, especially knowledge and self-knowledge, and other supreme ends have arisen in the heaven of the poet.

The Craving for Magical Knowledge and the Dismissal of Beauty

9. It was inevitable that somewhere a tragedy should occur. The origin of this tragedy can be traced back to Rimbaud. It was not the tragedy of modern art and poetry. But it was, in a small group of poets and poetry lovers, a tragedy of the human spirit.

Let us think of the nature of poetic knowledge, as we discussed it in the last chapter. An obscure knowledge through inclination—born in the preconscious of the spirit—in which the world is known *in and through* the subjectivity, grasped both together and inseparably by means of an emotion become intentional and intuitive. Such a knowledge is utterly different from what we ordinarily call knowledge, it is more experience than knowledge. It is neither conceptual nor conceptualizable; it is ineffable in itself, expressible only in signs and images and, finally, only in a work made. But precisely because it is not abstractive nor rational, it has no intelligible boundaries, and expands, as it were, to the infinite.

And now, suppose that this poetic knowledge not only becomes conscious of itself but takes itself as its own aim. What will the result be? Rimbaud gives the answer. The famous "Lettre du Voyant" says all that can be wanted on the subject. "The first study of the man who wants to be a poet is his own self-knowledge, total. He seeks his soul, he scrutinizes it, tempts it, learns it. As soon as he knows it, he must cultivate it. This seems simple. . . . But what is required is to make the soul monstrous. . . . I say that one must be a seer, make oneself a seer. The poet makes himself a seer through a long, immense, and reasoned out dislocation of all the senses. . . . He becomes beyond all others the great Invalid, the great Criminal, the great Accursed One—and the supreme Knower! For he reaches the unknown. And even if, demented, he loses at last the understanding of his visions, well, he has seen them! Let him be blasted while leaping among things unheard of and nameless: there will come other horrible laborers; they will begin at the horizons where the other collapsed."

I insisted, in the second part of this chapter, that poetry, though transcending art, is committed by nature to the productive activity of art, engaged by nature in a dynamic trend which is the dynamic trend of art tending to engender a work. No doubt one can be a poet without producing any work; but if one is a poet, one is virtually turned toward operation: it is essential to poetry, in the tendential movement through which everything created goes toward completion, to move in the direction of operation, as the sap of a tree moves toward the fruit. But when it becomes conscious of itself, and of its power to know, poetry is released, in some measure, and for a time, from this dynamic tendency, to the extent that knowing oneself means turning back upon oneself. And then, at that moment, poetry enters into a kind of conflict with art, with art to which it is committed: whereas art demands to shape an object, poetry demands to be passive, to listen, to descend to the roots of being, to the unknown which no idea can circumscribe. All that is simply natural—one of the natural tensions and crises in the life of the spirit.

But if poetry yields to an invasion of vertigo? If it loses its footing? Then it is cut off from any operative end. Breaking its natural ties, and driven back on itself in an unnatural movement of inversion, it only yearns to *know*. This is, I think, what came about in the experience of Rimbaud, and gives it such crucial significance. If we do not take his state-ments as a romantic and juvenile exaggeration (a too easy way of escape, indeed), if we take them seriously, as we must do, we must say that what Rimbaud experienced—and taught—was a definite, perfectly conscious and reasoned out decision to turn poetic knowledge into absolute knowledge, and to make of poetry, contrary to its nature, a means of *science*. And then, since the process is unnatural, and since poetic knowledge, which does not proceed by objectivization, is ignorant of any objective limitation, poetry thus out of joint will develop a monstrous appetite for knowledge, a vampire's appetite which will drain man body and soul. It will claim for itself all the living springs and the gift of heroic life, it will wish to be all things and to provide all things—act, holiness, transubstantiation, and miracle; it will assume the burden of humanity.

10. Rimbaud had too great lucidity. He ceased to write. Other laborers came, who began at the horizons where he had collapsed. His technique of dislocation of all the senses was succeeded by Breton's various techniques of disinte-gration or Dali's theory of "critical-paranoiac activity." If I am speaking, once again, of the Surrealists, it is because they offer to us a particularly typical experiment, showing what poetic knowledge can become when, cut off from its natural ends, it turns into a means of science, and is trans-formed into absolute knowledge.

The first implication of the event is that poetry and poetic knowledge reject henceforth the natural necessity which causes them, because they have no object, to make an object for themselves, and thus to enter the operative dynamism of art and the working reason. Poetry, henceforth, yearns to know, not to make. It breaks with art as a practical virtue of the intellect. Art itself is no longer interested in the work as an end, the work becomes only a means of communicat-ing knowledge, a kind of miraculous preaching.

The second implication is that poetry and poetic knowl-edge, which naturally demand to engender in beauty, refusing now to engender, have no longer any interest in beauty. They repudiate their tendency to and their relation of co-equality and connaturality with the transcendental which is their correlative and their end beyond any end. The end, henceforth, is absolute knowledge, not beauty. Poetry proceeds decidedly to the dismissal of beauty. The divinity which Baudelaire adored is cast down. It would be a shame for the poet even to think of beauty. He is the revealer of absolute knowledge.

Thus, poetic knowledge tends no longer to an object to be produced. And it does not tend to an object made intelligible in a concept and grasped by the logical instruments of reason, since it is by itself knowledge through inclination, not through concepts and reason. As a result, *science,* the kind of science unnaturally required of poetic knowledge, is identified with *power*. Furthermore, in poetic knowledge things are known as resounding in the subjectivity, and as one with it, and this knowledge—essentially obscure—is expressed, not through abstract ideas, but through the images awakened by intuitive emotion. As a result, science, the kind of science unnaturally required of poetic knowledge, is to be ruled by the law of images for which there is no principle of noncontradiction, and for which the sign contains and conveys the very reality of the thing signified. In other words, poetic knowledge transformed into absolute knowledge is magical knowledge.[24] Hence it is that Surrealism is so basically intent on magic, sorcery, fortune-telling, crystal-gazing, trance-speaking, as well as on occultism and any kind of hermetic gnosis; this passion for magical knowledge is in no way accidental; and it is with as much seriousness as credulity that André Breton states that the only incentive of surrealist activity is a hope to determine, and reach the *point suprême* in which *yes* and *no* are fused together, and from which, for the Cabbala, the entire world is engendered.

Surrealism has separated poetic knowledge from beauty, and from any transcendental end. The final end and center, then, can only be man, and the revelation of man, to be brought about by the disorganization of all his psychic and moral organism, releasing the magical powers of the unconscious. And the genuine revelation aimed at by poetry—that revelation, in a work of art, of the spiritual depths of the human subjectivity awakened to the world by intuitive emotion—becomes the message of the *hasard objectif*—of the mysterious intentions ascribed to chance, and the torrent of dark forces in which man and the world communicate—transmitted by automatic writing.

And through the way of destruction man, like the mythical phoenix, will finally be transfigured into light, be given back all the power he was capable of ascribing to God. Thus the achievement of a work, which is the genuine glory of the artist, is replaced by the quest for the human subject's omnipotence.

And the delectation that beauty gives is replaced by the delight of experience of supreme freedom in the night of subjectivity. Are not the first fruits of the future transfiguration to be attained in that state which Breton describes as "an annihilation of being into an internal and blind glittering which is no more the soul of ice than that of fire"? A strange sentence, which in its cryptic way points to the great secret of magical gnosis—that spiritual experience of the blind glitter of nothingness, in which all differences are abolished and all contradictions made one, by virtue of the void, and in which the soul believes it is transferred above everything and enjoys infinite liberty. This is the black mysticism in which poetic knowledge transformed into absolute knowledge finally winds up.

The dismissal of beauty is dearly paid. Poetry is used for ends contrary to its nature, and subdued to a craving for a false knowledge of which it is supposedly the source. For all that, poetry is not destroyed, poetry still exists, in a state of feverish exaltation of the dreaming faculty, I don't mean only in the artists more or less engaged in Surrealism, who in actual fact, when they produce, don't care very much for the doctrine, I mean in Surrealist experience itself. But, as I observed in a previous chapter, the poetic workings have been displaced to the outside, they are expected from the *hasard objectif* and the marvelous of the world. Within the soul, poetry has become but an empty perceptivity; and the power of the void, which it enjoys, is able to develop in the senses a wonderfully acute *taste,* and to foster perfect despair, and to kill a number of young men with remarkable accuracy.

11. The case of Surrealism is interesting because it provides an outstanding opportunity to test any philosophy of poetic knowledge. It is, moreover, a quite exceptional case. The world today does not risk perishing through an excess of poetry, even poetry gone mad. And the big forces which tend both to the deification and the destruction of man, and of which Surrealism is a particular symptom, are in possession of singularly larger and more powerful means of realization.

In one respect especially the Surrealists were prophets of the modern world—namely with regard to the repudiation of beauty. But they dismissed beauty for the sake of magical knowledge, whereas the modern world, with infinitely greater success, dismisses beauty for the sake of nothing except hard labor. Let us consider this fact. The dismissal of beauty is quite a dangerous thing—if not for art, which *cannot* in reality divorce beauty, at least for humanity. For, as Thomas Aquinas puts it, man cannot live without delectation, and when the spiritual delectations are lacking, he passes to the carnal ones.

One of the vicious trends which outrage our modern industrial civilization is a kind of asceticism at the service of the useful, a kind of unholy mortification for the sake of no superior life. Men are still capable of excitation and relaxation, but almost deprived of any pleasure and rest of the soul—a life which would seem insane even to the great materialists of antiquity. They flog themselves, they renounce the sweetness of the world and all the ornaments of the terrestrial abode, *omnem ornatum saeculi,* with the single incentive of working, working, working, and acquiring technological empire over matter. Their daily life lacks nothing so much as the delectations of the intelligence-permeated sense; and even the churches in which they pray are not uncommonly masterworks in ugliness. Then, since we cannot live without delectation, they have no other resource left but those arts and pleasures which satisfy "the brute curiosity of an *animal's* stare"—all the better as they produce stupefaction and obliviousness, as a substitute for Epicurean ataraxy. No wonder that other kinds of drugs, from alcohol or marijuana to the cult of carnal Venus, occupy a growing place in the process of compensation.

The dehumanizing process I just mentioned can be overcome. Art in this connection has an outstanding mission. It is the most natural power of healing and agent of spiritualization needed by the human community.

Yet not only are the opposite forces now quite strong, but there are some serious impediments in relation to art itself, especially to the free or self-sufficient arts, the arts of *mousikè,* which matter above all. On the one hand the creative research of modern art seems to carry it along further and further from the capacity of appreciation of what we call today the masses (though if a work, especially a picture, is blessed with poetic intuition, it has a chance to face less prejudice in the simply uneducated man than in an educated man who is an ignoramus in art). On the other hand art, as our previous analyses have shown, has its own difficulties with beauty, which are in no way slight. The subject of the present chapter obliges us to insist on this latter point.

As regards, not our culture as a whole, but art in its actual operation, the dismissal of beauty is an accident, and, to a large extent, wishful thinking and self-delusion. Art, as long as it remains art, cannot help being intent on beauty. The great modern artists are, to be sure, as intent on beauty as their predecessors, though in another manner. But many of them, especially in the field of poetry and literary creation, are divided unto themselves. They have not dismissed beauty, but they are at the same time under the sway of another passion and craving. What I said a moment ago about Surrealism related to an out-and-out effort to get rid of the division by rejecting one of the two terms in mutual conflict. Modern literature as a whole has simply accepted its state of inner division, as a result of a general trend which remained confused and multiform and which the Surrealists alone carried to an extremity by throwing both art and poetry out of gear, and simply proceeding, at least in their dogma, to the dismissal of beauty.

To have the artist himself become, as Blackmur puts it, the hero manifested through the work, was the final result toward which this general trend tended. A phenomenon which can be described as a shift toward the human ego, and an overturn or "catastrophe" of that advent of the creative Self in art which I tried to outline in the first chapter. In its pure line and genuine direction, this advent of the Self had to do with the act of poetic knowledge and the creativity of the spirit grasping obscurely, through the Self, both Things and the Self, and revealing both in the work, for the sake of the work. To prevent such a considerable spiritual adventure from deviating toward *amor sui,* and a confession or rather an epiphany of the ego offered to the world, for the sake of the human subject, not of the work, required, to tell the truth, a great deal of fortitude in the artist. Even those to whom we are most indebted risked being more or less wounded. Rousseau's *Confessions* have in this respect the value of a tremendous signpost. We remember his celebrated hymn to himself:

"I want to show my fellows a man in all truth to nature. And that man will be myself. Myself alone. I feel my heart and I know men. I am made like none of those whom I have seen; I dare to think that I am made like none that are. If I am not of more account, at least I am different. Whether Nature did well or ill to break the mould in which she cast me, can only be judged when I have been read.

"Let the trumpet of the last judgment sound when it will, *I shall come to appear before the sovereign judge with this book in my hand. . . .*" The poor man! A book in his hands.

Yet this astonishing sentence is perhaps the deepest disclosure of the heart, and the desolate grandeur, of the modern artist. Proust died correcting the proofs of his last book.

"I shall say boldly," Jean-Jacques went on to state, "this is what I have done, what I thought, what I was. I have told with equal candor good and ill . . . have shown myself just as I was. . . . Gather round me the countless multitudes of my fellow creatures; let them hear my confessions, let them lament my infamies, let them blush for my meannesses. Let each of them in his turn disclose his heart at the foot of Your throne *with the same sincerity,* and then let but one of them say, if he dare, 'I was better than that man.' "

Thus was to make its appearance the shibboleth of *sincerity,* Gidian sincerity, in modern art. And at the same time the true kind of heroism—*in relation to the work*—which is required from the poet and to which the greatest modern artists have been incomparable witnesses, was to be usurped and superseded in many cases by the fraudulent heroism of the self-centered ego, and the poet's delusive endeavor to perform an heroic function *in relation to his own Self* as image of man and mankind's liberator. "With the Romantic period, when the historical sense came in, a new decision was taken: that the artist himself might be a hero, as Byron, Goethe, Hugo were themselves heroes greater than any of the heroes in their works. Motive and conscience had got outside the works. . . . Arnold was making his claims that poetry might save the world by taking on the jobs of all the other functions of the mind at the expressive level." [25] After a while "the artist became the hero-*manqué,* the *poète-maudit,* and celebrated himself, or prototypes of himself, in his works. Then with the rise of Symbolism and of Art-for-Art's-Sake the heroes of a considerable body of works began to be portrayed as artists. The subject of the artist and of the special sensibility of the artist began to be the heroic subject and the heroic sensibility which best expressed society itself. The hero was expression, without need either of motive or of conscience. . . . Hence it is that the problem of the artist became a version of the problem of man and that the proper human heroism should seem to find itself in the heroism of the artist. . . . Not only is the artist isolated and the hero of all his knowledge, but he finds that he has upon his hands the task of the deliberate creation of conscience in a conscienceless society." [26]

In his essay on "La Crise du concept de littérature," [27] Jacques Rivière had similarly pointed out: "It is only with Romanticism that the literary act began to be conceived as a kind of assault on the absolute, and its result as a revelation"—not the genuine "revelation" involved in poetic knowledge, but rather a pseudoprophetic revelation, bound up with magic and the search for transmuting reality through the power of words, [28] which was to be made in the Surrealist theory into the magical revelation of absolute knowledge. "The writer," Rivière went on to say, "has become a priest. . . . All of nineteenth-century literature is a vast incantation towards the miracle."

I have previously noticed the basic ambivalence of the spiritual experience of modern poetry. At this point we are confronted with a new sort of ambivalence. On the one hand the work is so magnified that it must call forth the miracle. On the other hand the search for the miracle makes the work of no interest. On the one hand beauty becomes the great provider of the miracle. On the other hand the search for the miracle supplants the search for beauty. The consequence, observable in a number of modern writers, has been not a dismissal of beauty nor of the work, but a weakening in the movement toward beauty, together with a weakening in the movement toward the work, or a kind of desertion of the work as master object to which the operative intellect is vowed. The hero writer is more interested in constructing his own image as an example, for the generations to come, of a martyr in printed paper—at least this was so some decades ago. Now he seems concerned with less arduous forms of devotion, and prefers either using printed matter for the psychotherapeutic release of the repressed dreams and sex obsessions of his tormented reader or fostering, in the service of mankind and his ego together, that confusion of art and partisanship to which the *littérature engagée* seems committed.

On the other hand, the initial cause of the trouble heralded by Rousseau—the accidental shift from the creative Self to the self-centered ego—has naturally entailed another shift: from creative emotion as intentional means or vehicle of poetic knowledge, to brute or merely subjective emotion as sheer psychological phenomenon become the matter of the work and a *thing* to be expressed by it. As a result modern literature, in its lower moments, has been invaded by a double disease: emotionalism (that is, search after and communication of brute emotion blurring or replacing the creativity of the intellect and the purity of poetic intuition) and, at the same time, shallow intellectualism (that is, falling back on the empty contrivances of a merely constructive or critical reason estranged from the heart, to make up for the weakening of intuitive reason and of the intellect's genuine creativity stirred by creative emotion and poetic experience).

Let us not forget, nevertheless, that all above-mentioned shifts and swervings are accidental disorders which thwart, conceal, and obscure in modern culture the great essential fact: the spiritual advent, not of the self-centered ego, but of creative subjectivity. Given the misery of the human condition, these disorders appear as a ransom paid to our weaknesses for the invaluable advance achieved in the self-awareness of art and poetry. The basic significance of modern art lies in this advance, and in the effort to discover and penetrate and set free the active mystery of poetic knowledge and poetic intuition. There would be no more unfortunate error than to mistake the wounds from which modern art is suffering for the substance of the élan that they threaten and mask.

SIX

BEAUTY AND MODERN PAINTING

New Thresholds, New Anatomies

1. Painters as well as writers are exposed to suffer the inner division whose symptoms were a particular feature of the nineteenth century, and to be deceived by the myth of the artist as a hero; but less so, I think, than poets and writers: because they can less easily shift toward the spiritual glorification of the ego, being bound, willy-nilly, to the world of visible matter and corporeal existence, to *Nature*. Yet this very fact is for modern painting a source of unheard of difficulties in the very line of its own creative development. The obligation to recast the visible fabric of things in order to make them an expression of creative subjectivity entails now inevitable drawbacks, now accidental failures, and causes many victims.

The first victim was the human figure. The impotency of modern art to engender in beauty except at the expense of the beauty of the human figure is a disquieting symptom. If it is true that the human body is the most beautiful work in natural creation; and that the human face is naturally sacred, because it is the visible sign and the natural sacrament of human personality, and because in it an immortal soul shows through—then the impotency I just mentioned, and which can be found, to one degree or another, in all great contemporary painters, cannot be considered a slight defect. The fact was, no doubt, inevitable: precisely because the human figure carries the intrinsic exigencies of natural beauty to a supreme degree of integration, it is particularly difficult to recast its visible fabric except in deforming it. Will this difficulty be overcome some day? As long as it is not, that is, as long as the recasting in question has not become, as it was in El Greco, a change into something more human than the human appearance, modern painting will be in possession of every means to express spirituality, save the most normal one.

I just spoke of the great contemporary painters. In them the impotency not to impoverish or damage the form of man, either by blotting out its richness in significance, or by brutalizing or distorting it, is only a lack as a rule.

In the later manner of Picasso, it has become the expression of a positive aggressiveness, but always subordinate to the liberty of the creative line, and to that other kind of poetic freedom which is *black humor,* and to an inherent sense of beauty (not as to these disfigured human bodies, but as to the work as a whole). Yet we have also to do today with a particularly unfortunate, and illegitimate, progeny of great contemporary painters—the School of Degradation, I would say—and with the avid followers who mistook Picasso's cruel hieroglyphs for animal frenzy. They have found in his lesson a means of releasing the resentments of a boorish soul and of getting at little cost the admiration of an idiotic public. They cling furiously to the human figure, but to make it into a putrid foetus or a disintegrated lizard or kangaroo armed with pincers and topped by a stupid eye or a fiendish set of teeth. Where Heraclitus had said, "The most beautiful of the apes is hideous in comparison with the human race," they offer us a human race hideous in comparison with the ugliest of the apes. These painters, without being Surrealists, enforce in practice, not only with regard to man's face and body, but with regard to the very work, the surrealist dismissal of beauty, and they probably believe they convey a prophetic message to mankind. They are of interest mainly to anthropologists, who may compare their mental processes with that through which, in Tantrist or in Aztec sculpture, the human countenance became a magical instrument for fright and terror, and contempt for man. (But then, at least, the work itself had sometimes its own beauty.)

2. What matters to us is that there are other painters, who really count in the movement of creative research, and who keep on being intent on doing a work, and being intent on beauty. These painters have been confronted with a growing difficulty inseparable from the advance of modern painting: namely the fact that, in proportion as the creativity of the spirit strives for greater and greater liberation in order for the Self to be revealed in the work, Nature discloses greater obstacles, or rather demands from poetic intuition a ceaselessly growing power, in order for things to be grasped, and expressed in the work, without hampering or thwarting the simultaneous expression of subjectivity and the freedom of the creative spirit. What was twenty years ago an invaluable conquest over naturalism will seem now still tainted with naturalism. Any representation whatever of natural appearances is seen as an obstacle to the free creativity of the spirit. And it is, in actual fact, as long as it has not yet been purified and transfigured in the pungent night of creative intuition. The road of creative intuition, however, is exacting and solitary, it is the road to the unknown, it passes through the sufferings of the spirit. Artists are always tempted to prefer the road of technical discoveries.

Cubism set out to transpose natural appearances by decomposing and reshaping them in reference to the free expansion of forms and volumes in a newly organized space, which depends on the construction requirements of painting-as-painting, and makes our vision less bound to the limitations and opacity of matter (may it be possible to have all the sides of an object simultaneously present to the eye!). It provided us in this way with a number of admirable paintings.

Futurism, less fortunate as a rule in its achievements, except for some remarkable pictures of Severini's,[1] attempted a similar transposition in reference to the lively shiftings and mutual interpenetration of visual impressions produced by motion.

While dislocating natural appearances, neither Cubism nor Futurism did actually break with them. They tried to bring out from them a new visual significance—but by making this effort only with respect to external sensibility, and by relying finally on the discovery of a new technique, new tricks and means. It was possible for a Chagall or a Malevich to denounce Cubism's obdurate naturalism.

Then there was, for a few years, another school—a one-man school, to tell the truth—which I should like to call the School of Transmutation. I am alluding to Marcel Duchamp's[2] radical experiment. I take it here as an instance of a possible theory which it is of philosophical interest to disengage in its generality. I imagine that, from this point of view, we might express this attempt at integral transmutation in the following way.

The painter looks at Things, at the universe of visible Being—intent to grasp in it some reality beyond appearances and some hidden meaning. He receives the poetic spark (even though charged perhaps with a somewhat sadistic electricity). Then he sets out to express what he has grasped, not by simply transposing the natural appearances of the objects involved, but by using the totally different appearances of other objects belonging in a totally separate sphere—without any flash of intuitive similarity springing forth between these distant objects: so that the secret reality grasped in Being will be expressed, enigmatically, through a totally new creation totally contrived by his own spirit. A bride will become an insidious machine whose anatomy displays an ironical and icy complication of cylinders, pipes, and bevel gears.

Natural appearances will be totally transmuted into forms which pertain to another world of objects. The painter is an alchemist. He transmutes lead into gold, or gold into lead, kings, queens, and nudes into the volumes and surfaces of imaginary engines in motion, through which the ambiguous reality intended by him and the successive moments of its manifestation in time and movement are spread out in space.

Such an attempt was logically conceivable. It had an exceptional theoretical interest. It was indeed an attempt at the impossible. For the entire process runs against the nature of our spiritual faculties.

Creative intuition and imagination do not proceed in an angelic or demonic manner. They are human, bound to the alertness of sense perception. They grasp a certain transapparent reality through the instrumentality of the eye and of certain natural appearances—they cannot express or manifest it except through the instrumentality of these same natural appearances, recreated, recast, transposed of course, not cast aside and totally replaced by other appearances proper to another realm of Things in the world of visible Being. It's as good as having the soul of a flower in an elephant. In genuine metaphor the illuminating image arrives from another world, as a bird through the window of your room, to quicken the transposition of natural appearances and their power of significance: it supersedes them only for an instant, it does not suppress them. Here, on the contrary, there is no illumination, nor illuminating image. The Thing within which creative intuition has caught its diamond is not illuminated, it is killed. The other Thing which has been conjured up does not suggest it, it absorbs it, and expresses it only in secret cipher. The process cuts off in human art the intellect from its inescapable connection with sense perception. It is unnatural in itself.

As a matter of fact, notwithstanding the homage paid by Neoromantic and Surrealist critics to Marcel Duchamp, we must observe that in his own work poetic intuition, strong as it may have been at the start, is in reality quickly superseded by pure intellectuality. Even at the initial moment, in the germinal grasping, there is more of an intellectual scheme or an idea (the craftsman idea) than of poetic knowledge. The spiritual spark was less revealing than contriving—contriving the ironical or cynical concept of a formula of transmutation. And what appears striking in the execution of the work is not attentiveness to the impalpable spirituality of creative emotion, but rather—together with a half sarcastic obsession with machinery and the devices of engineering—an extremely careful elaboration, a patient preparation of sketches and well-calculated essays, winding up in the production of some shady sophisticated myth, like that myth of the "celibate machine," doubtless highly typical of our time, which has captured the imagination of high-browed gapers fond of hermetic marvels.

Be that as it may, an attempt at the impossible is apt to win admirers, not followers. Only Marcel Duchamp, with the enigmatic gifts of a searching mind, was able to instruct us about the significance of transmutation as a solution to the difficulties of modern painting. His experiment was bound to remain solitary. Even he himself stopped painting. After the few works which for some years impassioned Paris's esoteric circles, he gave up creative art [3] for another art of calculation, in which he had always been interested. He is now playing chess in New York.

Nonrepresentative Beauty

3. It is still in a prolongation of Cubism that painting has continued to seek the seemingly unattainable way out of its present predicament. Is some other solution possible? Is there not a short cut? It is no longer a question of attempting the impossible, but rather of rejecting part of too heavy a burden. Let us turn away from Things, and from any concern for grasping in them any transapparent reality and hidden meaning. Let us by the same token give up completely, or as completely as possible, natural appearances as transposed and transfigured as they may be, and any representation of

Things. Let us renounce the existential world of Nature completely, or as completely as possible. Will not art be revealed at last in its true essence, be freed at last from any trace of naturalism, express at last freely the free creativity of the spirit and the release of creative subjectivity?

It is in this way, I think, that the notion of nonrepresentative art imposed itself on the initiators of the School of Abstraction. And here we have what I would call the genuine concept of abstract art. Modern abstract art is subjective in intention, quite contrary to the objective abstract art of Islam. But modern abstract art, in so far as it is true to its original concept, implies in no way a repudiation of beauty. On the contrary, if it divorces itself from the Things of Nature, it is with a view to being more fully true to the free creativity of the spirit, that is, to poetry, and therefore to tend toward beauty, the end beyond the end of poetry, in a manner more faithful to the infinite amplitude of beauty. That's why I would say in this connection nonrepresentative or nonfigurative beauty as well as nonrepresentative or nonfigurative art.

"Suprematism"—another word for abstract art—"Suprematism," wrote Malevich, "is the rediscovery of that pure art which in the course of time, and by an accretion of 'things,' had been lost to sight. . . . The happy liberating touch of nonobjectivity drew me out into the 'desert' where only feeling is real. . . . From the suprematist point of view, the appearances of natural objects are in themselves meaningless; the essential thing is feeling—in itself and completely independent of the context in which it has been evoked.[4]

At least nonfigurative art delivers us radically from the ugliness and stupidity in the image of man which have invaded contemporary painting. It does so by getting clear of the human figure. And at least it has—I mean in its most genuine representatives—a sense of the beauty of rhythm and harmony, and of the pleasure of the intelligence-permeated eye. I know that abstract art presents itself in a multiplicity of contrasting forms, and that it is sometimes infected by the animal frenzy and the aggressive resentment of which I spoke a moment ago. Be that as it may, I remain grateful for the thoughtful effort of Mondrian and Kandinsky toward perfect and restful balance. Abstract art is able to provide us with an element of contemplation, and repose of the soul—only, it is true, by quitting the realm of the human, even of the living, even of the existential reality of being, and by offering to our eyes, along the lines of some Platonic ideal, the peace of geometrical surfaces, wire constructions, or wooden artifacts.

4. Yet in actual fact the theory rests on false premises, and this attempt at a new solution—so disinterested and earnest in its beginnings—involves a basic illusion. The short cut was a blind alley.

Abstract painters are right in telling us that they are not "opposed to nature" [5] and do not break away from nature in the sense that they use and combine prime elements and various kinds of pure units or sensory determinants which they have extracted and singled out from nature, and that they are essentially concerned with laws of dynamic equilibrium, laws of proportional correspondences, optical laws, psychophysical laws which are grounded on nature; and even that the spontaneous gushing forth of arbitrary forms on their paper or their canvas depends on a nature which is their own subjective nature.[6] But all that is beside the point. The point is that nonrepresentative painting breaks away from Nature as an existential whole, turns away from Things and the grasping of Things, and renounces seeing into the inner depths of the world of Nature, of visible and corporeal Being.

Now if it is true that creative subjectivity awakens to itself only by simultaneously awakening to Things, in a single process which is poetic knowledge; and that the way by which the free creativity of the spirit enters into act is essentially poetic intuition, and that poetic intuition is nothing but the grasping of Things and the Self together through connaturality and intentional emotion—then it must be said that in breaking away from the existential world of

Nature, from Things and the grasping of Things, nonrepresentative art, by this very fact, condemns itself to fall short of its own dearest purposes and the very ends for the sake of which it came to life. Cut off from the mystery of integral reality to be obscurely attained in some of its transapparent aspects—in other words, cut off from poetic intuition—any effort to express freely the free creativity of the spirit, and to reveal the depths of creative subjectivity is bound to slow extinction. In actual fact, instead of tending more faithfully to the infinite amplitude of beauty, all lunges and efforts of poetry cannot prevent nonrepresentative art from tending of itself to the most limited form of beauty, the mute beauty, with almost no echoing power, of the best balanced objects produced by mechanical arts. There is no exercise of the free creativity of the spirit without poetic intuition. Painting and sculpture cannot do without poetic intuition. The crucial mistake of abstract art has been to reject—unwittingly—poetic intuition, while rejecting systematically the existential world of Things.

There is a curious sentence in the passage from Malevich I quoted a moment ago. "The appearances of natural objects," he said, "are in themselves meaningless; the essential thing is feeling"—feeling "completely independent of the context in which it has been evoked." He did not perceive that through feeling the intellect obscurely grasps the meanings in which Things abound, and which are conveyed to an attentive eye through the appearances of natural objects. Feeling for him remained merely subjective feeling, was not raised to spiritual intentionality. He remained secluded from the infinite meaningfulness of the existential world of Nature.

I would hate to be too systematic myself. Poetry is capable of worming its way in anywhere. I do not deny that in the most strictly nonrepresentative painting there are still possibilities for poetry. Even when an artist closes his eyes to things, he has still seen them, his soul is unconsciously inhabited by the forms of the universe. And thus it is possible that, while turning away from the existential world of things, the unconscious presence of this very world in the secret recesses of the painter may be enough to load some subjective feeling, unrelated to any given thing, with the spiritual élan of poetic intuition. It is possible for a painter who obeys only his merely subjective feeling (merely subjective at least in appearance), or else a free impulse of the unconscious (both the automatic and the spiritual unconscious intermingled), to trace, in total freedom from any representation whatever, lines and forms which are instinct with beauty and poetry—melodic as it were, and apt to move the heart, just as music can. My point is that such possibilities remain exceptional—and, in the last analysis, very limited; and that one cannot try to develop therefrom a specific form of art without pushing painting farther and farther away from the very sources of poetic intuition and creative emotion.

All in all, abstract art, taken as a system, is in the same predicament as idealist philosophy. Both are walled in. Even all the psychophysical laws with which nonrepresentative painting is so much concerned, and which deal with the most complex and subtle and fluent effects produced on sensation by elementary sense stimuli in relation to one another and to the environment, cannot be known in a separate manner and applied in the aprioristic way for which abstract art is looking. Painters know them only in their concrete and factual results, and in the very Things to be manifested in the work, and through creative experience intent on the existential world of Nature.

Turning away from the difficult task of grasping more and more profoundly and expressing more and more revealingly the transapparent aspects of Things, it is not surprising that, in the course of time, abstract art should appear to the growing flock of its adepts a mere way to escape poetic intuition. As a matter of fact it was to wind up in a new sort of academicism. At last it becomes again possible to take painting easily. A new eagerness for recipe and formula spares people the self-abnegation and the ordeals imposed by poetic creativity. Thus it is that we are now offered in exhibitions, art magazines, and modern art museums—together with infrequent works whose genuine poetry recalls that of the originators, and with valuable achievements and inventions in the field of merely decorative painting—a gaudy multitude of convolutions, angles, or cobwebs and amoeboid or filiform mucosities, all of them meant to express the originality of the creative self, in pictures which lack personality to such a point that they can scarcely be distinguished one from another. Everyone joins in willy-nilly, spurred by the noble iron rod of imitation, fashion, and the art dealers.

5. Practicing scales is not giving a concert. As an exercise or an experiment, nonrepresentative painting has, I think, unquestionable value. It unbinds the imagination, discloses to the eye of the painter a world of unforeseen possibilities, relationships, correspondences, rhythms, and equilibria, enables him more perfectly to master the prime elements of his means of expression; and over and above all it teaches him himself, in complete freedom, through the release of his own singular inventive resources as a sensitive instrument. All that, nevertheless, has to do with technique, not with poetry, or at best with making technique more supple and tractable to poetry. In this particular order, practice in abstract art has perhaps been made by the very development of modern painting a necessary moment in the individual painter's self education. And with regard to the general evolution of painting, it was also, perhaps, and for the same reasons, an unavoidable moment. Yet in relation to art's real life, and to the progress in creativity and self-awareness achieved in the last hundred years, the irruption of nonrepresentative art can hardly be considered an advance in the process. Of itself it points rather at a period of stagnation or regression.

It must be noticed, furthermore, that in what is commonly labeled abstract art today, there are trends which already step in reality out of abstract art. When a painter happens— contrary to the theory—to be actually intent on the existential world of Nature and put in motion by poetic intuition, but uses abstract or nonrepresentative forms as means of expression, these forms are not in reality purely abstract or nonrepresentative. They make present on the canvas, they *represent*—be it in the most bare and dematerialized manner —some vital element, a rhythm, a contrast, a contour which has been seen in Nature and which is just enough to suggest some natural appearance with the significance it is laden with, even if this meaningful appearance moves you without your being able to recognize or identify the Thing to which it belongs. Condensed and simplified as they may be, natural appearances are there. Through them the existential world of Nature is there. It is there with that particular inner depth and those particular meanings which knowledge through connaturality and intentional emotion have disclosed to the painter together with his own subjectivity. By way of forms still impoverished and half-mute, but derived from Nature in actual fact, the work expresses, not a merely subjective feeling symbolized according to the requirements of psychophysical laws, but, together with an intuitive feeling, some diffident aspect of the reality of the visible world. Such painting, which is, it seems to me, characteristic of the effort of some contemporary painters still designated as abstract painters,[7] is in reality no more purely abstract art than cubism was.

May we believe that in this way a new development will come about, and finally set free contemporary painting from the academicism of the nonrepresentative system? No doubt a spontaneous process progressively reintegrating Nature in the inner movement of abstract research would be of greater interest than that kind of compromise, extrinsically mixing pieces of dull natural forms with nonfigurative formulas, which can also be observed today here and there.

Natural Appearances and Creative Intuition

6. In any case the truth of the matter is that creative intuition is today, and has always been, and will ever be, the primary power of authentic renewal. Salvation in art comes only through creative intuition.

The great mistake has been to put the instrumental and secondary before the principal and primary, and to search for an escape through the discovery of a new external approach and new technical revolutions, instead of passing first through the creative source, and thus taking a risk, but having a chance to find a real solution. Another mistake, connected with the first, has been to conceive of forward movement only in terms of a flight from Naturalism, as if it were enough to run farther and farther away from an error to get at the truth. The mistake has been to look for freedom *from* something—first from an error: servile imitation or copy of natural appearances, but then from the existential world of Nature itself, and from any kind of representation whatever of natural appearances—instead of looking for freedom *to* achieve in one's work a more and more genuine revelation both of Things and the Self, and *to* obey creative forces in a manner truer and truer to a deeper and deeper poetic intuition.

Everyone must in the end consent to be led into the desert. But we should not mistake the desert of emotion and feeling cut off from Nature for the desert of man's spirit in its struggle with the Angel.

To tell the truth, there is a need for a restatement of the old question of imitation (though the word itself is hopelessly wrong). It is perfectly clear that imitation in the sense of a sheer copy of natural appearances achieved in such a way that the image deceives the eye and is taken for the thing is a wrong notion, directly opposed to the nature of art.[8] But Aristotle never had such a notion in mind. He meant that delight in seeing (or beauty) is all the greater as the object seen conveys a greater amount of intuitive knowledge: thus in art and poetry the object is also a sign—through which some transapparent reality is made intuitively known. Does not dance "imitate mores"? What is "imitated" —or made visibly known—is not natural appearances but secret or transapparent reality through natural appearances. Furthermore St. Thomas insisted that art imitates nature *in her operation*—not in respect to natural appearances, but in respect to the ways in which nature herself operates. To create his work of lines and colors the painter imitates nature as he would imitate another painter. He does not copy nature as an object, he steals from nature, he extracts from his observation of, and connivance with her, the operative ways through which nature manages her own raw materials of form, color, and light to impress on our eye and mind an emotion of beauty. This is quite a peculiar type of imitation indeed, which consists in the act of making oneself instructed by a reluctant and jealous master: pilfering rather than imitation. Here we have such secrets as that of the flamelike form detected by Michelangelo, or that of inherent irregularity detected by Renoir, or that of the cylinder, sphere, and cone structure detected by Cézanne. One day, after a walk in the wintertime, Rouault told me he had just discovered, by looking at snow-clad fields in the sunshine, how to paint the white trees of spring. Such a genuine concept of "imitation" affords a ground and a justification for the boldest kinds of transposition, transfiguration, deformation, or recasting of natural appearances, in so far as they are a means to make the work manifest intuitively the transapparent reality which has been grasped by the artist.

Yet the fact remains that this genuine concept of imitation, correctly understood, expresses a necessity to which human art is bound: first, with regard to the transapparent reality to be "imitated" or intuitively manifested; second, with regard to natural appearances themselves as to be used *instrumentally* (or as means mastered by art, and thus as transposed and recast with a view to the end): for without the instrumentality of natural appearances made present or "represented" in such a way, the intended manifestation cannot be *intuitive*, that is, the work falls short of the essence of art. As I have previously noticed, it is through the instrumentality of natural appearances that things reveal some of their secret meanings to the artist's intuition: it is also through the instrumentality of natural appearances—necessarily recast, and perhaps drastically so—that the same secret meaning can be intuitively revealed in and by the work.

Taken in this correct philosophical sense, the law of "imitation" (misleading as this unhappy word may be), the law of transference or re-production is inescapable.

7. Modern art obeys an essential necessity of growth made more exacting by self-awareness, when it claims greater and greater freedom with respect to natural appearances: not, I say, freedom *from* any representation whatsoever of natural appearances, but freedom *in* this very representation, and freedom *to* transpose and recast natural appearances at its own pleasure, on the condition that the recasting in question causes the work to manifest intuitively, or reveal, a transapparent reality grasped in the existential world of Things. In abstract painting this condition is lacking, to one degree or another.

Contemporary painting will get out of its predicament when it understands that the only way to effective transposition, deformation, recasting, or transfiguration of natural appearances passes through poetic intuition. Poetic intuition does as it pleases with natural appearances. It catches them in its own inner music. In its expansion toward the work it takes them away from their material existence in nature, and makes them attuned to itself. Then it is not by any technical trick of decomposition of forms, it is by virtue of the inner pressure, in the natural forms thus quickened by creative emotion, toward going beyond themselves, and telling more than what they are, and becoming parts of a total song laden with meaning and significance, that natural forms are deformed and transposed, transfigured and recast.[9]

It is also by virtue of poetic intuition, embracing the total organization of the work and imposing on it its requirements for unitary objective expression, that each form is sensed and determined in relation to all others, and that the picture expands with harmonic plenitude in the total inner space which is proper to it as a self-sufficient unit.

This internal *number* of the work answers a basic necessity which ancient masters were perfectly aware of—Cubism and abstract painting only put a new emphasis on it. I think that there is more real novelty in a particular element which contemporary research is bringing out, and which refers directly to the poetic sense. Modern art, it seems to me, has become exceptionally aware of the importance of the *metaphorical interference* that poetic intuition naturally releases, in other words of the impact of that "illuminating image"—a form, an object, a glimmer, a bit of a world, emerging from elsewhere into the center of the stage—by which the intuitive significance of the work is increased, as it were, boundlessly. Note the fact in passing—it is in relation to poetry that I shall try to analyze further[10] the nature of the illuminating image. To have laid hands on this proper asset of poets is one of the authentic conquests of modern painting.

Painting, in reality, is not trapped today in a blind alley. Roads are open, there are signposts, precisely in relation to the points I just discussed. If I were asked to mention some names, I would say the Romanesque primitives, Hieronymus Bosch, Tintoretto, El Greco, Piranesi, Georges de Latour, Claude, Goya in the past; and, in our age, Cézanne, Rouault, Braque, Chagall, what is best and most durable in Picasso, and certain findings of the Surrealist painters.

In doing so I do not mean at all, of course, to point to any particular way out, but to point to a certain inspiration to find a way out—an inspiration to which, I believe, significant and liberating testimonies have been given. Every great painter blocks the way he himself has opened, and exhausts, as it were, the possibilities which this way might offer. The question, to be sure, has never been to walk in the footsteps of such masters; the question is to scrutinize them with such love as to become free from them, and to feed on their experiences and inner flame humbly and stubbornly enough to discover new directions without even thinking of it.

Despite the conditions of our present state of civilization, so hostile to creative freedom, there will always be artists who have fortitude enough to turn toward the inner sources, and trust in the power of the small translucid cloud of poetic intuition. They will be able to get out—by walking, rather than by reasoning—of the various entanglements I have tried to analyze in this chapter, and to be unselfish in the very awakening of creative subjectivity. For the painter as for the poet there is no other way to regain interior unity, being entirely turned toward the end beyond the end, and thus being perhaps also given, in addition, a new possibility of communion with his fellow men in this modern world of ours which is sick with a repressed, brutally frustrated longing for unity, beauty, and poetry.

SEVEN

POETIC EXPERIENCE AND POETIC SENSE

Magic and Poetic Knowledge

1. I referred, in a previous chapter, to Rimbaud's statement: *"Je est un autre,"* *"I* is another." Curiously enough, it occurred that Lautréamont said just the contrary: *"Si j'existe, je ne suis pas un autre."* "if I exist, I am *not* another." In the interval between these two statements, proffered by two poets who are both the recognized prophets of contemporary French poetry, an entire philosophy is contained.

I know that in actual existence, with respect to the concrete meaning they had for Rimbaud and Lautréamont themselves, the statements in question are not as contradictory as it seems. For in saying *"Je est un autre,"* Rimbaud laid himself open to a kind of transmutation of his own being invaded and inhabited by *all things,* by the mysterious powers wandering in the world, by the *anima mundi.* And in saying *"Si j'existe, je ne suis pas un autre,"* Lautréamont locked himself up within himself, against the invasion of this Another—God, who was his enemy. Yearning for magical transmutation and refusal of transcendence are not incompatible positions.

But I should like to consider, for a moment, these two statements *in themselves.* "If I exist, I am not another." Take this at the level of Being, or of ontologic reality: you have the principle of identity, the primary law of being.

"I is another." Take this at the level of Knowing, or in relation to the universe of knowledge, especially as objectivizing things in concepts and attaining its perfect state in rational science: you have the primary law of knowledge, for in the act of knowing I am identified—spiritually—with another; I, while keeping my actual identity, become immaterially or "intentionally" the other in so far as it is another, *aliud in quantum aliud.* Only the object is grasped, miraculously pure of any interference of the subjectivity.

"I is another." Take it at the level of Poetry, and poetic knowledge: you have the primary law of poetic knowledge, which, in so far as it is knowledge, also means immaterial or intentional identification;[1] but now this identification comes about through poetic intuition, by means of emotion; and it is with and through the subjectivity, and in order to reveal it, that the thing grasped is grasped.

"I is another." Take it at the level of Being: it is only at this level that such a statement is opposed, and diametrically opposed, to the other statement, "If I exist, I am not another." Then it means that identification with another in actual reality—and that identification of any thing with any thing by means of the signs which represent them—which are characteristic features of magic.

The distinction between these three planes, the plane of abstract knowledge, the plane of poetry, the plane of magic, is fundamental. And we see that the plane of poetry is intermediary between the plane of abstract knowledge and the plane of magic. Poetic knowledge is spiritual and intentional; of itself it bears no trace of magic in the strict sense (referring to magical operation) in which I am using this word, and has nothing to do with any dissolution of the Self into things, or any adulterous confusion with them, or any claim to creative power over them. But poetic knowledge implies that kind of invasion of things into the preconscious night of the spirit, near the center of the soul, through emotion and affective union, by means of which poetic intuition is born; and it knows things as one—intentionally one, but one—with the Self, as resounding in the subjectivity. Fur-

thermore, poetic knowledge, considered in its most connatural, pure, and primary requirements, expresses itself
through images—or through concepts which are not carried
to the state of rational thought, but are still steeped in images, being used in that nascent state where they are emerging from images as Venus from the sea. And the thought of
the poet, in so far as it is centered on poetic knowledge,
escapes to a certain extent the sunlit regime of the logos,
and participates to a certain extent in the nocturnal regime
of imagination, in which the principle of noncontradiction
does not come into force and things are at the same time
themselves and another, because their presence in a sign—
as known through it—is mistaken for a real and physical
presence.[2] Thus the thought of the poet (at least his subconscious thought) resembles somewhat the mental activity
of the primitive man, and the ways of magic in the large
sense of this word (referring to magical thought as studied
by anthropology).

It is easy to slip from magic in the large sense to magic in
the strict sense, and from the intentional or spiritual union
to the material or substantial one. I think that poetry
escapes the temptation of magic only if it renounces any
will to power, even and first of all in relation to the evoking
of inspiration, and if there is no fissure in the poet's fidelity
to the essential disinterestedness of poetic creation.

2. Poetry, in our time, is all the more exposed to the attraction exercised by magic, as the rational knowledge with
which our culture provides the intellect of the poet is an abstract knowledge which has got clear of wisdom for the sake
of the mathematical analysis of phenomena and, by the same
token, has estranged the human mind from itself.

Such an abstract knowledge offers the poet, instead of an
articulate universe answering in some way the yearning of
reason for intelligible being, a dislocated picture of conflicting appearances in which all the laws of reason are seemingly made questionable, but through which science succeeds
in performing on matter wondrous achievements. Thus

abstract knowledge, engulfed as it is today by physicomathematical science, can only, if no superior wisdom is at play, give an appearance of sanction, afforded by the pseudo-philosophical *Weltanschauung* it seems to favor, to that Irrational Marvelous which poetry dreams of; it can only jeopardize a little more the universe of thought of the modern poet, and make the temptation of magic grow stronger for him.[3]

I submit, therefore, that poetry become self-aware can restore its normal state of stability and autonomy in the universe of the spirit only if the allurement of magic is counterbalanced for it by the attraction of a rational knowledge which itself has refound the full scope of its domain and a true reflective understanding of its own degrees of vision—one of which, and an invaluable one, but only one, is physicomathematical science. Only the magnet of what St. Augustine called *ratio superior,* the "superior reason," which looks at and adheres to things that are eternal, can keep the soul of the poet in some kind of unity and ensure in him the freedom of poetic knowledge at its own proper level. Never has poetry been in greater need of reason, and of genuine human wisdom—I mean in the realm of abstract knowledge, which pertains to the poet not as a poet, but as a man, and on which depends the universe of thought *presupposed* by his activity as a poet. And beyond genuine human wisdom, he is fortunate if he also feels the attraction of genuine contemplation.

Poetry, Mysticism, Metaphysics

3. In the discussions on the true nature of poetry which occupied Frenchmen before the second World War, particular interest was shown in the relations between poetic experience and mystical experience. Henri Bremond offered some half-truths, Claudel some excessive truths on the matter. Finally a sensible conclusion arose from the controversy. Poetic experience and mystical experience are distinct in nature: poetic experience is concerned with the created world and the enigmatic and innumerable relations of beings with each

other; mystical experience with the principle of things in its own incomprehensible and supramundane unity. The obscure knowledge through connaturality which is peculiar to poetic experience comes about by means of emotion stirring the human recesses of the subjectivity; but the more obscure yet more final and more stable knowledge through connaturality which is peculiar to mystical experience comes about either, in natural mystical experience, by means of merely intellectual concentration producing a void through which the Self is ineffably touched or, in grace-given mystical experience, by means of charity, which connatures the soul with God, and which transcends both emotion and the human recesses of the subjectivity. Poetic experience is from the very start oriented toward expression, and terminates in a word uttered, or a work produced; while mystical experience tends toward silence, and terminates in an immanent fruition of the absolute.

But different in nature as they may be, poetic experience and mystical experience are born near one another, and near the center of the soul, in the living springs of the preconceptual or supraconceptual vitality of the spirit. It is not surprising that they intercross and communicate with one another in an infinity of ways; that poetic experience naturally predisposes the poet both to contemplation and to confusing all manner of other things with it; and that mystical experience naturally prepares the contemplative to make the silence of love sometimes superabound in poetic utterance, responsible for some of the most admirable poems ever written, and for some of the worst.

Poetry is spiritual nourishment. But it does not satiate, it only makes man more hungry, and that is its grandeur.

Poetry is the heaven of the working reason. Poetry is a divination of the spiritual in the things of sense—which expresses itself in the things of sense, and in a delight of sense. Metaphysics also pursues a spiritual prey, but metaphysics is engaged in abstract knowledge, while poetry quickens art. Metaphysics snatches at the spiritual in an idea, by the most abstract intellection; poetry reaches it in the flesh, by the very point of the sense sharpened through intelligence. Metaphysics enjoys its possession only in the retreats of the eternal regions, while poetry finds its own at every crossroad in the wanderings of the contingent and the singular. The more real than reality, the superreal (I would not give up this word to the Surrealists), the superreal which both seek, metaphysics must attain in the nature of things, while it suffices to poetry to touch it in any sign whatsoever. Metaphysics gives chase to essences and definitions, poetry to any flash of existence glittering by the way, and any reflection of an invisible order.

Poetry Transcends Art

4. I have insisted, throughout this book, that Poetry is naturally attached to Art, and is by essence oriented in the direction of art. I have also insisted that in the very order of creativity poetry transcends art. If it is permissible to lay stress once again on this transcendence of poetry, I would say that it is the consequence of two facts: first, poetry is essentially a release and actuation of the free creativity of the spirit, and, as I suggested in a preceding chapter, it has as such, of itself, *no object;* for beauty, for it, is neither an object to be made nor an object to be known, but only a transcendental correlative, and an end beyond any end. In art, on the contrary, the creativity of the spirit is not free, but *bound* to the making of the work, which is an *object* enclosed in a particular genus and category. As soon as the poetic intuition enters the sphere of operation, it enters the sphere of art and of the bound activity of the spirit, yet it still remains free, because it always commands, and is the primary rule of art; it does not obey the rules, the rules obey it.

Secondly, poetry is knowledge, knowledge essentially oriented toward expression and operation, but not practical knowledge in the strict sense of the word. It is only in a remote manner, from afar, that poetic knowledge pertains to the practical realm. Truth, in it, is not, as in art or in prudence, conformity with the straight or undeviating appetite, but conformity with Being (Being grasped through emotion). Poetic knowledge analogically participates in the contemplative character of philosophy, for it is knowledge of the very interiority of things—though experiential knowledge totally different from the theoretical knowledge proper to science and philosophy. And thus, because it is, in its own way, spiritual communion with being, poetry transcends art, which is entirely encompassed in and committed to practical knowledge in the strict sense of this word, knowledge only to make.

It is because of this transcendence that poetry, like Platonic *mousikè,* enjoys a universal dominion over all the arts which have to do with beauty—over all arts to the extent to which a concern for beauty dwells in or creeps into them.

5. At this point it can be observed that (since the energies of the soul, however distinct from one another in their essence, involve dynamically one another, and are commingled as to their exercise in concrete existence) poetry, though essentially linked with art and oriented toward artistic activity, extends in a certain manner—accidentally—beyond the realm of art. Then poetry lives in regions and climates which are no longer natural to it, it lives in foreign parts, and it is no longer free, but kept in subjection. What I mean is that a kind of poetic intuition can come into play everywhere—in science, philosophy, big business, revolution, religion, sanctity, or imposture—when the mind of man attains to a certain depth or mastery in the power of discovering new horizons and taking great risks.

There is poetry involved in the work of all great mathematicians. Secret poetic intuition was at work in the primary philosophical insights of Heraclitus and Plato, Aristotle and Thomas Aquinas, Plotinus, Spinoza, or Hegel; without the help of poetry Aristotle could not have extracted from experience the diamond of his fundamental definitions; in the background of all the ideological violence of Thomas Hobbes there was something which poetry had taught him, his awareness that he was the twin brother of Fear. Poetry helped Francis of Assisi, and Columbus, and Napoleon, and Cagliostro.

I am aware of all that, but I say that, in all that, poetic intuition, caught up and entangled in the workings of some activity of the soul, is subdued to the specific purposes and the specific laws of this foreign activity. It secretly labors, in the underground of imposture, sanctity, politics, or philosophy, for the specific object of the one or the other. As soon as in the margin left available by the iron discipline of master qualities which are not the virtue of art, the free creativity of the spirit has stirred and quickened imagination, it is captured and mastered for ends which are not its own; that is why poetry—restrained, though hiddenly at play in the specific work of great scientists—finds sometimes a way out, and captures them in its turn in its own nets. For all that, the fact remains that by essence poetry, in the preconceptual life of the intellect, is the firmament of the virtue of art; and that the essential universality of poetry is only the universal dominion it enjoys over the arts.

Poetic Experience. Exit the Platonic Muse, Enter Real Inspiration

6. I have spoken in preceding chapters of poetic knowledge and poetic intuition. The expression "poetic experience," which I used in the first part of the present discussion, has, it seems to me, a somewhat different, more complex, and more comprehensively psychological significance. It refers to a certain state of the soul in which self-communion makes the ordinary traffic of our thinking stop for a while, and which is linked with particularly intense poetic intuition.

At this point the best that a philosopher can do is to try to follow the testimony of the poets. The first thing, I think, which we have to mention in this connection is the essential requirement of totality or integrity to which I have already alluded. Poetic experience brings the poet back to the hidden place, at the single root of the powers of the soul, where the entire subjectivity is, as it were, gathered in a state of expectation and virtual creativity. Into this place he enters, not by any effort of voluntary concentration, but by a recollection, fleeting as it may be, of all the senses, and a kind of unifying repose which is like a natural grace, a primordial gift, but to which he has to consent, and which he can cultivate, first of all by removing obstacles and silencing concepts. Thus poetic experience is, emerging on the verge of the spiritual preconscious, a state of obscure, unexpressed and sapid knowing— the expression of which, when later on it will come about in a work, will also be sapid. Do we not read, in an old Sanskrit text, that "Poetry is a word whose essence is Savor"? In such a spiritual contact of the soul with itself, all the sources are touched together, and the first obligation of the poet is to respect the integrity of this original experience. Any systematic denial of any of the faculties involved would be a sort of self-mutilation. Poetry cannot be reduced to a mere gushing forth of images separated from intelligence, any more than to a discursus of logical reason, as Raïssa Maritain put it in an essay which I am largely using here.[4]

There is no poetic experience without a secret germ, tiny as it may be, of a poem. But there is no genuine poem which is not a fruit growing with inner necessity out of poetic experience. According to a text from the above-mentioned essay to which I attach particular importance, "The brooding repose provided by such an experience acts like a refreshing, rejuvenating, and purifying flood in which the mind is bathed. . . . The depth of the quiet which all the faculties then enjoy cannot be overvalued. It is a concentration of all the energies of the soul, but peaceful and tranquil concentration, with no tension; the soul enters its repose, in this place of refreshment and peace superior to any feeling. It dies as Angels die—but to live again, in exaltation and enthusiasm, in that state which is wrongly called inspiration —wrongly, for inspiration was nothing else indeed than this very repose, in which it escaped from sight. Now the mind invigorated and vivified enters a happy activity, so easy that everything seems to be given it at once, and, as it were, from the outside. In reality everything was there, kept in the shade, hidden in the spirit and in the blood; all that which will be manifested in operation was already there, but we knew it not. We knew neither how to discover nor how to use it, before having gained new forces in those tranquil depths."

Carlyle also spoke of those "quiet mysterious depths." [5] In the same way Hölderlin, according to an essay by Heidegger, thought that "in poetry man concentrates or retires into the inmost depth of human reality. There he penetrates through quietude: not indeed through the illusory quietude of idleness and the void of thought, but through that infinite quietude in which all energies and relations are at play."

Another, yet concordant aspect of the inner experience with which we are concerned is disclosed to us by T. S. Eliot. Speaking of "this disturbance of our quotidian character which results in an incantation, an outburst of words which we hardly recognize as our own (because of the effortlessness)"—"to me," he says, "it seems that at these moments, which are characterized by the sudden lifting of the burden of anxiety and fear which presses upon our daily life so steadily that we are unaware of it, what happens is something *negative:* that is to say, not 'inspiration' as we commonly think of it, but the breaking down of strong habitual barriers—which tend to re-form very quickly. Some obstruction is momentarily whisked away. The accompanying feeling is less like what we know as positive pleasure, than a sudden relief from an intolerable burden." [6] This description gives us, in a tone which is typically Eliot's, significant testimony on the negative aspect of poetic experience. Yet the question remains how the sudden breaking down of strong habitual barriers is produced and what is the invisible force, blowing from the unconscious, which whisks them away.

7. Shall we try to discuss at this point the notion of inspiration, already alluded to more or less explicitly in all the previous remarks? Poetic experience implies, it seems to me, two phases, a first phase of systole and a second phase of diastole; and in the second phase, as was observed above, everything seems to be given at once and, as it were, from

the outside, though in reality everything was already there, hidden. Such a fact is probably what misled Plato, and caused him to believe that poetic inspiration came *from above the soul*. There is no Muse outside the soul; there is poetic experience and poetic intuition *within the soul*, coming to the poet *from above conceptual reason*.

As to the first phase, it depends on the one hand, I think, on a presupposed psychological condition in which, by some lucky conjunction of circumstances, the external world and external perception lose their grip on the soul, but at the same time the soul's inner balance and the interconnections between the intellect and the internal senses remain intact (a dreamlike condition, as it were, but integrated, with intelligence neither bound nor disconnected); it depends, on the other hand, on a determining cause, which is the attracting and absorbing action exercised—in the manner of a shining particle that puts you to sleep if you keep staring at it—by a preconscious poetic intuition present in the mind. For poetic intuition first causes poetic experience and is, in its turn, fortified by it, and so they grow together.

In the first phase, then, in the phase of systole and unifying repose, all the forces of the soul, gathered together in quietude, were in a state of virtuality and dormant energy. And poetic intuition, still preconscious, was the only act formed within the preconscious life of the intellect, and was the secret reason for this silent concentration. It is not surprising that at a given moment this same poetic intuition, acting no longer in the manner of an hypnotic but rather of a catalytic agent, should make the virtual energies concentrated around it pass also to the act. Then, from the single actuation of all the forces of the soul withdrawn into their root vitality, a single transient motion will result, which manifests itself either negatively, by a breaking of barriers, or positively, by the entrance of poetic intuition into the field of consciousness.

Thus it is that after the silent gathering a breath arises, coming not from the outside, but from the center of the soul —sometimes a breath which is almost imperceptible, but compelling and powerful, through which everything is given in easiness and happy expansion; sometimes a gale bursting all of a sudden, through which everything is given in violence and rapture; sometimes the gift of the beginning of a song; sometimes an outburst of unstoppable words.

That is the phase of diastole, and of "inspiration" as it manifests itself in its most apparent and usually recognized forms.

Bad Romanticism[7] made of "inspiration" an excuse for facility, or simple release of brute emotions and passions, or uncontrolled flux of shallow words and sentimentalism. It is unfortunate that both the reaction (sometimes one-sided) of a sound and strict criticism against such a fraud and the blind prejudices of our "scientific" psychology have resulted in the strong and strongly unintelligent contemporary loathing for the very word and notion of inspiration. Nothing is more real, and more necessary to poetry, and to any great work, than inspiration. And nothing is more natural, and more *internal*.

Inspiration is natural, but neither continuous nor frequent as a rule. Furthermore, it takes on all sorts of forms and disguises. It may come in happiness and exaltation, it may come in distress and misery; it may force itself on the poet only as a pang of conscience, obliging him to struggle again and again with the deficiencies of expression. Sometimes inspiration remains unperceived when it is especially deep and steady. Sometimes it must be paid for by hard labor and thankless digging in an arid soil. If the above remarks on poetic experience are true, it appears that poetic intuition is the most essential and spiritual, the primary element and catalytic agent of inspiration, and that all the other features which characterize inspiration develop by a happy chance (what Aristotle called good fortune), dependent on an unforeseen moment of psychological suspense but intact dynamic integrity, and also on the temperament of each individual, his natural inclinations, and his capacity for and fidelity to spiritual repose. I would say, consequently, that inspiration is always *necessary* as poetic intuition, or in its

primary seed, and always supremely *desirable* as fully unfolded, or as all-pervading motion (that is, moving all the
powers of the mind to superior freedom and action, but
neither expelling and replacing nor binding and blinding
them). Transports, rapture, delirium, and frenzy are none
of its essentials; they are only a token of the weakness of
nature and can proceed moreover from spurious sources.
The real blessing is poetic intuition, and not any kind of
thrill.

The distinction just indicated between inspiration in its
primary seed or as poetic intuition and inspiration as
all-pervading motion, may perhaps help us to reconcile
two seemingly conflicting truths: on the one hand no poem,
as a rule (especially if it is a long piece of poetry) can proceed in its entirety from inspiration—that is, inspiration
in the second sense, or as all-pervading motion which gives
wings to the intellect and imagination; on the other hand,
every part of the poem must cling to inspiration—that is,
inspiration in the first sense of the word, or as poetic intuition.

We are similarly enabled correctly to understand the
distinction made by John Keble, on the basis of Aristotle, between the two classes of poets (if there is any sense in looking for categories in poetry) whom he designated as *ecstatic*
and *euplastic* poets. In the "ecstatic," or those endowed with
a strain of madness, we would have mainly inspiration fully
unfolded or as all-pervading motion. In the "euplastic," or
those endowed with *a happy gift of nature,* we would have
mainly inspiration in its primary seed or as poetic intuition.
Of course a "euplastic" poet may be a greater poet, and
truer to inspiration, than an "ecstatic" one. But those who
lack both kinds of inspiration are no poets at all.

8. In one sense—as to the meaning of the work, and the
degree to which it *exists*—inspiration gives all, and is even
too rich. In another sense—as to the ways of execution—it is
disarmed and in search of tools. Precisely because it is transcendent in nature and intangible, arising from the spiritual
night of subjectivity, and because it is only a breath, inspira-

tion cannot *give form* without that operative reason which it transcends and uses as an instrument. Inspiration's power is the power of a source—not only a source which is at the beginning, as the source of a river is, but also a source which is, or should be, as far as the human condition permits, simultaneous with the entire process, from beginning to end, as is the eternal source on which all the moments of time depend. No instant in the making of the work should escape it, at least, as we have seen, inasmuch as inspiration is made identical with poetic intuition. Thus inspiration requires of necessity the steady attentiveness of a purified mind. But having only the power of a source, inspiration also requires of necessity—as a means—the rational toil of the virtue of art and all the logic and shrewdness, self-restraint and self-possession of working intelligence.

To claim to have inspiration expel intelligence and take charge of the work alone is an illusion similar to that of the *illuminati* in the order of mystics. It was but normal that such an attempt—both to give up everything, including reason and freedom, for total passivity under inspiration, and to obtain this very passivity at will, from the power of man and magical recipes—should wind up in illusory transports and in the Surrealist hopes in automatic writing: of itself it leads to the renunciation of the work. To the extent to which Surrealist poets and painters produce poems and pictures that exist, sometimes in a superior manner, the alertness and elective power of intelligence are at play in them. To the extent to which André Breton is a poet, and singularly gifted, his works give the lie to his system. "The spirits of the prophets are subject to the prophets," St. Paul said. And commenting on this sentence, John of St. Thomas warns us not to "err in thinking that those born of the Spirit are carried along by a frantic impulse, like those possessed by an evil spirit. . . . Birth from the Spirit does not take away, it brings and strengthens freedom of election." The Spirit does not work in man "by violence" but "by breathing and by quickening his inclination," "contrary to what occurs with delirious ravings." [8]

Thus it is that poets are the first to lay stress on the essential need for lucidity and choice, and for that freedom which depends on conscious intelligence, in the making of the work. "There is a great deal, in the writing of poetry, which must be conscious and deliberate." [9] Did not Novalis write: "It is impossible for the poet to be too cool, too collected"? And Arnim: "There has never been a poet without passion. But it is not passion which makes the poet. No poet has ever done lasting work in the instant when he was dominated by passion." Baudelaire similarly observed: "The construction, the armature, so to speak, is the most important guarantee of the mysterious life of the works of the mind." And, after Edgar Poe, he repeatedly insisted, as all teachers of literary criticism know, that "everything that is beautiful and noble is the result of reason and calculation."

Let us not be misled, however, by such statements. When Baudelaire spoke in this way, or when Paul Valéry declared, "Enthusiasm is not the cast of mind of a writer," they were offering us only one facet of the truth, and in one sense they were deceiving us—and themselves—through that kind of self-detached and self-chastising knowledge, ironical in nature, which is linked with feigning, repressed suffering, and anger against a superior gift too dearly paid for or too rarely enjoyed. For reason and calculation in the poet are there only to handle fire, and if "enthusiasm" means fire, there is no writer without enthusiasm (touched with reason-gloved hands). So much the better if in the handwriting the pen is controlled and diligent: the words will burn all the more. It is not, furthermore, with regard to inspiration and poetic intuition, it is with regard to passion, "brute" passion, associated with them but not spiritualized (made "intentional") in the creative fire, that Novalis and Arnim demand cool-headedness. "The role of consciousness, in the poet, consists in the act of constantly, doggedly seeing to it that *only* the gift penetrates into the poem, and nothing else but this gift and only into the poem." [10] Essential as the part played by intelligence may be, did not Pushkin, the most intelligent of Russian poets, write: "I think, God forgive me, that the poet must be a little stupid"? And Baudelaire, the most intelligent of French poets: "Great poetry is essentially *stupid,* it *believes,* and that's what makes its glory and force. Do not ever confuse the phantoms of reason with the phantoms of imagination: the former are equations, the latter are beings and memories." [11]

Just, then, as the most dangerous criminals are lucid maniacs, so the most perfect poets are madmen using unfailing reason. But poets are not really mad. Consequently, they are aware in themselves of a torturing division, a rending of their own human substance, which they are condemned to bring to unity—enigmatic, unstable, never satisfying unity—not in themselves, but in their work. Hence their connatural torment. They are obliged to be at the same time at two different levels of the soul, out of their senses and rational, passively moved by inspiration and actively conscious, intent on an unknown more powerful than they are which a sagacious operative knowledge must serve and manifest in fear and trembling. No wonder that they live in inner solitude and insecurity.

> *To feel me in the solitude of kings,*
> *Without the power that makes them bear a crown,*

as Byron put it.[12] And today, a French poet: *"Magicien de l'insécurité, le poète n'a que des satisfactions adoptives. Cendre toujours inachevée."* [13]

The Experience of the Composer and the Painter

9. Poetic experience can be—is in general, I believe—a transient and fleeting experience (fleeting, because emotive). The poets, at least in modern times, have given us invaluable information about it. Must we suppose that it takes on its full dimensions only in them? What about the composers? Particularly, what about the painters and the other artists more concerned with the external senses and with matter? In one way or another they also experience the creative repose, the sudden breaking down of barriers, and the sudden gratuitous gifts of the poetic state, and know how deeply

art is in need of it. Yet composers and painters, because they do not deal with language and the natural instruments of thought, are less interested than poets in reflectively scrutinizing and putting into words their inner experience. This experience remains for them, to a large extent, hidden in the preconscious.

Poetic experience is still freer, still more immersed in the internal recesses of subjectivity, still closer to the need and longing of the spirit for utterance, in the composer than in the poet—"where the word stops, there starts the song, *exultation of the mind bursting forth into the voice*," as St. Thomas puts it.[14] But it is not as attainable and expressible through introspection, it is as enveloped in the musicality of creative imagination and the birth of melody that such experience emerges into the consciousness of the composer. And as concerns the painter, I would submit that poetic experience in him is snatched away from the heart and absorbed by the eyes, and made captive both of his intentness on working and of that universe of visible matter which is his primary object.

Thus when we look for some verbal expression bearing witness to the inner experience of composers and painters, we are more often than not obliged to satisfy ourselves with external, indirect, and so to speak oblique indications, whose complete meaning it is up to us to infer.

10. "What I produce is due to my understanding of music and to my sorrows," Schubert said.

In Schumann's correspondence, there is this passage: "Anything that happens in the world affects me; politics, for example, literature, people; and I reflect about all these things in my own way—and these reflections then seek to find an outlet in music. This is also the reason for which so many of my compositions are hard to understand. . . . For this reason, too, so many other recent composers do not satisfy me, because—in addition to all their lack of professional skill—they enlarge on lyrical commonplaces. The highest level reached in this type of music does not come up to the point from which my kind of music starts. The former may be a flower. The latter is a poem; that is, belongs to the world of the spirit. The former comes from an impulse of crude nature; the latter stems from the consciousness of the poetic mind." [15]

Are not the presence and power of poetic experience implied in such "reflection" which transforms into music "anything that happens in the world," in such a way that music, then, "stems from the consciousness of the poetic mind"? They are also implied in the "inspiration" of which Chopin spoke to Delphine Potocka: "Every creator has moments when his inspiration weakens and when only brainwork is done. When one picks up musical notes, one can point out such parts with the finger. The main thing is that there should be the greatest amount of inspiration and the least possible amount of work. Liszt does plenty of work, but has little inspiration. In Mozart you seldom find any amount of work. In Bach there is contrapuntal work but of such a perfection and so closely knit with inspiration that you cannot separate them. Don't talk to me of composition; creation is not a thing one can learn. Every man sleeps, eats, and moves differently, and you wish that all would create the same way. I am tormenting myself devilishly over every piece." [16]

Yet it is in the following text, where Arthur Lourié defends against contemporary constructivism the genuine value of melody and, by the same stroke, of inspiration, that I find the most significant testimony of the way in which poetic experience manifests itself in the composer: "Every melody," Lourié puts it, "has the property of revealing some intimate truth, and of discovering the original reality, both psychological and spiritual, of the one who creates the melody. *Melody discloses the nature of the subject, and not that of the object.* To be sure, it can espouse the object, and become the expression of it, but its essential predestination lies in the revelation of the very nature of the subject from whom it proceeds. . . . The quality of the melody depends on categories of moral-aesthetic unity. . . . Melody is inaccessible to the logic of our consciousness (contrary to harmony and rhythm); in the face of it our reason remains powerless, for melody is essentially irrational. There can be an angelic melody, but not an angelic rhythm, because in eternity there is no longer time, but there is and there will ever be praise. . . ."

As against the motif, which is, so to speak, "an abortive melody, stopped at a certain moment of its growth," and the theme, which is, on the contrary, "a melody at a secondary stage of its development," and embodied in the musical action, "melody itself is linked to no action, and leads to no action. It is a kind of *thing in itself*. The motif serves to justify the action. The theme is a means of developing a thought. But melody is of no use at all. Melody gives *liberation*. At any moment whatever of a logically complex musical situation, the advent of melody immediately brings liberation, to the very extent of the importance of the melody which arises. Melody is one thing, and all the 'music' is, in the last analysis, quite another thing. For with melody 'one can do nothing.'

"Melody is, as it were, an instant where the conditions of time and space are brought to naught, and the musical being is perceived as free from them. Melody gives the illusion of being a stopped instant, and so gives the impression of belonging to the category of the eternal. . . . It is a good through itself, being an expression of the truth of the one who produces it. It appears as a purification by confession, from the fact that it reveals the nondisfigured essence of that which is, and not any lie imagined by its author." [17] What is told us here is indeed that melody is the pure and direct expression of poetic experience in the composer.

11. On the side of painters, nowhere do we find richer insights about their own poetic experience than in Chinese tradition. If we are looking for evidence from our modern Western artists, we may remember this statement of Robert Henri: "The object, which is back of every true work of art, is *the attainment of a state of being*, a state of high function-

ing, a more than ordinary moment of existence. In such moments activity is inevitable, and whether this activity is with brush, pen, chisel, or tongue, its result is but a by-product of the state, a trace, the footprint of the state." We may (if we are not afraid of the Romantics) take into consideration the aphorisms of Caspar-David Friedrich: "Close your physical eye, in order first to see your picture with the eye of the spirit. Then make what you have seen in your night rise to daylight, in order for your action to be exercised in turn on other beings, from the outside toward the inside." "The painter must not paint only what he sees before himself, but also what he sees within himself. If he sees nothing within himself, let him give up painting what he sees without." We may hear Rouault speaking of the painter's "Interior promptings," or Picasso asserting that "a painter paints to unload himself of feelings and visions." Yet I think that, if we are interested in the unexpressed bearing of the simplest expressions, when they are used in the unsophisticated style proper to painters, we shall especially enjoy Cézanne's exclamation to Ambroise Vollard: "I damn well have to be let alone when I *meditate*." A deep "meditation," to be sure, since the only possible revenge for having been troubled in it by some pest was to destroy the nearest of his paintings at hand.

I would conclude this attempt at an analysis by saying that poetic experience, though the motion it involves terminates "in an arrangement of words on paper," [18] or of notes on a score, or of colors on a canvas, is of itself a sort of natural contemplation, obscure and affective, and implies a moment of silence and alert receptivity. Without this moment of contemplation there is no poetic activity.

Self-awareness and the Search for Self-purification in Modern Poetry

12. There has been in modern poetry a remarkable search for self-purification. I do not mean to say a search for intellectual or moral purification. Modern poets have treated intelligence with no less disrespect than have modern philos-

ophers, and they have proved to be very well prepared for all kinds of diseases of the intellect.

In speaking of a search for self-purification, I think of a search for the purification of poetry itself of all extraneous or adventitious elements, or of a search after the pure essence of poetry. This search, I think, is one with the search for self-awareness; both have developed together.

At this point I would submit that the French language being naturally an exceptionally remarkable instrument for prose, not for poetry—and the most obtrusive tradition of the French mind being Cartesian and rationalist—and French classical poetry having been too often (I don't speak of Villon, or Scève, or Racine) a rhymed discursus of reason —the outburst of poetic self-awareness which has come about since Baudelaire has produced in France a most extraordinary crisis and most extraordinary results: a kind of heroic struggle with the language, rendered by force a surprisingly powerful poetic instrument, whose very intellectuality swarms with burning signs; and a kind of heroic effort of poetic intelligence to discover at any price and lay bare its own hidden substance.

I realize that it would be presumptuous of me to air opinions about English poetry. May I say, nevertheless, that, to my mind, because the English language (which makes philosophy miserable) lends itself to poetry in the most connatural manner, and offers it such admirable facilities that they absolve it from worrying about its own nocturnal depths— perhaps also because English poetry has, it seems to me, a speech of its own born in high places above prose, whereas French poetry steals its speech from prose, either inconspicuously diverting the ways of prose or mining into its rock—English poetry has developed in a more continuous way, and has not been driven in modern times to such a need for metamorphosis, nor led by self-awareness to so revealing a convulsion.

As a result, I would say that, although between English or American and French modern poetry there is an external similarity—a similar approach to images, words, the means

of expression, and a similar behavior of the sensibility—
nevertheless the primary experience, the sort of collective
revolutionary experience on which all has depended for
modern French poetry, has not been felt elsewhere, it seems
to me, with the same cogent necessity, nor has it played the
same central part, both in the sense of center of disturbance
and of center of gravity. I think that Mr. Blackmur's profound analysis of Hart Crane's tragic lack of integration,
and of the perfect but too perfect perhaps and too clever
ambiguity of Wallace Stevens remarkably illustrates this
situation with respect to two significant instances.[19] In short,
English poetry continued its song—with modern inflections.
It did not go mad on the subject of knowing what poetry is.

13. All previous observations I submit to the verdict of
more competent judges. Taking up now the thread of my
remarks, I note that in the seventeenth and eighteenth centuries art advanced in an invaluable way its consciousness of
itself *in so far as it is art,* thanks to grammarians and masters in rhetoric and prosody.

As to the *prise de conscience* of *poetry as poetry,* it was
only in the course of the nineteenth century that the phenomenon came about. Then, for some decades, one was able
to contemplate a series of discoveries, failures, catastrophes,
and revelations which were extraordinarily illuminating. I
believe that what occurred after Baudelaire with respect to
poetry had in the domain of art as much historic significance
as, in the domain of science, the greatest crises of renewal
and revolution in physics and astronomy.

As has been observed in other parts of this book,
self-awareness has brought to poetry both unheard-of possibilities for precious disclosures and, when reflective introspection disregards or distorts the essence of poetic knowledge,
serious risks of perversion. In itself self-awareness is an
incomparable spiritual gain. We may believe that the conquest and discovery of the immense fields contained in poetic knowledge, and revealed by its becoming self-aware, will
make the fortune of poetry if the poets are thus quickened

in their *work of creation,* that is, if their spiritual experience
is deep enough, and their operative reason strong enough, to
turn self-awareness into a superior sort of simplicity, through
an *esprit d'enfance,* of disinterestedness, and of voluntary
poverty. For the virtues required of the modern artist—I
mean, in the very sphere of art, as aesthetic, not moral virtues—are, as Max Jacob put it, evangelic in nature. "One
must be a very great poet to be a modern poet," he said.[20]
And he went on to say: "Voluntary poverty is an aesthetic
virtue. Soberness is an aesthetic virtue. Chastity is an aesthetic virtue. Respect is an aesthetic virtue." "Fortitude,
renouncement, obedience, order, humility" are aesthetic
virtues in the realm of art, as they are Christian virtues in
the realm of moral life.

The Poetic Sense

14. The poetic sense, in the work, corresponds to the poetic experience, in the poet.

That is enough to make us realize the essential difference
which separates the poetic sense from the logical sense.

We have already observed that the poetic sense is to the
poem what the soul is to man—it is the poetic intuition
itself communicated to the work in its native, pure, and
immediate efficacy. What it means, through the complex
fabric of all the elements and qualities of the work, is subjectivity obscurely grasped in its very night together with
some transapparent reality resounding in it. Such a primordial sense or meaning gives to the poem its inner consistency, its necessary configuration, and first of all its very
being and existence. "The poetic sense" of a poem "cannot
be separated from the verbal form it animates from
within," [21] from the whole fabric of words it causes to exist.
And the words, there, are not only signs of concepts or ideas,
but objects also, objects which are endowed with their
proper sonorous quality. Their function as signs, in their
mutual interrelation, depends at the same time on this
physical sonorous quality itself—and on the images they
convey—and on the fog or aura of unexpressed associations

they carry with them—and on their intelligible or logical meaning (only a part of the whole).

So the poetic sense is a meaning which is immanent in that object which is the poem or consubstantial with it, and which the reader intuitively perceives, perhaps after a time of careful rereading, and either of intellectual concentration (especially when the poem is "difficult") or (especially when the poem is obscure in nature) of passive attention opening his mind and feelings to significant emotion. It might be said that the poetic sense is the inner melody—perceptible to the mind, not to the ear—of the poem, for in music also the melody is the native, pure, and immediate life force—this time perceptible to the ear—of poetic intuition, the poetic sense of the musical work.

As to the logical or intelligible sense, it is only one of the elements or components of the poetic sense. With respect to the poetic sense it is but a kind of fluid and variegated matter. So that the poetic sense is an immanent meaning made up of meanings: the intelligible meanings of the words (carried either by concepts or by images)—and the *imaginal* meanings of the words—and the more mysterious meanings of the musical relations between the words, and between the meaningful contents with which the words are laden. Thus the intelligible sense, through which the poem utters ideas, is entirely subordinate to the poetic sense, through which the poem exists.

It is with respect to the intelligible sense that a poem is *clear* or *obscure*. A poem may be obscure or it may be clear, what matters is only the poetic sense. The law of intelligible clarity imposed by the classical tradition has not only been an occasion for innumerable mediocre poems, where the logical sense was prevalent over the poetic sense, but it has often concealed, obscured for theoretical reflection, the necessary primacy of the poetic sense, which was, of course, enforced in practice by all great poets. In modern poetry a swarming of obscure poems, good and bad, has been the price paid for the full recognition of this necessary primacy.

15. Now I hasten to say that no poem can be *completely* obscure, for no poem can completely get rid of the intelligible or logical sense. Poetry does not refer "to a material object closed in itself, but to the universality of being and beauty, perceived each time in a singular existence. It is not in order to 'communicate ideas,' it is in order to keep contact with the universe of intuitivity" [22] that the poem must always, in one way or another, be it in the dark, convey some intelligible meaning. No poem can be completely mute, in spite of the beautiful poem by MacLeish, which itself is far from mute:

> *A poem should be palpable and mute*
> *As a globed fruit*
>
> *Dumb*
> *As old medallions to the thumb*
>
> *Silent as the sleeve-worn stone*
> *Of casement ledges where the moss has grown—*
>
> *A poem should be wordless*
> *As the flight of birds*
>
> *A poem should be motionless in time*
> *As the moon climbs*
>
> . . . .
> *A poem should not mean*
> *But be.*[22a]

A poem must only be, yes, but it cannot be except through the poetic sense; and some intelligible meaning, subordinate or evanescent as it may be, at least some atmosphere of clarity, is part of the poetic sense. It has been observed that when a poet reads aloud a poem which is on the verge of nonsense, and which he loves, he attunes himself so perfectly to the feeling which has generated it, and to its poetic consonance, that he gives to it, willy-nilly, an appearance of logical sense.[23] A similar remark can be made with regard to the records of Joyce's readings. However darkly, however instinctively, intelligence is at play when the poet writes. Even his nonsense he writes, despite all and despite himself, "with a certain secret measure, a certain music, a rhythm of the phrase which, if they are kept to by the reader, will provide the poem with an intelligible resonance." To one degree or another, even in the most obscure poems, even when the poet turns his back completely on intelligence, the intelligible sense is always there. No poem can be absolutely obscure.

Conversely, no poem can be absolutely clear, since no poem can receive its being from the intelligible or logical sense uniquely. "The poetic sense is not the logical sense, and the poem born in the obscurity of self-communion is necessarily obscure to some degree, be it only by reason of *'quelque méprise,'* of 'some' instinctive 'slip' in the choice of words." [24] When we speak of clear or obscure poems, we always mean *to a certain extent*. A clear poem is comparatively clear; an obscure poem, comparatively obscure.

As regards obscure poems, a distinction, moreover, must be made. Mallarmé's, Valéry's, Hopkins', Pound's, Eliot's, Tate's, poems are not "obscure" in essence, but rather in appearance. Let us call such poems "difficult" or "hermetic." Their obscurity comes in reality either from the heavy concentrated intelligibility and the complexity of logical connotations with which they are burdened, or from so tense a concern for the power of significance of the logos that one would want to make of the whole fabric of the poem one single intelligible word. With St.-John Perse it is different: the intellectuality of the word is treasured only as a richer and more pungent vehicle of the subconscious rush of poetic knowledge.

Other poems are obscure in essence—though the reflective analysis of the critic still can bring out, more or less painfully, the trace at least of intelligible sense which, as we have seen, is necessarily there. They are obscure in essence— I would say "nocturnal"—because they are obscure with the obscurity of feeling. Here the poet is not concerned with the intellectual mystery of the significative and constructive power of the Word, but with the mysterious screen or obstacle that thwarts in every sign the function of signification. He wants to get free from this inherent screen by humbling and dislocating the words, so as to make them more flexible and more transparent (though in darkness) instruments of intuitive emotion. It is this second category of obscure poems that I have in view in the present analysis, precisely because they are obscure in essence, and because they oblige us to enter more deeply into the secret workings of poetry.

16. Baudelaire's poems are clear. He did not change any of the ways and laws of expression of the poetic language. He seems to speak like the others. Yet a revolution has taken place, invisibly. What seems to me the token of his exceptional greatness is the fact that with him, through an incomparable power of intellectualization and spiritualization of sensuality, and the implacable strength of his introverted vision, the poem has been transformed into a single missile conveying a single irresistible intuition—with an immensely increased power of penetration. Its external structure remains the same, but its inner concentration is not the same; all its parts, in reality, are only joined together by the fire of the poetic intuition, because the logical sense has been burned from within, and is now only a channel for this fire.

Many modern poems are also clear poems. May I quote two, chosen to my liking? First, the beginning of "Sailing to Byzantium":[25]

> *That is no country for old men. The young*
> *In one another's arms, birds in the trees,*
> *—Those dying generations—at their song,*
> *The salmon-falls, the mackerel-crowded seas,*
> *Fish, flesh, or fowl, commend all summer long*
> *Whatever is begotten, born, and dies.*
> *Caught in that sensual music all neglect*
> *Monuments of unageing intellect.*
>
> *An aged man is but a paltry thing,*
> *A tattered coat upon a stick, unless*
> *Soul clap its hands and sing, and louder sing*

> *For every tatter in its mortal dress,*
> *Nor is there singing school but studying*
> *Monuments of its own magnificence;*
> *And therefore I have sailed the seas and come*
> *To the holy city of Byzantium.*

The second poem is by Apollinaire (I remember his head bandaged in white; he had been wounded on duty during the first war, and his death was indeed arriving—as a whistling hurricane):

Je n'ai plus même pitié de moi
Et ne puis exprimer mon tourment de silence
Tous les mots que j'avais à dire se sont changés en étoiles
Un Icare tente de s'élever jusqu'à chacun de mes yeux
Et porteur de soleil je brûle au centre de deux nébuleuses
Qu'ai-je fait aux bêtes théologales de l'intelligence
Jadis les morts sont revenus pour m'adorer
Et j'espérais la fin du monde
Mais la mienne arrive en sifflant comme un ouragan.[26]

Such poems are condensed, the expression is purely restricted to the essentials, any discursive or oratorical development and liaison has been replaced by allusive streaks. But they are clear poems: the intelligible sense is *explicit,* either expressed by conceptual utterances clearly *circumscribing* it—or carried by images, without the intermediary of any expressed concept (though a great many virtual concepts are involved), in which case the intelligible sense, although still explicit, is, as it were, *not circumscribed,* I would say, open.

17. Let us consider now more or less obscure poems (obscure in essence).[27] In certain of them—sometimes the most obscure—the concepts and conceptual utterances may take up a great deal of room, but, because they are then submitted to the mental regime of imagination, not of logical connections, and to the nocturnal law which presides over the stirring of images, they hardly convey any explicit intelligible sense.

> *It was sweet to drown in the readymade handy water*
> *With my cherry capped dangler green as seaweed*

Summoning a child's voice from a webfoot stone,
Never never oh never to regret the bugle I wore
On my cleaving arm as I blasted in a wave.
Now shown and mostly bare I would lie down,
Lie down, lie down and live
As quiet as a bone.[28]

A l'expiration de mon enfance, je m'enlisai dans un
marais. Des aboiements éclataient partout. "Tu ne les
entendrais pas si bien si tu n'étais toi-même prêt à aboyer.
Aboie donc." Mais je ne pus.

Des années passèrent après lesquelles j'aboutis à une terre
plus ferme. Des craquements s'y firent entendre, partout des
craquements, et j'eusse voulu craquer moi aussi, mais ce
n'est pas le bruit de la chair.

Je ne puis quand même pas sangloter, pensais-je, moi qui
suis devenu presque un homme.[29]

In other more or less obscure poems, the conceptual utterances have either disappeared or they are reduced to a
minimum or are merely allusive. Here again, there is no
longer any *explicit* intelligible sense, even carried by the images. The intelligible sense dawning in the images is only
implicit.

Sometimes[30] this implicit intelligible sense is still *determined,* I mean pointing to an object (though in a merely
implicit manner):

> *High in the noon of May*
> *On cornices of daffodils*
> *The slender violets stray.*
> *Crap-shooting gangs in Bleecker region,*
> *Peonies with pony manes—*
> *Forget-me-nots at windowpanes.*[31]

Only images. Is it, however, a mere visual description of the
flowering spring? No, all this carries an implicit intelligible
sense, and this implicit sense points to the mysterious big
city by which the poet's emotive intuition was stirred.

Sometimes the implicit intelligible sense is *undetermined,*
I mean pointing to no object, and only pushing our intellect
in a certain direction; nothing in the poem makes this di-

rection clear, we are only prompted toward it in actual fact. We see nothing, yet we feel there is something to be looked at.

> Nevertheless I dislike
> The way the ants crawl
> In and out of my shadow.[32]

> Sur une mer en l'air de maisons et de vide
> Rappelez-vous le bal: un bateau fait en fil.[33]

There is an intelligible meaning, but we don't know what this meaning is; only through reflective afterthought shall we be able to surmise something about it. But reflective afterthought has nothing to do with the direct perception of the poem.

> I see a distance of black yews
> Long as the history of the Jews

> I see a road sunned with white sand
> Wide plains surrounding silence. And

> Far-off, a broken colonnade
> That overthrows the sun with shade.[34]

The intelligible meaning is not only implicit, but *undetermined.* Our intelligence is aware of the existence of a signification, but the signified remains unknown. And it is enough for the poem to have radiance, as a black diamond has, and for the intellect to receive a delight, still more insidious perhaps as the signified is unknown: since the fact that what is signified by a sign is unknown is almost the fact that the sign signifies the unknown.

In the same way it can happen that in ritual dances and folklore solemnities or in the rites of those fancy-dress brotherhoods which have such appeal even for businessmen, in royal coronations, in judicial ceremonies, or in carnival processions, all of which are a kind of collective poetry of the people, the significance of the sign is forgotten in the course of time, or remains obscure and indistinct." [35] The essential thing is that there should be a sign and signification. If I do not know exactly what a given sign signifies, well, it is then free to signify *everything* for me. In a sense, poetical joy and affective exaltation will then only become vaster in becoming more indeterminate.[36]

Finally, the following excerpts from *Ash Wednesday*[37] offer to us, it seems to me, an instance in which clarity and obscurity, explicit abstract meanings and implicit undetermined significations intertwine to compose a complex radiance of an admirable quality.

Lady of silences
Calm and distressed
Torn and most whole

Rose of memory
Rose of forgetfulness
Exhausted and life-giving
Worried reposeful
The single Rose
Is now the Garden
Where all loves end
Terminate torment
Of love unsatisfied
The greater torment
Of love satisfied
End of the endless
Journey to no end
Conclusion of all that
Is inconclusible
Speech without word and
Word of no speech
Grace to the Mother
For the Garden
Where all love ends.

Under a juniper-tree the bones sang, scattered and shining
We are glad to be scattered, we did little good to each other,
Under a tree in the cool of the day, with the blessing of sand,
Forgetting themselves and each other, united
In the quiet of the desert. This is the land which ye
Shall divide by lot. And neither division nor unity
Matters. This is the land. We have our inheritance.

18. In all the observations I just proposed, we were already beginning to consider the poem, no longer from the point of view of the one who produces it, but from the point of view of the one who reads it or listens to it. A new issue is thus raised, which I shall try to discuss in the next chapter.

In another connection, we might ask ourselves whether it is possible to find in modern painting trends similar to those which modern poetry discloses. Such comparisons are always risky. It could be said, however, it seems to me, that to the triad concept-image-word, with which the poet has to do, what corresponds in painting is the triad *natural appearances-sensation-line and color.*

Now, on the one hand, whereas the image and the concept belong to two different realms, the realm of the senses and that of the intellect, sensation and natural appearances, on the contrary, pertain to the same general order—both relate to the senses. As a result modern painting—while turning from natural appearances to sensation, and definitely realizing that the sensations of the eye at the spectacle of nature, seized in their immediate freshness and intuitivity, and used for a new creation in which they become the very object offered on the canvas, are the chosen instrument or vehicle for conveying more freely the painter's vision (the poetic sense) —nevertheless modern painting could not liberate sensation from natural appearances as completely as modern poetry has liberated the image from the concept. Even impressionists could not produce in painting an equivalent for imagist poetry. Cézanne is, in my opinion, the greatest representative of painting living on sensation and speaking through sensation (*"Les sensations faisant le fond de mon affaire, je crois être impénétrable"*). This sensation-speaking painting, which, from the point of view of the language used, characterizes most of the nineteenth-century schools, recasts and transfigures natural appearances, but it is far from getting rid of them. If painting wants totally to get rid of natural appearances, it must go beyond this point, and become abstract painting, which no longer speaks.

On the other hand, whereas the elementary unit, the

word—any word whatever, even disconnected, even *"les mots en liberté"*—is by nature a sign as well as an object, and always makes present something other than itself, lines and colors, on the contrary, are not signs by themselves, they are made into signs only when they are arranged so as to suggest some sort of thing in nature. As a result, when modern painting, prodded perhaps by a desire to follow in the footsteps of modern poetry, set out to free itself absolutely from natural appearances, it was possible for it to wind up in the stage of abstract or nonrepresentative painting. But the same is not possible for poetry, because poetry uses words. There can be in poetry no equivalent for abstract painting.

These remarks are directly concerned with the means and technical vocabulary of painting and poetry, that is, with something subordinate, and, after all, secondary, however indispensable. We are more interested in the poetic sense. What makes modern painting (I am not speaking of abstract art) singularly dear to us, is the fact that its means are incomparably appropriate for the liberation of the poetic sense. Thus it is that the least bit of modern painting, when it is simply good, awakens in us deeper emotion and resonance, and delight, and love, than many masterpieces of the past. To liberate the poetic sense in their work, the old masters, given the obstacle created by their respect—feigned as it may have been, and yielding to freedom—for natural appearances, were obliged to resort to a science of means, an inventive labor of operative reason, a cleverness and perfection of the virtue of art to which modern painting hardly attains. When they succeeded, the result remains unequalled. Look at the best paintings of Poussin. It was by dint of intelligence and self-restraint, and by avoiding anything which might "debauch" [38] the eye or the mind, that he made the poetic sense prevalent and sovereign in the work, so as to captivate us forever.

EIGHT

THE INTERNALIZATION
OF MUSIC

Poetic Intuition and the Beginning of a
Wordless Musical Stir

1. When Albert Béguin, in his essay on "Poésie et Mystique," [1] speaks of the images which "ascend from the depths of the being and *compose a song*" not yet expressed in words, he points out something which is, I think, common experience among poets. Thus a remarkable fact, on which I should like to lay stress, is the fact that the very first effect, and sign, of poetic knowledge and poetic intuition, as soon as they exist in the soul—and even before the start of any operative exercise—is a kind of musical stir produced in the depths of the living springs in which they are born. It is of the utmost importance, I believe, to distinguish between the musicality of the words (even inner words not yet externally uttered)—and that musical stir, linked with poetic intuition itself, of which I am now speaking and in which the words play no part. By itself it *precedes,* at least as to natural, if not always as to chronological priority, the outpouring of words, and we must consider it apart and for its own sake.

A kind of musical stir, of unformulated song, with no words, no sounds, absolutely inaudible to the ear, audible only to the heart, here is the first sign through which the presence of poetic experience within the soul is recognized. How can we try to give account of this fact? If all our preceding analyses are true, we can say, it seems to me, that on the one hand we have an actual flash of knowing—poetic experience, poetic intuition—born, through spiritualized emotion, in the preconscious, nonconceptual life of the intellect. On the other hand, we have a spiritual milieu—a kind of fluid and moving world, activated by the diffuse light of the Illuminating Intellect, and seemingly asleep but secretly tense and vigilant—which is this preconscious life of the intellect, and of the imagination and of emotion, empty of any actual concept or idea, but full of images and full of emotional movements, and in which all the past experiences and treasures of memory acquired by the soul are present in a state of virtuality. It is within this fluid and moving milieu that poetic experience and poetic intuition exist, not virtually, but as an act or actuation definitely formed.

How would it be possible that they would not awaken and stir this vital milieu, and produce, as it were, waves in it? Poetic intuition expands in it, and this expansion comes about in time, wave after wave. This is a kind of primal expression, though in no way by means of words: a merely psychic, so to speak congenital expression, which originates in the indivisible unity of the poetic intuition. I submit that in the relationship between this indivisible unity of the poetic intuition and the successive partial units of its expansion or expression in its own vital milieu a kind of music is involved.

At this point I should like to introduce a new concept, which seems to me necessary but for which it is not easy to find a name—I would say dynamic charge or *intuitive pulsion*,[2] both imaginal and emotional. Each of the partial units of which I just spoke is a complex of virtual images and emotion, stirred in the fluid and moving world of the creativity of the spirit, and essentially tendential, dynamic, and transient. This complex I call a dynamic charge or intuitive pulsion, awakened by poetic experience under the activating light of the Illuminating Intellect. None of these various pulsions is a total expression of the poetic intuition, all of them essentially depend on its indivisible unity. Between them there is movement and continuity. And this moving continuity between partial units (which originates in the indivisible unity of poetic intuition, and through which poetic intuition passes) is nothing but a *meaning* set free in a *motion:* that is to say, a kind of melody—in the state of a source, a primeval melody—this word being taken in a merely analogical sense, having in no way to do with sounds, but only with inaudible psychic charges of images and emotion. At the moment of which we are now speaking, at the moment of the initial expansion which is one with the existence of the poetic intuition, the images involved in the pulsions are almost unconscious and imperceptible, only in a nascent state; and the emotion involved is the very emotion, spiritualized and intentional, through which the poetic intuition arises, and which now begins to awaken emotional overtones. Such is, as I see it, the *musical stir* immediately produced by poetic experience and poetic intuition.

The Music of Intuitive Pulsions

2. But the expansion of the poetic intuition in its vital milieu develops, and at the same time the intuitive pulsions also expand and become more and more distinct; explicit images awaken, more distinct emotions resound in the fundamental emotion. Then there is in the soul of the poet an enlarged musical stir, a music no longer almost imperceptible, but more and more cogent, in which the soundless rhythmic and harmonic relations between intuitive pulsions, together with their soundless melody, merge into consciousness. This enlarged musical stir is the spontaneous start of operative exercise; with it the process of expression begins, in a first transient and tendential stage. Yet this music is still an inaudible music—not the music of the words, but the music of the intuitive pulsions, within the soul. Mallarmé alluded to it, I think, when he wrote: *Le chant jaillit de*

source innée, antérieure à un concept, si purement que re-
fléter au dehors mille rythmes d'images"; and Coleridge
too, when he insisted that " 'The man that hath not music
in his soul' can indeed never be a genuine poet."

> *O pure of heart! thou need'st not ask of me*
> *What this strong music in the soul may be!*

But it is not enough to speak of the "music in the soul,"
or, as Carl-Gustav Carus put it, of "that song," which
is a "wondrous confidence of the Unconscious to the Conscious," and which is "feeling." We must try to look more
closely at the "innate source," and to understand how

> *Music is feeling then, not sound.*[3]

As a matter of fact, if we know the existence of this inaudible music, within the soul of the poet, it is because in
listening to the poem—especially to "modern" or post-
Baudelaire poems—a similar music is awakened within
our own soul. Yet I am not following now the order of discovery, but that of logical exposition, and so I am obliged
to speak of the poet before speaking of the poem and of the
one who listens to it. Furthermore I am confronted with a
special difficulty, because I am dealing with something which
I must look for *behind* the words, *as if* I were in the presence of the emotional movements within the imagination of
the poet, *before* the production of words: well, no philosophical analysis is possible in this domain without such an effort
at introspective reconstruction.

Here, then, we have, I think, a first stage, merely imaginal and emotional, in the expression of poetic experience.
It is transient and tendential, it tends to verbal expression,
and as a matter of fact it may now and then take place at
the same time as the outpouring of words and their "arrangement on the paper" (or the arrangement of colored
spots on the canvas, or the arrangement of sounds on the
score), which is the second and final stage. Yet my contention is that these two stages in poetic expression are distinct
in nature, and that the transient expression through those

natural signs which are the imaginal and emotional pulsions comes first, and precedes in nature the expression through those *social* signs which are the words of the language.

3. As a result, I would say that there are two essentially distinct musics, in the designation of which the word music has only an analogous sense, the music of the intuitive pulsions, within the soul, and the music of words—and of the imagery contained in words—which will pass outside the soul, into the external world: as there are two essentially distinct stages in poetic expression, the transient expression through the intuitive pulsions, and the final expression through the words. All this is given, in one sense. For poetic intuition *is given*. And poetic intuition *gives* the transient expression through intuitive pulsions; and poetic intuition *gives* the final expression through words. But with the first stage of poetic expression the operative exercise has already started; and as soon as the operative exercise starts, the virtue of art begins to be involved. Already in the first stage of poetic expression, through intuitive pulsions, intelligence is on the alert, only, I mean, to listen, to listen to poetic intuition, and to what is given by it, the music of imaginal and emotional pulsions; and it may happen, now and then, that at the same time the first line of the future poem is also given.

In the second stage of poetic expression—through words—intelligence is on the alert more than ever; it listens both to poetic intuition and to the music of intuitive pulsions, and it waves aside—among all the words spontaneously emerging from the unconscious—everything which is not consonant with this primary rule.

Let us observe at this point that the intuitive pulsions are, as it were, partial and secondary sparks of intuition depending on the central poetic intuition, and awakened in the poet's mind all along the road to creation with its various accidents. And they can be minute emotional-imaginal charges, toward which the poet turns in need of one single line or one single word. Here again the primary task of creative intelligence is, as we have said, a task of *choice* between the words spontaneously offered.

But in this second stage, and in proportion as the process of production develops, creative intelligence is also at play as working reason, accomplishing a properly so-called artistic task, applying the secondary rules of making, taking care of the arrangement of words, weighing and testing everything. Here all the patience and accuracy, all the virtues of craftsmanship are involved, and intelligence works and works again, takes up the task anew, uses all that it knows, displays the most active sagaciousness to be true to its own superior passivity, to the indivisible inspiring actuation received—poetic intuition and wordless meaning or melody—to which it does not cease listening.[4] And this effort of supreme loyalty can be resumed even after years.

For the poem is an object made of words, the most ungrateful and treacherous material—sounds which are poor in color and variety, signs which are worn out by social use, haunted by swarms of adventitious associations, and stubbornly fixed in the least connotations of their meaning. The more transcendent is the inner revelation—ineffable in itself, contained in the poetic intuition, within the creative night of the poet's soul—which a work of words has to express through signs and symbols, in irritating the senses and seducing reason—the more exacting and, as it were, crucifying is the task imposed on the virtue of art. No one is expected to do the impossible; that is what the poet is required to do.

The Transmission of Poetic Intuition through the Poem

4. We are now in a position, it seems to me, to tackle another issue, which I touched on at the end of the preceding chapter, and which has to do with the poem no longer as proceeding from its creative sources in the poet, but as perceived by, and acting on, the one who reads it or listens to it.

Here I should like to observe, in quite a general way, that

the poem is essentially an end, not a means. An end as a new creature engendered in beauty; not a means as a vehicle of communication. "The one all-sufficing motive for a great poet's singing is that expressed by Keats:

> *I was taught in Paradise*
> *To ease my breast of melodies.*

Precisely so. The overcharged breast can find no ease but in suckling the baby-song." [5]

The poetic intuition demands to be objectivized and expressed in a work. It is enough that the work exists, that this kind of a world is created. The fact that it makes the poet communicate with other human beings, even the fact that it is seen, or listened to, is in itself an effect of superabundance, terribly important for the poet, for he is a man, but additional with respect to the prime essential requirement of poetry. And in the last analysis it is fortunate for the poet. For if the prime essential aim were for him to be understood, to have the experience and vision of his heart completely conveyed to, and genuinely received by others, he would be the most unhappy of men. *"On est toujours seul,"* Picasso said.

Yet the effect of superabundance of which we just spoke, the function of conveying something to men, as additional as it may be, plays, in actual fact, a secondary but crucial and necessary role. And it is absolutely essential from the point of the reader, or the listener. What is it which is thus conveyed? Since the work is the final objectivization of poetic intuition, what the work tends finally to convey to the soul of others is the same poetic intuition which was in the soul of the poet: not precisely as creative, but as cognitive, both of the subjectivity of the poet and of a flash of reality echoing the world. Any poetic work is a revealer. A good work delights the sense and the intellect, but the radiance, in its beauty, is first of all the radiance of the ontologic mystery grasped by the intuition of the poet; then, when the work strikes the eyes of another, it causes a communication of intuition, a passage from creative intuition to receptive intuition.

Of course a great many things, and often the most important, the dearest to the poet, are lost and wasted in the process. Furthermore, because of the ambiguity essential to existence and to any great existential achievement, the significance of the work is larger in one sense, and more diversified, in the minds of men than in the mind of its author; a great work lives a life of its own throughout generations— admired, detested, forgotten, rediscovered; and the facets of its message are perpetually changing. What matters is that something be perceived of what was contained, even virtually, in the inexhaustible intuition from which it proceeds. And it is our good fortune if the smallest bit of it is really conveyed to us. Then we may experience somewhat the truth of Shelley's flaming sentence: "Poetry arrests the vanishing apparitions which haunt the interlunations of life, and veiling them or in language or in form, sends them forth among mankind, bearing sweet news of kindred joy to those with whom their sisters abide—abide, because there is no portal of expression from the caverns of the spirit which they inhabit into the universe of things."

The fact remains, in any case, that not only those who glancing at a work expect from it a mere pleasurable mirroring of their own customary feelings, habits of thought and trite perceptiveness simply live in barbarous parts, but also that a mere external contemplation of a work, appreciating its qualities even with trained intelligence and aesthetic discernment, but from the outside, remains on the threshold of poetry. We must listen to the interiority of the work and to the poetic sense, be open to what it conveys, let ourselves be attracted by the magnetic ring of which Plato spoke. And this requires a sort of previous, tentative *consent*—to the work and to the intentions of the poet—without which we cannot be taken into the confidence of the poem.

Now what we receive when we make ourselves thus open is not a participation in the subjectivity or the subjective feelings of the poet. The process of which I am speaking is quite different from such a kind of *Einfühlung*. We keep our identity, we are not interested in commingling ourselves with the self of another; a mixing of subjectivities is by no means attractive—it would be a kind of spiritual unchastity. We are even more interested in what the poet has grasped in things than in his grasping of himself (which however was the most important thing for him). What we receive, though it may be partially or deficiently, is an *intellectual gift*,[6] a participation in the poetic knowledge and poetic intuition through which the poet has perceived a certain unique mystery in the mystery of the world; then, it is true, since poetic intuition is knowledge through emotion, we receive a participation in the poet's emotion—not in his feelings, I mean, but in his spiritualized and intentional emotion, in his emotion as *causing to see*. We receive a transient and incomparable knowing, a vision, a fleeting revelation. And thus it is that it can be said, as C. E. M. Joad puts it: "In the appreciation of music and pictures, we get a momentary and fleeting glimpse of the nature of that reality to a full knowledge of which the movement of life is progressing. For that moment, and so long as the glimpse persists, we realize in anticipation and almost, as it were, illicitly, the nature of the end. We are, if we may so put it, for a moment *there*, just as the traveller may obtain a fleeting glimpse of a distant country from an eminence passed on the way, and cease for a moment from his journey to enjoy the view. And since we are for a moment *there*, we experience, while the moment lasts, that sense of liberation from the urge and drive of life, which has been noted as one of the characteristics of aesthetic experience." [7]

Classical Poetry and the Music of Words

5. How then, is poetic intuition thus conveyed? I do not intend to discuss this problem in all its aspects, I should like only to emphasize a point which is of special importance for me: that is, the internalization of music as manifested to us by modern poetry.

In order to make things clearer, I shall consider, in a purposely oversimplified manner, first, the case of a classical poem as produced by the poet; second, the case of the same poem as perceived by the reader.

Let us bring our attention to bear on the general structure of the activity of the mind. As we saw in a previous chapter, its various functions envelop one another. Yet in relation to our purpose, and as regards the prevailing influence at play, three different regions or areas can be distinguished in this activity. First, the region of the Preconscious life of the Intellect, where poetic intuition is born. Second, the region of the Imagination. Third, the region of Conceptual and logical Reason.

Now let us consider our first case, the production of the classical poem. Near the center of the soul, on the verge of the spiritual preconscious, poetic experience is awakened, poetic intuition has captured in things a flash of reality, and points to it. Then a first expression, with no words or concepts, comes about in the region of the imagination, through those natural signs which are the intuitive pulsions, both imaginal and emotional.

All this is common to modern and classical poetry. But, in classical poetry, when it comes to the second stage in expression, the expression by words—the creative impulse enters the sphere of authority of conceptual reason, and conceptual reason claims its rights to sovereignty. The intuitive content which puts pressure on the poet must be translated into concepts, and this translation into concepts must comply with the absolute primacy of the rational connections and the logical objectivity to be expressed through the signs of this social instrument which is language. A set of conceptual units rationally assembled is built in order to *communicate notions*. The classical poem, thus, is, if I may put it so, a *bound* (logically bound) form; and it is necessarily clear, the intelligible sense which is an element of the poetic sense is *explicit* intelligible sense. Furthermore, the first stage in expression, the expression through the music of intuitive pulsions, has been most often repressed and superseded by the sovereign claims of the rational expression and the conceptual unfolding, which prevent this inner music from being conveyed by the words.[8]

6. In our second instance, we have the reader confronted with this poem. And let us remember that, according to the old saying of Logicians, *words signify concepts* and *concepts signify things.* The reader is confronted with a work of words which signify, through concepts subjected to the sovereignty of rational connections and logical objectivity, a definite set of things, standing as objective realities before the mind—for instance a lamp which is shattered, a cloud scattered, a lute broken, and a love forgotten—or the fact that a girl named Rose Aylmer had all gifts and died. Well, if this were all, where would be the difference between poetry and a piece of information—a piece of information which, moreover, would let the essentials escape? It is not this definite *set of things* that the poem is intended to signify, this definite set of things is only a means, and an intermediary, even an obstructive intermediary. Far beyond it, what the poem signifies is the flash of reality to which the poetic intuition points, and which it has captured obscurely in the mystery of the world, for instance the unique pity of Rose Aylmer's death as intuitively grasped by Walter Savage Landor, or the frailty of love as intuitively grasped by Shelley. Thus, in reality, the reader is confronted with a work of words which signifies, first, as an intermediary, and through concepts subjected to the primacy of logical connections, a *definite set of things* standing as objects of thought—and second, as the final aim, a mysterious *flash of reality* which has been grasped without concept and which no concept can express. How can the reader be made aware of this second signification, the true signification of the poem? Only by being brought back toward the original intuition. And this can be accomplished only through a magnetic, supraconceptual power, which is the *music of the words* (including that of the proffered notions and images) strong enough to overcome the obstacle

created by the intermediary signification, the definite set of things, and to put the eyes of our logical reason to sleep, and to lead us, captive, to a participation in the poetic intuition which was born in the spiritual night of the preconceptual activity of the poet.

> *Ah, what avails the sceptred race,*
> *Ah, what the form divine!*
> *What every virtue, every grace!*
> *Rose Aylmer, all were thine.*

> *Rose Aylmer, whom these wakeful eyes*
> *May weep, but never see,*
> *A night of memories and of sighs*
> *I consecrate to thee.*[9]

> *When the lamp is shattered*
> *The light in the dust lies dead—*
> *When the cloud is scattered*
> *The rainbow's glory is shed.*

> *When the lute is broken,*
> *Sweet tones are remembered not;*
> *When the lips have spoken,*
> *Loved accents are soon forgot.*[10]

Thus it is that the music of words is of absolute necessity for the classical poem; and together with the music of words, the rhyme, and all the prosodic requirements of a regular form. All these laws and exigencies are but the instruments of liberation of the poetic sense.

Let us take another instance, say Blake's "The Sick Rose." The original music of intuitive pulsions is merely latent, it has been repressed by the weaving of rational expression; but the music of the words is there, and does the whole job.

> *O Rose, thou art sick!*
> *The invisible worm,*
> *That flies in the night*
> *In the howling storm,*

> *Has found out thy bed*
> *Of crimson joy:*
> *And his dark secret love*
> *Does thy life destroy.*

Modern Poetry and the Internalization of Music

7. Let us read now a modern poem—I choose at random —for instance some lines from "The Hollow Men":[11]

> *This is the dead land*
> *This is cactus land*
> *Here the stone images*
> *Are raised, here they receive*
> *The supplication of a dead man's hand*
> *Under the twinkle of a fading star.*
> *It is like this*
> *In death's other kingdom*
> *Waking alone*
> *At the hour when we are*
> *Trembling with tenderness*
> *Lips that would kiss*
> *Form prayers to broken stone.*

Modern poetry has undertaken completely to set free the poetic sense. In the double signification of the poem, it endeavors to extenuate, if possible to abolish the intermediary signification, this *definite set of things* whose presence is due to the sovereignty of the logical requirements of the social signs of language, and which is, as it were, a kind of wall of separation between the poetic intuition and the unconceptualizable flash of reality to which it points. The poem is intended to have, not a double, but a single signification— only this flash of reality captured in things.

Thus, in our third case, the case of the production of the modern poem, the poet is intent on the intuitive pulsions stirred by poetic intuition in the region of the imagination. There, in the preconscious life of the intellect, the images, instead of being used for the birth of ideas in the process of abstraction, are moved and quickened by poetic intuition, under the light of the Illuminating Intellect: and the unconceptualizable intelligibility involved in poetic intuition passes through them in an *intentional* or immaterial manner, so that they are made into the vehicles of an intelligible meaning, which will never terminate in a concept, and can remain implicit, even sometimes undetermined, but still is an intelligible meaning, capable of obscurely touching and moving the intellect. And it is from the imaginal-emotional pulsions, and the intelligibility conveyed by the images, that the poet receives the supreme organizing law of his words; it is with respect to these pulsions that he makes concepts and words connected with one another. He sometimes even completely dispenses with explicit concepts, and passes immediately from the images to the words.

Yet this is a particular case, and modern poetry is in no way concerned with being merely imagist poetry. It uses concepts, not only implicit concepts carried along by the images, but explicit concepts as well, and highly abstract concepts, and so much the better if its concepts are loaded with the richest content of thought! But the supreme law of expression is no longer the law of rational and logical connections, it is the law of the inner connections between intuitive pulsions, and of the unconceptualized intelligibility of which the images quickened by poetic intuition are the vehicles. Even in the clearest modern poem, in which the expression develops along pure rational channels, the secret law which commands everything remains the law of obedience to the movement of intuitive pulsions, the verbal expression remain ceaselessly sustained and permeated by the experience of this inner emotional and imaginal movement. And this is still more apparent in the many poems which do not develop along pure rational channels. In any case the sovereignty has shifted from the rational connections to the experiential and internal ones. Let us say, then, that now the poem is a *free form,* I mean not logically bound, and it may be clear but it may also be obscure, that is, involving a merely implicit, even undetermined intelligible meaning.

8. And thus, when it comes to our fourth instance—the case of a modern poem as perceived by the reader—the reader is confronted with a work of words which does not signify first a *definite set of things*—the wall of separation has fallen. The poem signifies only the unconceptualizable flash of reality obscurely grasped in the mystery of the world by the intuitive emotion of the poet.

The words, which signify no longer concepts subjected (as is normal in science) to the sovereignty of rational connections and logical objectivity—and which, therefore, signify no longer things as a set of objective realities standing before the mind—the words now signify concepts (implicit or explicit concepts) and images (images carrying explicit or implicit intelligible meaning) as obeying the law of intuitive pulsions, and connected together with respect to intuitive pulsions. And thus the words immediately bring the reader back to the inner music of the intuitive pulsions stirred in the imagination of the poet, and finally, through this music, to a participation in the poetic intuition naturally expressed by this music. For there there is music, as I pointed out at the beginning. And this inner music plays its essential part in classical as well as in modern poetry with respect to the *birth* of the poem in the soul of the poet. But with respect to the *expression* it remained most often unexpressed in classical poetry, because it was *displaced,* repressed, or obliterated by the royal law and privilege of the rational expression, and was *replaced* by the music of words. Now, on the contrary, the music of intuitive pulsions appears in the foreground, it is revealed in full, it has become the royal instrument of poetic expression. The reader immediately listens to it, and in his soul are awakened intuitive pulsions akin to those in the poet's soul. There has been a reversion, or introversion; poetry cannot do without music, but the primary role has shifted from the music of words to the internal music of the intuitive pulsions. Such is that internalization of music which I wanted to point out. I do not believe that without modern poetry we could have become fully aware of the importance of this inaudible, wordless, and soundless music.

It is easy, I think, to verify such observations if we read modern poets,[12] exercising at the same time our power of introspection, and paying attention not only to the words but to what they produce within ourselves.

Here again we must first invoke Baudelaire, who, as I observed in the preceding chapter, seems to speak the language of classical poetry, and who in reality has already changed everything, by virtue of the exceptional force of his gaze turned inwards, and of his extraordinary power of intellectualization of sensuality, bringing everything back toward the internal sources. There are sometimes surprisingly platitudinous and prosaic pieces in his lines: they pass unnoticed: they do not matter. The visible form of the poem is eclipsed by the violence of the intuition. At the same time, the rhythm of the charges of intuitive emotion has been made absolutely prevalent.

I find a similar prevalence of the music of intuitive pulsions in all the poems I quoted in the Texts for this chapter under heading II.

Sous le pont Mirabeau coule la Seine/
  Et nos amours./

I am gall, I am heartburn./
                God's most deep decree
Bitter would have my taste./
                My taste with me./

We have lingered in the chambers of the sea
        By sea-girls wreathed with seaweed red and brown/
Till human voices wake us/
                And we drown./

I have put division marks in these lines, not to stress the scansion, but to indicate the dynamic charges or intuitive pulsions with which they are laden, and to beg the reader to lend himself to an experiment, and to listen *within himself,* each time, to the awakening of these soundless, purely mental units of image and emotion.

In the following lines of Yeats (from "The Blessed") there is, it seems to me, a simple melody of intuitive emotional charges, each one expressed in one line:

> *And blessedness goes where the wind goes,|*
> *And when it is gone we are dead;|*
> *I see the blessedest soul in the world|*
> *And he nods a drunken head.|*

In other lines of Yeats ("After Long Silence" [13]), there is a more complex harmony. After a brief pulsion comes a long cadence of five lines, in which other pulsions are involved, as integral parts of one single motion. And then two final pulsions mysteriously one. The whole rhetorical movement of the poem is but the expression of the complex internal movement and music of all these imaginal-emotional pulsions:

> *Speech after long silence;||*
>   *it is right,*
>   *All other lovers being estranged or dead,|*
>   *Unfriendly lamplight hid under its shade,|*
>   *The curtains drawn upon unfriendly night,|*
>   *That we descant and yet again descant*
>   *Upon the supreme theme of Art and Song:||*

> *Bodily decrepitude is wisdom;||*
>   *young*
> *We loved each other and were ignorant.||*

9. To sum up, I would say that a poem is an engine to make us pass *through* or *beyond* things, and that the process of spiritual production and, consequently, the structure of such an engine are typically different in classical and in modern poetry. This I have taken the liberty of expressing by means of two diagrams, for those readers (if there are any) who are fond of this innocent hobby. Of course these diagrams make things more absolute and more sharp-edged than they are in reality. I think nevertheless that in both cases they point to the essential directions.

The first diagram refers to classical poetry.

It represents, first, the process of spiritual production of the poem in the mind of the poet (area I being that of the Preconscious life of the Intellect; area II, that of the Imagination; area III, that of Concepts and Reason); second, the structure of the poem; third, the reality attained. And, in the fourth place, the thick line is a symbol of the return movement, or of the significance of the poem, as conveying to the mind (no longer of the poet, but of the reader) the reality attained by the poet.

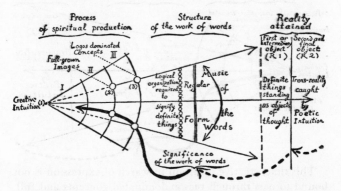

Creative intuition (1) in search of expression passes mainly through full-grown and definitely formed images (2)—what we called in Chapter IV the externals of imagination—and through concepts existing under the regime of the logos (3) (the images are even, more often than not, sought and picked up to illustrate explicit concepts after the latter have been elicited).

The poem aims to express and signify the transreality (R^2) caught by creative intuition, but in order to do so it must use the instrumentality (and the screen) of definite things which stand as objects of thought (R^1), and are signified by logically organized concepts. The work of words, bound to this logical organization, has, thus, a *double signification* (R^1 and R^2), the first of which (R^1) belongs to the realm of rationalized and socialized communicability. To compensate for this extrapoetic burden, the music of the words is of absolute necessity.

Finally the poem is also subjected to a *double regulation*. The first regulation is that of creative intuition and of the secondary rules of the making which are at the service of creative intuition. The second regulation is that of the regular form of the poem.

Our second diagram refers to modern poetry.

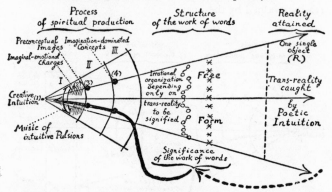

This time, creative intuition in search of expression is not bound to pass through reason-dominated concepts and full-grown images which have been logically organized. The creative process is free to start developing in the nest of dynamic unity of image and thought where the music of intuitive pulsions takes place, and where emotion and nascent images are pregnant with virtual intelligibility. Creative intuition (1) passes mainly through those spiritual germs which are the intuitive pulsions (2) through preconceptual images (3) and through concepts (4) which, whether explicitly formed, or just emerging from mother images, are subject to the regime of imagination more than to their own logical regime.

The poem signifies only the transreality (R) caught by poetic intuition, without being bound first to signify a definite set of things standing as objects of thought. It has, thus, *one single significance,* which has to do with poetic intelligence, not with rationalized and socialized communicability. St. Paul says that those who are unmarried have only a single care, how they may please God, having not to please a wife or husband too.[14] So the virgin poem tends to its unique object without division.

The music of the words, still necessary as it may be, yields the foremost place to another, more internal, music. Music is pushed back inwardly. What matters essentially now is the music of intuitive pulsions, which passes into the work of words freely—without being repressed or obliterated by the exigencies of the logos—and to which the reader in his turn is taken by this work of words.

Finally the poem is subjected to *one single regulation*— that of the creative intuition and of the rules of the making which are at the service of creative intuition. The form of the poem is free, which does not mean free from any rule, but free from any regular pre-established pattern.

10. Thus it is that modern poetry had to dispense with the regular form of the poem, and the necessity of the rhyme, and the other requirements of classical prosody. Modern poetry is bound to obey more exacting laws and rules, for they are free and contingent rules, depending at each moment on the correctness of the ear, and on the fact of each and every word, measure and period in the poem being exactly in tune with the soundless music stirred by poetic intuition within the soul. "These mysterious rules," as Cocteau puts it, "are with regard to the old rules of versification what ten games of chess played at once are with regard to a game of dominoes." [15]

Even modern poetry often dispenses, or believes it dispenses, with the music of words. In so doing, either it searches in reality for a tougher, not pleasurable, broken music, but still music, or it loses and gets clear of an indispensable element, because it believes that the music of words prevents or masks the pure expression of the inner pulsions of images. This is only an effect of too weak a power in the poet himself. For the music of words is in the work of words the necessary response of the words to the inaudible music stirred by poetic intuition. In the best modern poems, this internal music is all the more expressed and cogent as the music of words is purer and truer.

Although, in classical poetry, which was too talkative, as a rule, the sovereign claims of rational expression and conceptual unfolding most often left unexpressed the music of the intuitive pulsions, this internal music, nevertheless, found expression at the most radiant moments—rare indeed, at least in French classical poetry—and in great poets it was muted or made far away rather than completely repressed. Sometimes it even risked escaping our inattentive mind only because it was too perfectly fused with, and expressed by, the music of words. Such is the marvel of some famous lines of Racine:

> *Ariane, ma sœur, de quel amour blessée*
> *Vous mourûtes aux bords où vous fûtes laissée*

or of Webster:

> Cover her face; mine eyes dazzle; she died young.

Let it be observed, to avoid any misunderstanding, that the fact of modern poetry's being primarily concerned with the intuitive pulsions of images and emotion, and overlapping, so to speak, the area of sovereignty of conceptual reason, means in no way that modern poetry is a merely affective and sensory poetry. For this fact has to do only with poetic expression. The richness in thought, in intellectual knowledge, in rational depth, may be as great in modern poetry as in classical poetry. It is expressed otherwise, through freer and more intuitive means, that's all.

I have said that in its process toward expression modern poetry has freed itself from the sovereignty of the logical organization of concepts. I do not mean that it is empty of concepts, and sweeps away concepts from the mind! Here I should like to insist on what I have already pointed out. The intellect cannot do without concepts. On the one hand, in the very process of expression, there are concepts, either concepts in a nascent state, and virtual, as it were, carried along by the images; or implicit, unapparent concepts, serving only as supports for the expression of images;[16] or concepts which are explicit and used with their full intellectual meaning: in any case, and this is the essential point, they remain indispensable instruments of meaning, but they are no longer the masters of the work, and in this sense they have all been dethroned; poetic expression does away with their well-off descriptive garrulity, as well as with the necessity of making prevalent their own regime of rational articulation and logical objectivity. On the other hand, before the process of poetic expression, and with respect to that knowledge which is *previous* to poetic knowledge, a modern poet is as full of concepts, right or wrong, as a classical poet. They are part of the treasure of memory which is present, in a virtual state, in the preconscious life of the intellect, and which is used by poetic intuition.

A Parenthesis about the Critic

11. To finish this discussion of the poem as perceived by man, or the poem as speaking to the reader, I should like to add a few words about the critic. In the second chapter I quoted the passage where Baudelaire declares that it would be unnatural, a kind of monstrosity, for a critic to become a poet. But Plato, quoted in another chapter, insists that any rational criticism is null and void if the critic has not first been attracted by the rings of inspiration, and invaded by the same madness which is in the poet. The critic must perceive much more purely and deeply than the ordinary reader all that which, conveyed by the poem, makes contact, intuitively, with the creative intuition of the poet. In other words, the critic is a poet, and has the gifts of a poet, at least virtually. Before judging of the work as to its ways of execution he must discover the creative intentions from which it proceeds and the more secret things which stirred the soul of its author. He must be able to receive "instantly" the "immortal wound" of which Robert Frost once spoke.

Baudelaire was dealing with a figment of the mind, a critic who would be possessed *only* of the critical gifts, that is, who would not be really a critic. The whole question comes down to the greater or lesser development of reflective faculties. There are critics, it is true, and remarkable critics, who are unable to compose a poem: poetry in them has migrated to their critical work. Charles Du Bos, whom I consider the greatest of French critics, was obliged to give up, after some vain attempts, even the idea of any creative work: I am sure he was a poet, and admirably gifted; but poetic activity had been paralyzed by a prodigious development of the reflective faculties.

I do not forget, for all that, in some writers, who are simply deprived of the poetic gift, criticism is but "the satisfaction of a suppressed creative wish." [17] But I insist that such writers are not really critics. "Their reaction is that of the ordinary emotional person developed to an exceptional degree." "The reading sometimes fecundates" their "emotions to produce something new which is not criticism, but is not the expulsion, the ejection, the birth of creativeness." In other words, they are abortive critics, just as they are abortive poets.

*Purposive Comparison and Immediately
Illuminating Image*

12. I have discussed the question of the internalization of music and the notion of intuitive pulsion, both imaginal and emotional. A particular problem dealing with the images remains to be examined.

"The image," John Crowe Ransom writes, "cannot be dispossessed of a primordial freshness, which idea can never claim. An idea is derivative and tamed. The image is in the natural or wild state, and it has to be discovered there, not put there, obeying its own law and none of ours. We think we can lay hold of image and take it captive, but the docile captive is not the real image but only the idea, which is the image with its character beaten out of it." [18] Poetry, especially modern poetry, manages to have the image's character *not* beaten out of it.

As was observed at the beginning of Chapter IV, there are for the images three possible states or existential conditions. First, they can be part of the "externals of the imagination" —I mean engaged in the ordinary, quotidian, and more or less superficial life of the imagination as centered on sense perception and the needs of our conscious daily activity, as well as of our rational knowledge of the external world (Category number one).

Second, they can be part of what we called the automatic or deaf unconscious, where they are cut off from the intellect and engaged in the structures and dynamism of the separate world in which instincts, repressed memories and tendencies, dreams, and libido lead a life of their own (Category number two).

Third, they can be part of the preconscious life of the intellect in which they are illuminated by the Illuminating Intellect—either to be used in the genesis of concepts and abstract ideas or to be stirred and activated by poetic intuition (Category number three). The problem I should like to take up deals with the metaphoric use of images, considered from this particular angle. Here again, I believe, we are indebted to modern poetry for a new awareness of an old truth.

Let us refer to the statement of Reverdy which is cited in the Texts for this chapter and which is of special interest for French modern poetry; French poets paid great attention to it, at the time it was written. Unfortunately, while pointing to something he felt to be decisively important, Reverdy expressed himself rather obscurely, and neglected to define what he meant by the word *comparison*. "The image," he says, "is a pure creation of the mind; it cannot be born from a *comparison,* but from the *bringing together* of two realities more or less remote from one another." But is not any comparison such a bringing together? Where is the difference? I think that in this statement, and when he goes on to say that the poet creates "a strong image, new for the mind, by bringing together *without comparison* two distant realities whose relationship has been grasped by the mind alone," he understands, by the word *comparison,* a *purposive* comparison brought about by looking for similarities already given in nature—in other words, the act of seeking among things, in order to illustrate an idea, a reality whose concept is *naturally* joined with this idea (for both are united in a more general concept): as the concept of youth and the concept of spring, for instance, are united in the more general concept of rising vitality. In other words, the bringing together was already done in nature (or rather in the concepts brought out from nature), and the mind does not "create" it, rather it takes notice of it.

There are, thus, two typically different ways of using images metaphorically.

On the one hand, there is the way of logical thought. We know a thing in a concept: for instance the fragility of worldly felicity. Then, in order to illustrate or clarify this object known, and definitely formed or expressed in our mind, or to make it more easily communicable, we look at our inner world of ready-made images (in Category number one, images organized in view of our rational knowledge of the external world); and we pick up among these images another thing which participates in the same common idea of fragility, say glass, the fragility of glass. And we say that the first thing is like the second.

> *Et comme elle a l'éclat du verre*
> *Elle en a la fragilité.*[19]

That is what I call *purposive comparison.* Everything, here, comes about at the level of the externals of reason and the externals of the imagination. The comparison takes place between two things known, each one expressible and expressed on its own account; it brings one thing already known near to another thing already known, in order better or more strikingly to express the former, by superimposing the latter on it. Poetry, of course, may use such a way of expression.

But of itself this purposive comparison is a rhetorical mode pertaining to the discursus of reason; not a creative mode pertaining to the intuitive ways of poetry.

On the other hand, there is the intuitive way of poetry, the way of the preconscious, nonconceptual activity of the intellect. Poetic intuition is born in this preconscious activity, it involves an obscure, emotive knowledge, ineffable and unconceptualizable in itself. It stirs the intuitive pulsions, both imaginal and emotional, of which I spoke at the beginning, so as to make its mysterious content known or seen in a manner, and brought to consciousness. The images thus stirred are themselves in a state of fluidity—not organized but movable by every wind—and part of the preconscious life of the spirit. They are images in Category number three, illuminated by the diffuse light of the Illuminating Intellect, and instruments for some intelligibility to be brought out— while keeping their own wild life, beneath the threshold of the abstractive process of formation of ideas. Thus an image is seized upon as the vehicle of some intelligible meaning, radiating from poetic intuition, and in being expressed in a word, it conveys this intelligible meaning and makes a certain thing intelligibly, though not conceptually, grasped. As when Yeats said:

> *The winds that awakened the stars*
> *Are blowing through my blood.*[20]

Here we may observe that the image is rationally, or astronomically, rather questionable, for in nature no star has ever been awakened by any wind. But this is precisely, I think, a confirmation of my point. Yeats did not write, and could not have written, according to the classical pattern: "Just as the winds awakened the stars" (one term in a purposive comparison), "so, etc." (the other term in a purposive comparison). In reality his image was not taken from the facts of astronomy and the externals of the imagination, it came from the *preconceptual imagination,* and was used only, irrespective of any truth already known about the winds and the stars, to make known and expressed something which is not even named, say, the poet's passionate exaltation. And so it is all the more meaningful.

Be it added that of course it is not only with respect to the central creative intuition, it is also with respect to any particular intuitive pulsion, any fleeting flash awakened during the production of the work and dealing with any of its parts, minute as it may be, that the images can be used in this way. Thus it is for instance that in order to make known and expressed what is totally singular and conceptually inexpressible in the deliciousness of having "nothing but the blanket between you and your snugness and the cold of the outer air," Melville wrote: "There you lie like the one warm spark in the heart of an arctic crystal.

That is what I call the *immediately illuminating image,* without the intermediary of any concept—illuminating because it is illuminated both by the Illuminating Intellect and by poetic intuition or spark of intuition. Everything, here, comes about in the depths of the preconceptual life of the intellect and the imagination. Two things are not compared, but rather one thing is made known through the image of another. One thing already known is not brought near to another thing already known. One thing which was unknown—only contained in the obscurity of emotive intuition—is discovered, and expressed, by means of another already known, and by the same stroke their similarity is discovered: all that, as Reverdy put it, as a result of the creativity of the spirit. The second thing (the warm spark in the heart of an arctic crystal, or the winds that awakened the stars) is brought near the first (what is ineffable, and not yet made known, either in the snugness of the sleeper or in the exaltation of the poet) not because both are the objects of two concepts naturally joined together, but because, in the preconscious ocean of images, the image of the second thing has been moved and lifted by the common activity of emotive intuition and the Illuminating Intellect, in search of an intuitive expression for some pressing and obscure intelligibility. And just because it is a question of making intelligible something still unexpressed, in this primeval nebula where nothing is ready-made, but everything is to be engendered and the spirit is in travail; because the whole operation comes about irrespective of the conceptual organization of things according to their natural similarities, but only with respect to the intuitive power of the intellect, the fact that the two things brought together are naturally *distant* from one another, and that their bringing together is utterly new, and fresh, and unforeseeable, is but a natural effect of this free power of the intellect—not of any deliberate effort of the will and frowning research. Thus, to quote another example of which, I believe, Mr. Blackmur is particularly fond,[21] could Miss Marianne Moore speak of

The lion's ferocious chrysanthemum head.

13. I have considered what is, to my mind, the prime and most genuine way in which the immediately illuminating image arises—I mean as drawn by poetic intuition from the ocean of images which are part of the preconscious life of the spirit and connatural instruments of the Illuminating Intellect. Now it must be added that, in a secondary or complementary way, all images, from whatever region of the imagination they may come, either from the externals of the imagination (our Category number one) or from the automatic unconscious (our Category number two), may play the role in question, from the moment when, and on the condition that, in emerging into consciousness they are touched and quickened by the creative activity of the intellect and of poetic intuition. Then they are furnished from outside the native place of poetic activity, but poetic activity makes them its own. It may even happen that a poet appropriates to himself images born outside himself, in the mind of another person who may perhaps be nothing of a poet. In this other person they were only wandering images, with only potential, no actual poetic meaning or value. But once the poet's intellect lights upon them, they may become for him really poetic or immediately illuminating images. If I am not mistaken, Hart Crane, in "Emblems of Conduct," availed himself of the

gift of the last lines written by Samuel Greenberg, in a hospi
tal bed before his death. The objection may be raised, no
doubt, that Samuel Greenberg himself was a poet. But he was
another poet, whose images Crane appropriated, this is my
point. Moreover we may turn to the case of insane persons,
and to the interest that poets take sometimes in their writings and in the images which arise in them.

To complete our observations on the immediately illuminating image, we might note that in using this way of expression, and in conveying through it some intuitive pulsion
to our own conscious or preconscious powers, poetry can follow two different paths. Either the words, though possibly
endowed with the purest musical quality, will be as simple
and naked as possible, so that only their meaning, not their
own sonorous structure, is the vehicle of the image:

> *Je suis seul sur la lèvre tremblante du rivage*
> *Seul sur le roc glissant des fièvres de la mort.*[22]

Or they will be rich and elaborated words, and their own sonorous structure will have an essential part in the expression
of the image. Such is the case, I think, with Hopkins' poems.

> *Or a jaunting vaunting vaulting assaulting trumpet*
> *telling.*[23]

I assume that the poets who prefer the second path are
those whose poems I characterized above as "difficult" rather
than "obscure," and who dream of raising words to a supreme power of significance, by reason of their inherent dignity.

Was I more able than Reverdy to make clear the distinction between *purposive comparison* and *immediately illuminating image?* I have no doubt, in any case, about its
importance. And what seems to me particularly noticeable
is the fact that we are confronted here, not with any merely
technical difference, but with a difference which depends on
the very manner in which the vitality of the powers of the
soul is at play.

Modern poetry, by the fact of its particular approach to

images and to intuitive pulsions, and by the fact that most often it does not express the thing itself which calls forth the image, but only suggests it through the image, obliges us to become aware of this difference. This in no way means that it is new in itself. I think that what I call the immediately illuminating image has been the instrument of all great poets. Is it necessary to quote Dryden:

> *while within your arms I lay,*
> *The world fell mould'ring from my hands each hour,*

or to stress the powerful spontaneity which despite the discursive and symmetrical form runs through Blake's "A Divine Image"? And what could not be said of Shakespeare and Dante! All their lines are permeated with the force of the immediately illuminating image. When Dante describes the yellow of the eternal rose, or when he shows us Leah—the active life—moving her fair hands around to make herself a garland, while her sister Rachel—the contemplative life—

> *non si smaga*
> *del suo miraglio, e siede tutto giorno,*

when Shakespeare writes:

> *She looks like sleep,*
> *As she would catch another Antony*
> *In her strong toil of grace,*

or makes King Lear exclaim:

> *But I am bound*
> *Upon a wheel of fire, that my own tears*
> *Do scald like molten lead,*

it is not the purposive comparison, it is the immediately illuminating image which is at work.

The question, moreover, does not concern only poetry. I have previously pointed out the part that the illuminating image—analogically understood—similarly plays in painting. And what about the remarks made in this chapter on the internalization of music, and the notion of intuitive pulsions? These remarks also apply to painting, *mutatis mutandis*. If a picture possesses that quality of "melody" of which Baudelaire spoke, it is, in the last analysis, by reason of the music of intuitive pulsions which the painter's vision and his creative intuition have awakened in the preconscious regions of his mind. The picture brings us back to this inner music at one go, simultaneously—not in the successive way proper to music or poetry. But the wordless song that develops within us, while we are dreaming in the contemplation of the work, is, I believe, the main and deepest factor in our emotion.

TEXTS WITHOUT COMMENT
(for Chapter Eight)

I

1. COLERIDGE, in *Biographia Literaria* (Ch. XIV):

The poet, described in *ideal* perfection, brings the whole soul of man into activity, with the subordination of its faculties to each other, according to their relative worth and dignity. He diffuses a tone and spirit of unity, that blends, and (as it were) *fuses,* each into each, by that synthetic and magical power, to which we have exclusively appropriated the name of imagination. This power, first put in action by the will and understanding, and retained under their irremissive, though gentle and unnoticed, control (*laxis effertur habenis*) reveals itself in the balance or reconciliation of opposite or discordant qualities: of sameness, with difference; of the general, with the concrete; the idea, with the image; the individual, with the representative; the sense of novelty and freshness, with old and familiar objects; a more than usual state of emotion, with more than usual order; judgment ever awake and steady self-possession, with enthusiasm and feeling profound or vehement; and while it blends and harmonizes the natural and the artificial, still subordinates art to nature; the manner to the matter, and our admiration for the poet to our sympathy with the poetry.

2. FRANCIS THOMPSON, *Coleridge:*

Around Coleridge the clamor of partisans is silent: none attacks, none has need to defend. *The Ancient Mariner, Christabel, Kubla Khan, Genevieve,* are recognized as perfectly unique masterpieces of triumphant utterance and triumphant imagination of a certain kind. They bring down magic to the earth. Shelley has followed it to the skies; but not all can companion him in that rarefied ether, and breathe. Coleridge brings it in to us, floods us round with it, makes it native and apprehensible as the air of our own earth. To do so he seeks no remote splendors of language, uses no brazier of fuming imagery. He waves his wand, and the miracle is accomplished before our eyes in the open light of day; he takes words which have had the life used out of them by the common cry of poets, puts them into relation, and they rise up like his own dead mariners, wonderful with a supernatural animation.[1]

3. JOHN CROWE RANSOM, in *The World's Body:*

Poetry distinguishes itself from prose on the technical side by the devices which are, precisely, its means of escaping from prose. Something is continually being killed by prose which the poet wants to preserve. But this must be put philosophically. (Philosophy sounds hard, but it deals with natural and fundamental forms of experience.)

The critic should regard the poem as nothing short of a desperate ontological or metaphysical manoeuvre. The poet himself, in the agony of composition, has something like this sense of his labors. The poet perpetuates in his poem an order of existence which in actual life is constantly crumbling beneath his touch. His poem celebrates the object which is real, individual, and qualitatively infinite. He knows that his practical interests will reduce this living object to a mere utility, and that his sciences will disintegrate it for their convenience into their respective abstracts. The poet wishes to defend his object's existence against its enemies. . . .[2]

II

4. MALLARMÉ, *Divagation première:*

Tout ce qu'on reconnaît écrit dans l'acceptation technique, soit phrasé, comporte une mélopée: l'écriture n'étant que la fixation du chant immiscé au langage et lui-même persuasif du sens.

. . . Je me figure par un indéracinable sans doute préjugé d'écrivain, que rien ne demeurera sans être proféré; que nous en sommes là, précisément, à rechercher, devant une brisure des grands rythmes littéraires et leur éparpillement en frissons articulés proches de l'instrumentation, un art d'achever la transposition, au Livre, de la symphonie ou uniment de reprendre notre bien: car, ce n'est pas de sonorités élémentaires par les cuivres, les cordes, les bois, indéniablement mais de l'intellectuelle parole à son apogée que doit, avec plénitude et évidence, résulter, en tant que l'ensemble des rapports existant dans le tout, la Musique.[3]

5. SAPPHO, *The Moon has set:*

> Δέδυκε μὲν ἁ σέλαννα
> καὶ Πληΐαδες, μέσαι δὲ
> νύκτες παρὰ δ' ἔρχετ' ὥρα
> ἔγω δὲ μόνα κατεύδω.

(The moon has set, and the Pleiades; it is the middle of the night and time passes, time passes, and I lie alone.) [4]

6. SAPPHO, *Atthis:*

> Ἠράμαν μὲν ἔγω σέθεν, Ἄτθι, πάλαι ποτά.
> (I loved thee once, Atthis, long ago.)[5]

7. WEBSTER, *The Duchess of Malfi* (IV, ii):

Cover her face; mine eyes dazzle; she died young.

8. KEATS, in *La Belle Dame sans Merci:*

> O what can ail thee, knight at arms,
> Alone and palely loitering?
> The sedge has withered from the lake,
> And no birds sing!
>
> O what can ail thee, knight at arms,
> So haggard and so woe-begone?
> The squirrel's granary is full
> And the harvest's done.
>
> I see a lily on thy brow,
> With anguish moist and fever dew;
> And on thy cheeks a fading rose
> Fast withereth too.—
>
> I met a lady in the meads,
> Full beautiful, a faery's child;
> Her hair was long, her foot was light,
> And her eyes were wild.
>
> I made a garland for her head,
> And bracelets, too, and fragrant zone;
> She looked at me as she did love,
> And made sweet moan.

9. COLERIDGE, in *The Ancient Mariner:*

> The fair breeze blew, the white foam flew,
> The furrow followed free;
> We were the first that ever burst
> Into that silent sea.
>
> Down dropt the breeze, the sails dropt down,
> 'Twas sad as sad could be;
> And we did speak only to break
> The silence of the sea!
>
> . . . .

I looked upon the rotting sea,
And drew my eyes away;
I looked upon the rotting deck,
And there the dead men lay.

I looked to heaven, and tried to pray;
But or ever a prayer had gusht,
A wicked whisper came, and made
My heart as dry as dust.

. . . .

The loud wind never reached the ship,
Yet now the ship moved on!
Beneath the lightning and the Moon
The dead men gave a groan.

They groaned, they stirred, they all uprose,
Nor spake, nor moved their eyes:
It had been strange, even in a dream,
To have seen those dead men rise.

10. HEINE, *Ein Fichtenbaum steht einsam:*

Ein Fichtenbaum steht einsam
Im Norden auf kahler Höh'.
Ihn schläfert; mit weisser Decke
Umhüllen ihn Eis und Schnee.

Er träumt von einer Palme,
Die fern im Morgenland
Einsam und schweigend trauert
Auf brennender Felsenwand.

(A lonely pine is standing
  In the North where the high winds blow.
He sleeps; and the whitest blanket
  Wraps him in ice and snow.

He dreams—dreams of a palm tree
  That far in an Orient land

> Languishes, lonely and drooping,
>> Upon the burning sand.)[6]

11. BAUDELAIRE, in *L'Imprévu:*

> Reconnaissez Satan à son rire vainqueur,
>> Enorme et laid comme le monde!
>
> . . . .
>
> Il faut que le gibier paye le vieux chasseur
> Qui se morfond longtemps à l'affût de la proie.
> Je vais vous emporter à travers l'épaisseur,
>> Compagnons de ma triste joie,
>
> A travers l'épaisseur de la terre et du roc,
> A travers les amas confus de votre cendre,
> Dans un palais aussi grand que moi, d'un seul bloc,
>> Et qui n'est pas de pierre tendre;
>
> Car il est fait avec l'universel Péché,
> Et contient mon orgueil, ma douleur et ma gloire!
> —Cependant, tout en haut de l'univers juché,
>> Un Ange sonne la victoire
>
> De ceux dont le cœur dit: "Que béni soit ton fouet,
> Seigneur! que la douleur, ô Père, soit bénie!
> Mon âme dans tes mains n'est pas un vain jouet,
>> Et ta prudence est infinie."
>
> Le son de la trompette est si délicieux,
> Dans ces soirs solennels de célestes vendanges,
> Qu'il s'infiltre comme une extase dans tous ceux
>> Dont elle chante les louanges.

12. GERARD MANLEY HOPKINS, in *I wake and feel:*

> I am gall, I am heartburn. God's most deep decree
> Bitter would have me taste: my taste was me;
> Bones built in me, flesh filled, blood brimmed the curse.
> Selfyeast of spirit a dull dough sours. I see

The lost are like this, and their scourge to be
As I am mine, their sweating selves; but worse.[7]

13. JULES SUPERVIELLE, *Ce bruit de la mer:*

> Ce bruit de la mer où nous sommes tous,
> Il le connaît bien, l'arbre à chevelure,
> Et le cheval noir y met l'encolure
> Allongeant le cou comme pour l'eau douce,
> Comme s'il voulait quitter cette dune,
> Devenir au loin cheval fabuleux
> Et se mélanger aux moutons d'écume,
> A cette toison faite pour les yeux,
> Etre enfin le fils de cette eau marine,
> Brouter l'algue au fond de la profondeur.
> Mais il faut savoir attendre au rivage,
> Se promettre encore aux vagues du large,
> Mettre son espoir dans la mort certaine,
> Baisser de nouveau la tête dans l'herbe.[8]

14. HART CRANE, in *Atlantis* (*The Bridge*):

> O Thou steeled Cognizance whose leap commits
> The agile precincts of the lark's return;
> Within whose lariat sweep encinctured sing
> In single chrysalis the many twain—
> Of stars Thou art the stitch and stallion glow
> And like an organ, Thou, with sound of doom—
> Sight, sound and flesh Thou leadest from time's realm
> As love strikes clear direction for the helm.[9]

15. PIERRE REVERDY, *Au bas-fond:*

> Vierge et fière sur la lande animée
> Elle tamise l'argent de ses branches
> Elle sèche les roseaux qui chantent
> Sous les voûtes des ponts tournants
> Elle coupe court aux bruits qui mentent
> Elle tresse les nattes du vent
> Elle tisse la nuit qui l'enroule
> Elle émiette le pain noir

Elle étanche le sang qui coule
Sur la piste étoilée des larmes défendues
Et maintenant ombre détruite
Froissée dans les rafales du courant
Pêcheur de mort
Au ressac de la fuite
Allons plus loin
Plus personne n'écoute
Allons au fond des gouffres du remords[10]

16. ALLEN TATE, in *Idiot:*

The idiot greens the meadows with his eyes,
The meadow creeps implacable and still;
A dog barks, the hammock swings, he lies.
One two three the cows bulge on the hill.[11]

17. RAÏSSA MARITAIN, *La Chute d'Icare (d'après Breughel):*

Un rameau fleuri encadre la mer
Des navires songent à l'univers
Au rivage des moutons s'endorment
Icare est tombé du zénith
Comme une mouette qui plonge
Tout repose au soleil de midi
Rien ne trouble la beauté du monde[12]

18. T. S. ELIOT, in *The Love Song of J. Alfred Prufrock:*

Shall I say, I have gone at dusk through narrow streets
And watched the smoke that rises from the pipes
Of lonely men in shirt-sleeves, leaning out of windows? . . .
I should have been a pair of ragged claws
Scuttling across the floors of silent seas.

. . . .

And would it have been worth it, after all,
After the cups, the marmalade, the tea,
Among the porcelain, among some talk of you and me,
Would it have been worth while,
To have bitten off the matter with a smile,
To have squeezed the universe into a ball

To roll it toward some overwhelming question,
To say: "I am Lazarus, come from the dead,
Come back to tell you all, I shall tell you all"—
If one, settling a pillow by her head,
   Should say: "That is not what I meant at all;
   That is not it, at all."

. . . .

Shall I part my hair behind? Do I dare to eat a peach?
I shall wear white flannel trousers, and walk upon the beach.
I have heard the mermaids singing, each to each.

I do not think that they will sing to me.

I have seen them riding seaward on the waves
Combing the white hair of the waves blown back
When the wind blows the water white and black.

We have lingered in the chambers of the sea
By sea-girls wreathed with seaweed red and brown
Till human voices wake us, and we drown.[13]

19. GUILLAUME APOLLINAIRE, *Le Pont Mirabeau:*

   Sous le pont Mirabeau coule la Seine
      Et nos amours
      Faut-il qu'il m'en souvienne
   La joie venait toujours après la peine

      Vienne la nuit sonne l'heure
      Les jours s'en vont je demeure

Les mains dans les mains restons face à face
      Tandis que sous
     Le pont de nos bras passe
Des éternels regards l'onde si lasse

      Vienne la nuit sonne l'heure
      Les jours s'en vont je demeure

> L'amour s'en va comme cette eau courante
> L'amour s'en va
> Comme la vie est lente
> Et comme l'espérance est violente
>
> Vienne la nuit sonne l'heure
> Les jours s'en vont je demeure
>
> Passent les jours et passent les semaines
> Ni temps passé
> Ni les amours reviennent
> Sous le pont Mirabeau coule la Seine
>
> Vienne la nuit sonne l'heure
> Les jours s'en vont je demeure[14]

III

20. PIERRE REVERDY, *Image:*

L'image est une création pure de l'esprit. Elle ne peut naître
d'une comparaison, mais du rapprochement de deux réalités
plus ou moins éloignées. . . . Une image n'est pas forte
parce qu'elle est *brutale* ou *fantastique,*—mais parce que
l'association des idées est lointaine et juste. . . . On ne crée
pas d'image en comparant (toujours faiblement) deux réalités
disproportionnées. On crée, au contraire, une forte image,
neuve pour l'esprit, en rapprochant sans comparaison deux
réalités distantes dont *l'esprit seul* a saisi les rapports.[15]

21. MALLARMÉ, *Divagation première:*

Instituer une relation entre les images, exacte, et que s'en dé-
tache un tiers aspect fusible et clair présenté à la divination.
. . . Abolie, la prétention, esthétiquement une erreur,
malgré qu'elle régit presque tous les chefs-d'œuvre, d'inclure
au papier subtil du volume autre chose que par exemple
l'horreur de la forêt, ou le tonnerre muet épars au feuillage:
non le bois intrinsèque et dense des arbres. Quelques jets

de l'intime orgueil véridiquement trompetés éveillent l'architecture du palais, le seul habitable; hors de toute pierre, sur
quoi les pages se refermeraient mal.[16]

22. MARIANNE MOORE, in *Poetry:*

> . . . all these phenomena are important. One
>   must make a distinction
>   however: when dragged into prominence by half poets,
>   the result is not poetry,
> nor till the poets among us can be
>   'literalists of
>   the imagination'—above
>   insolence and triviality and can present
>
> for inspection, 'imaginary gardens with real toads in them,'
>   shall we have
> it. In the meantime, if you demand on the one hand,
> the raw material of poetry in
>   all its rawness and
>   that which is on the other hand
>   genuine, then you are interested in poetry.[17]

23. VERGIL, *Aeneid* (VI, 442-54):

> Hic, quos durus amor crudeli tabe peredit,
> secreti celant calles et myrtea circum
> silva tegit . . .
>   . . . Phoenissa recens a volnere Dido
> errabat silva in magna, quam Troius heros
> ut primum iuxta stetit adgnovitque per umbras
> obscuram, qualem primo qui surgere mense
> aut videt aut vidisse putat per nubila lunam. . . .

(Here those whom stern love has consumed with cruel wast-
ing are hidden in walks withdrawn, embowered in a myrtle
grove. . . . With wound still fresh, Phoenician Dido was
wandering in the great forest, and soon as the Trojan hero
stood nigh and knew her, a dim form amid the shadows—

even as, in the early month, one sees or fancies he has seen
the moon rise amid the clouds. . . .)[18]

24. DANTE, *Purgatorio* (Canto XXVII, 100-108):

> Sappia, qualunque il mio nome dimanda,
>   ch'i'mi son Lia, e vo movendo intorno
>   le belle mani a farmi una ghirlanda.
>
> Per piacermi allo specchio qui m'adorno;
>   ma mia suora Rachel mai non si smaga
>   dal suo miraglio, e siede tutto giorno.
>
> Ell è de' suoi belli occhi veder vaga,
>   com' io de l'adornarmi con le mani:
>   lei lo vedere, e me l'ovrare appaga.

(Know, whoso asketh my name, that I am Leah, and go moving my fair hands around to make me a garland.
To please me at the glass here I deck me; but Rachel my
sister ne'er stirs from her mirror, and sitteth all day.
She is fain to behold her fair eyes, as I to deck me with my
hands: her, contemplation; me, action, doth satisfy.)[19]

25. SHAKESPEARE, *Antony and Cleopatra* (V, ii):

>   Peace, peace:
> Dost thou not see my baby at my breast,
> That sucks the nurse asleep.

26. SHAKESPEARE, *Hamlet* (II, ii):

O God! I could be bounded in a nut-shell, and count
myself a king of infinite space; were it not that I have bad
dreams.

27. DONNE, in *The Extasie:*

> But as all severall soules containe
>   Mixture of things, they know not what,
> Love, these mixt soules doth mixe againe,

> And makes both one, each this and that.
> A single violet transplant,
> The strength, the colour, and the size. . . .

28. WILLIAM BLAKE, *A Divine Image*:

> Cruelty has a Human Heart,
> And Jealousy a Human Face;
> Terror the Human Form Divine,
> And Secrecy the Human Dress.
>
> The Human Dress is forged Iron,
> The Human Form a fiery Forge,
> The Human Face a Furnace seal'd,
> The Human Heart its hungry Gorge.

29. MALLARMÉ, *Le Vitrier*:

> Le pur soleil qui remise
> Trop d'éclat pour l'y trier
> Ote ébloui sa chemise
> Sur le dos du vitrier.

30. HART CRANE, in *Lachrymae Christi*:

> Whitely, while benzine
> Rinsings from the moon
> Dissolve all but the windows of the mills. . . .[20]

31. JULES SUPERVIELLE, in *Feux du ciel*:

> L'air demeure angoissé de mouettes immobiles
> Et leur cœur est une île de glace sous les plumes.[21]

32. DJUNA BARNES, *Watchman, What of the Night*:

The very constitution of twilight is a fabulous reconstruction of fear, fear bottom-out and wrong side up. Every day is thought upon and calculated, but the night is not premeditated. The Bible lies the one way, but the night gown the other. The night, 'Beware of that Dark Door!' . . .

His heart is tumbling in his chest, a dark place! Though some go into the night as a spoon breaks easy water, others

go head foremost against a new connivance; their horns
make a dry crying, like the wings of the locust, late come
to their shedding.[22]

33. PAUL CLAUDEL, in *La Perle:*

L'âme blessée et fécondée possède au fond d'elle-même un
appareil qui lui permet de solidifier le temps en éternité.
C'est la perle . . .

La perle, fruit de la mer et conception de la durée, n'a
d'autre valeur que sa beauté et sa perfection intrinsèque,
résultant de sa simplicité, de sa pureté et de son éclat, et que
le désir qu'elle inspire. . . . Elle est cette sagesse supérieure
que nous préférons à notre substance. . . .

Mais voici au flanc de cette autre perle une lueur qui croît,
quelque chose de gai, de vif et de vivant, que l'on appelle
l'orient, comme un cœur qui, du côté de l'amour, se découvre
une espèce de partialité. Comme un visage qui se tourne,
comme une joue sous le regard qui se colore de sensibilité
et de pudeur, un point lumineux s'est éveillé, un reflet rose
à quoi un vert ineffable n'est pas toujours étranger. Une
espèce de conscience virginale, une innocence ouverte à la
prédilection. Une fenêtre a éclos, une âme qui surmonte le
voile, la lampe qui répond au rayon, le mérite qui accueille
la grâce, la pureté qui épouse le pardon. . . .

Et je n'ai pas parlé des perles noires, de ces gouttes de nuit
liquide et mordorée qui, elles aussi, ont un orient et qui
rayonnent! Ce qui fait la gloire des Elus chez elles en est le
pressentiment. "Je suis noire, mais je suis belle," dit le
Cantique. C'est comme une voix qui s'est tue, mais le regard
est là qui trahit le chant. . . .[23]

34. ROBERT FROST, *The Silken Tent:*

>   She is as in a field a silken tent
>   At midday when a sunny summer breeze
>   Has dried the dew and all its ropes relent.
>   So that in guys it gently sways at ease,
>   And its supporting central cedar pole,

That is its pinnacle to heavenward
And signifies the sureness of the soul,
Seems to owe naught to any single cord,
But strictly held by none, is loosely bound
By countless silken ties of love and thought
To everything on earth the compass round,
And only by one's going slightly taut
In the capriciousness of summer air
Is of the slightest bondage made aware.[24]

35. T. S. ELIOT, in *Burnt Norton*:

Garlic and sapphires in the mud
Clot the bedded axle-tree.
The trilling wire in the blood
Sings below inveterate scars
And reconciles forgotten wars.
The dance along the artery
The circulation of the lymph
Are figured in the drift of stars
Ascend to summer in the tree
We move above the moving tree
In light upon the figured leaf
And hear upon the sodden floor
Below, the boarhound and the boar
Pursue their pattern as before
But reconciled among the stars.[25]

36. T. S. ELIOT, in *The Love Song of J. Alfred Prufrock*:

When the evening is spread out against the sky
Like a patient etherized upon a table[26]

37. GERTRUDE STEIN, in *What Happened*:

A blame what is a blame, a blame is what arises and cautions
each one to be calm and an ocean and a masterpiece.[27]

38. MARIANNE MOORE, in *A Grave*:

The firs stand in a procession, each with an emerald
turkey-foot at the top.[28]

39. MARIANNE MOORE, in *People's Surroundings:*
and the acacia-like lady shivering at the touch of a hand [29]

40. LAUTRÉAMONT, in *Chants de Maldoror* (VI):
Mais sachez que la poésie se trouve partout où n'est pas le sourire, stupidement railleur, de l'homme à la figure de canard.

41. LÉON-PAUL FARGUE, in *On dit: qu'il cache une partie de sa vie:*

> Un grand rouet d'or dévide son cœur aux crocs
> d'un buisson plein de fleurs.[30]

42. LÉON-PAUL FARGUE, in *La Lampe s'allume:*
Le phare qui tourne à pleins poings son verre de sang dans les étoiles traverse un bras de mer pour toucher ma tête et la vitre.[31]

43. ST.-JOHN PERSE, in *Anabase:*

> Un enfant triste comme la mort des singes.[32]

44. ST.-JOHN PERSE, in *Anabase:*

> Et les vaisseaux plus hauts qu'Ilion sous le
> paon blanc du ciel.[33]

45: RAÏSSA MARITAIN, in *Aux Morts désespérés:*
Notre deuil est si grand que le soleil m'étonne.[34]

46. RAÏSSA MARITAIN, in *Colonnes:*

> Le ciel et la terre et les îles
> Tout est fait de mon exil.[35]

47. PIERRE REVERDY, in *Grand Caractère:*

> Quand les lèvres du temps brûlées par le malheur
> Remuent dans la clarté mal assise des lampes.[36]

48. PIERRE REVERDY, in *Danse de terre:*

Les jours glissent comme des lettres dans la boîte
Les nuits sont au fond des cercueils.[37]

49. JEAN COCTEAU, in *Hôtel de France et de la Poésie:*

Le ciel est un marin assis sur les maisons.[38]

50. PAUL ELUARD, in *Poème perpétuel:*

Le soleil doux comme une taupe.[39]

51. PAUL ELUARD, in *Défense de savoir:*

Les astres sont dans l'eau la beauté n'a plus d'ombres.[40]

NINE

THE THREE EPIPHANIES OF
CREATIVE INTUITION

Poetic Sense or Inner Melody, Action and Theme,
Number or Harmonic Expansion

1. Modern poetry has made great discoveries in the realm of images, and of their mysterious life within the soul. It has made still greater discoveries as regards the internalization of music, the liberation of the poetic sense—first of all as regards self-awareness and poetic knowledge. On the other hand modern poetry is ordinarily reproached—and by those who are most knowingly and lovingly interested in it—with a serious, perhaps irremediable weakness in regard to the intellectual power which enables the work to encompass universal and objective values within the unity of a great purpose, let us say, in a word, in regard to the *theme*.

The remarks put forward by Waldo Frank in his Introduction to the *Collected Poems*[1] of Hart Crane have, I think, general import in this connection. Allen Tate, he observes, had already pointed out, in his own Introduction to *White Buildings,* that "a suitable theme" was lacking, and that "a series of Imagist poems is a series of worlds. The poems of Hart Crane are facets of a single vision; they refer to a central imagination, a single evaluating power, which is at once the motive of the poetry and the form of its realization." "This central imagination." Waldo Frank goes on to say, "wanting the unitary principle or theme, wavers and breaks; turns back upon itself instead of mastering the envisaged substance of the poem. That is why, in the first group [Crane's poems anterior to *The Bridge*], a fragmentary part of a poem is sometimes greater than the whole." And some pages further on, we read: "Dante's cosmos, imaged in an age of cultural maturity, when the life of man was coterminous with his vision, contains Time and persons. . . . Crane's cosmos (for reasons which we examined when we called Crane a child of modern man, a poet innocent of culture-words) has no Time: and his person-sense is vacillant and evanescent. Crane's journey is that of an individual unsure of his own form and lost to Time. This difference at once clarifies the disadvantageous aesthetic of *The Bridge,* as compared with that of broadly analogous Poems of cosmic search, like the *Commedia* or *Don Quixote*. It exemplifies the role played by the cultural epoch in the creation of even the most personal work of genius." We may add that it is difficult for a modern poet not to be a child of modern man.

Yet, before going further, it seems relevant to try to elucidate a few notions which—together with that of the poetic sense, analyzed in Chapter VII—relate to the essentials of the poetic work.

In the remarks of Allen Tate and Waldo Frank I just quoted, the importance of the theme is emphasized. What does this notion of the *theme* mean?

The word suggests something that is propounded or put forward. Experts in literature tell us that the theme, which must not be confused with the subject, is the "basic idea" or "general idea" which is presented in a poem,[2] and which can even be translated (while losing its very nature and poetic quality by the very fact) into an intellectual "statement." Yet this is far from sufficient to enlighten us. What is the relation of the theme to the creative emotion? What is its functional value in the poem? The first point to be noted, in my opinion, is that the theme does not precisely relate to what the poem *is,* but rather to what the poem intends or proposes, what the poem *wills*.

A poem, however, has no will of its own, unless metaphorically. But in things which have no will of their own, like physical agents, there is a property that corresponds to what the will is in voluntary agents—namely, action. Things have action. Is there not a concept of action which is appropriate to the realm of the things of art? Does not a poem have action? Let us, then, turn first to the notion of the action of the work.

2. It is not by accident that an eludication of the notion of action which is particularly helpful for our purpose is to be found in a book on the theater. *The Idea of a Theater,* by Francis Fergusson, is essentially concerned with this notion, and illustrates its significance by means of a rich comparative analysis. Quoting Aristotle: "Tragedy is the imitation of an action," Francis Fergusson points out that the action does not mean "the events of the story but the focus or aim of psychic life from which the events, in that situation, result." In other words the action must not be confused with the plot, which is either the "form" or "first actualization, of the tragic action," or, in a secondary sense, the means of producing a certain effect upon the audience.[3] The action is something much deeper and much more far-reaching—and much simpler too—which materializes at various levels of analogy; it is something basically spiritual, and essentially refers to "the changing life of the psyche" as projected in a certain direction.

It might be said, I think, that the dramatic action is the spiritual élan or motion which, emanating from a constellation of human agents gathered together in a certain situation, carries them along, and which, as a result, commands a certain development of events in time, permeating it with a definite significance. The central paradox of the theater is the fact that on the one hand these human agents are endowed with free will and can change, to some extent, the course of the events, while, on the other hand, the work itself, which has no free will, is all the more perfect as everything in it results from necessity, so that the action must also develop with unbending necessity. This paradox is but an effect and a sign of the *transposition* or recasting which nature inevitably undergoes when it passes into the work of art. It brings, moreover, our attention to bear on a particularly important point: the Aristotelian formula, the "imitation of the action," in which the tragedy, and, more generally, any dramatic work consists, does not refer to a merely successive *picture or image* of the actions performed in human life—merely successive, that is, made up, as Bergson put it, of immobile instants sewn to one another in time—as the picture of a race or a football game offered by the movies. The "imitation of action" *is itself an action,* which is *analogous* to the actions performed in human life, and which recasts them in a man-born pattern (originally ritualistic). And this action —analogous to the actions of human life—is the action of the work itself, the action of the play.

In other words the action that we are now discussing, the tragic or dramatic action, is a property of the dramatic work, not of the things that this work represents. In the same way, the "tragic rhythm of action"—the three moments which Kenneth Burke calls *Poiema, Pathema, Mathema,* and Mr. Fergusson, Purpose, Passion (or Suffering), and Perception— obviously belongs to the work as an inherent property of the latter, not to the human life "imitated" by it. Thus it appears —this is the point which matters for me—that the work itself is possessed of that property which is action. Action is a quality immanent in the work. The work does not only exist, it *acts,* it *does.*

3. Action is the formative principle of the dramatic work and is, therefore, manifested in it in a pre-eminent manner. But it is in no way a unique privilege of the theater. The concept of action is an analogous concept, which is valid in the whole field of art. Action is a necessary property of any work of art. Unity of action, Coleridge wrote, "is not properly a rule, but in itself the great and not only of the drama, but of the epic poem, the lyric ode, of all poetry, down to the candle-flame cone of an epigram,—nay of poesy in general, **as**

the proper generic term inclusive of all the fine arts as its species."

May we hope to get a better understanding of action in the field of poesy by casting our eye over metaphysics, and the philosophical theory of action in the primary and universal sense of this word? Philosophers distinguish between two kinds of action—"transitive action," through which one thing modifies another, and "immanent action," which belongs to the category of quality, and through which a living agent perfects its own being. Immanent action, which tends essentially to complete in actuation the agent itself, produces at the same time a certain effect or a certain fruit (the concept, for instance, in the intellect) which remains within the agent.

Assuming the Aristotelian notions of *act* as fullness or completion in being, and of *existence* as *actus primus,* primary act, and act of all acts, Thomist philosophy states that action or operation, either transitive or immanent, is an *actus secundus,* an emergent terminative act, or a superabundance of existence, through which being asserts itself beyond substantial existence. For things are and exist before acting. Everywhere except in God, action is distinct from the essence of the agent and from its act of existing.

It is of course in a merely analogical way that such notions apply to those spiritual qualities which are the "ontological" elements of the poem, or of the work *qua* work of the mind. In that mysterious organism of words and meanings which is the poem, there is no distinction between substance and accident as there is in beings of nature. It is by reason of their relation to the creative source, and of their *intentional value* (that is, of their value as conveying the creative source, in virtue of the immaterial and purely tendential existence proper to the meaning) that the difference of "ontological" function between the poetic sense and the action must be understood.

Let us say, then, that the prime and most basic intentional value in the poem is the poetic sense, because the poetic sense is closest to the creative source—a meaning which immedi-

ately signifies the inhabited subjectivity of the poet as revealed in the night of nonconceptual emotive intuition. The
poem receives its essence (that is, its intuitive communica-
tiveness and power of delighting the intellect) and its existence before the mind through the poetic sense—either purely
and simply (in the case of the poem strictly so called) or in a
merely inchoative way (in the case of the drama). As to the
action, it emanates from creative intuition as the second intentional value in the poem, presupposing therefore the
poetic sense and complementing it. The action is—analogically—an *actus secundus,* an emergent terminative act,
through which the poem superabounds in existence. The
poem has a kind of "transitive action"—which is extrinsic
and in addition—the action that it exercises upon the
reader (such is the "purgation of passions" produced by
tragedy). And it has a kind of "immanent action," which
is intrinsic and essential: like the tragedy, which is a paradigm in this regard, every work of art not only is, but does.
It moves, it acts. And this action is part of its very substance.[4] The "immanent action" I am pointing out, the
action of the poem, is what the poem *does*—an élan or
motion which develops in it, and through which within itself it asserts itself beyond itself. And through its action it
proffers something which is an ultimate fruit of intelligibility: the significance of the action, in other words, the *theme.*

4. At this point, we come again upon the theme. But we
realize that the theme is the term and *significance* of the *action*. On the one hand (though greater import can be given
by the poet either to the action itself or to what is signified
by it), the theme does not exist in the poem separately from
the action (as a *thesis* does, which is introduced into the
poem from without); the theme is immanent in the life of
the poem, because it is the meaning of the action. A poet
can use as many conceptual assertions as he pleases, the
moment they are required either by the poetic sense or by
the action: it is only through the action that they contribute
validly to the expression of the theme. On the other hand,

being the meaning of the action, the theme, like the action, presupposes the poetic sense, and originates in the creative intuition.

The proper effect of the action is to transfer poetic knowledge, from its own original state or level—where things and the Self are indivisibly grasped together, through emotion, and in darkness—to a more objective and more universal state or level, where creative knowledge is still, to be sure, unable to exist in terms of conceptual and logical reason (it exists in terms of action), but is disengaged from the night —the fecund and creative night—of subjectivity. Here we have to do with a process of relative depersonalization. But we have no longer an expression of the poetic knowledge and the creative emotion in their pure and original state, as the poetic sense is; we have an élan or motion into which creative emotion, losing its original state, objectivizes itself in some respect. The theme, or significance of the action, might be described as an objectivization and intellectualization—still implicit and concrete—of the content of creative emotion. It is irreducible to any merely logical statement, yet it can be subsequently translated—while losing its very nature by the fact—into such a statement.

Thus it is that the theme is in the poem the element which is the nearest to rational intellectuality. Through it, it is an objective content, pregnant with universal significance and laden with thought, that the poem embraces and offers. It is not surprising that the value and richness of the theme depend on, and are a token of, all the intellectual baggage of the poet—his more or less integrated universe of knowledge, his rational power and the energy of perception, comprehension, and command of his intelligence, the vastness and unity of his mental horizons—as presupposed condition.

Yet the central fact pointed out above holds true: the poetic sense or inner melody—prime and immediate expression, first-born of creative emotion—is prior to the action and the theme. The action and the theme are complements or objective reflections of the poetic sense: if they are not in consonance and unity with it, they mar the poem. They originate in creative emotion: without it they have no poetic existence. The idea of a theme can present itself to the mind independently of creative emotion: it gives nothing if it does not pass through creative emotion; the theme itself, the meaning of the action, exercises its function in the poem only by virtue of creative emotion.

Of course, in concrete psychological life, all things are at play together, in a way which may sometimes obscure the priorities in nature recognized by philosophical analysis. A poet, thinking of a certain theme, can be incited thereby to write a poem, just as he can be by the idea of a certain subject or by the fact that he has been commissioned by a publisher. Yet here we have simply psychological motivation, not the poetic process itself. Either the poet in question has already received the impact of some poetic intuition, which is the reason for his thinking of this particular theme; or he will wait for the coming of poetic intuition; or, if he does not wait for it, he will write a nonexisting poem. The theme has no creative power of its own. It receives its own unifying power from poetic intuition's creative power. All power comes from poetic intuition.

Let us read this poem of Donne:

> *If poisonous minerals, and if that tree*
> *Whose fruit threw death on else immortal us,*
> *If lecherous goats, if serpents envious*
> *Cannot be damned, Alas! why should I be?*
> *Why should intent or reason, born in me,*
> *Make sins, else equal, in me more heinous?*
> *And mercy being easy, and glorious*
> *To God, in his stern wrath why threatens he?*
> *But who am I, that dare dispute with thee,*
> *O God? O! of thine only worthy blood,*
> *And my tears, make a heavenly Lethean flood,*
> *And drown in it my sin's black memory;*
> *That thou remember them, some claim as debt,*
> *I think it mercy, if thou wilt forget.*

The theme, experts tell us,[5] may be summarized in "a flat prose statement": "Although it appears unjust that man, merely because he possesses the faculty of reason, should be damned for actions common to lower Nature and unpunished there, man should realize that God's treatment is not to be understood by human reason, and should therefore seek the remission of his sins through the double force of Christ's blood and his own repentance." "The handling of the idea," moreover, "is direct, in the form of argument. The question, then, is: how does the poet invest this argument with emotional force necessary to poetic effect?"

If this were the question, there would be no answer, and there would be no poem. The poet does not have to invest any argument with emotional force, because he does not begin with any argument. He begins with creative emotion, or poetic intuition, and the argument follows. Donne forcefully and eloquently developed his theme—because the creative spark and power came entirely, not from his theme, but from his creative emotion, which I would designate as the wound suddenly produced by some incomprehensible contrast—*poisonous minerals,* and *me*—and by virtue of which the whole poem exists.

Shall we take another example? Let us read William Blake's "The Scoffers":

> *Mock on, mock on, Voltaire, Rousseau,*
> *Mock on, mock on; 'tis all in vain;*
> *You throw but dust against the wind*
> *And the wind blows it back again.*

> *And every stone becomes a gem*
> *Reflected in the beams divine;*
> *Blown back, they blind the mocking eye,*
> *But still in Israel's paths they shine.*

> *The atoms of Democritus*
> *And Newton's particles of light*
> *Are sands upon the Red Sea shore,*
> *Where Israel's tents do shine so bright.*

No more objective and general theme could be desired: Voltaire, Rousseau, *Contra inanem philosophiam.* But where is the hidden creative power? In an invisible flash of intuitive emotion, which is obscurely conveyed to us—what can we say? dust of pride and God's glory—and by virtue of which the whole poem exists.

5. The action and the theme pertain to the second *intentional value* in the poem. Through them the poetic sense is complemented, or objectively reflected, in the same way— analogically speaking—as in the things of nature substance is complemented by quality. Another essential property, which I would call Number or Harmonic Expansion, constitutes a third intentional value, through which the poetic sense and the action are complemented, or externally reflected, in the same way—analogically speaking—as in the things of nature substance is extended by quantity.[6]

There is, for painting or music or dance or architecture as for poetry, a poetic *space* in which the unity of the work as spiritually conceived unfolds in the mutual extraposition of parts, extended either in time or in physical space. Not only are these parts all interrelated, but the very interrelation of parts depends on the whole which precedes them in the mind of the artist, and imposes on each of them its own exigencies of unity.[7]

This vital concurrence of the multiple, or vital order bringing to complex orchestral unity parts struggling to assert their own individual claims, is the number or harmonic expansion of the poem. The property in question, being the most perceivable to the senses, is also the most apparent, and has therefore so obvious an importance that the *arrangement* of the parts, the proportion, correspondence, and mutual impact between them, are what is first seen in the work, and the laws of this arrangement are what the working or discursive attention of the artist or the critic is most occupied with. Yet, essential as it may be, the number or harmonic expansion, being immersed in the materiality of the work, is only a kind of external reflection of the poetic sense and the action in the living and fertile mathematic of sense appearances. It is through number and harmonic expansion that the work is possessed of a kind of external music. For to the extent to which it has number, its visible or sonorous qualities, its impact on the senses and power of delighting them, its own charge of sensitivity and sensuousness are penetrated with the secret measures of reason and logic.

As opposed to the physical space, the poetic space proper to the number or harmonic expansion is not a pre-existing and empty milieu in which things take place, it results from the very expansion of the various parts of the work in their mutual concurrence and competition, so that it is, or should be, always *full*, filled with significative meanings, tensions, and pressures, either positive or negative (silences, voids, breathing spells, blanks reserved for the unexpressed and the nonexistent, which have as much impact on the mind as what is actually expressed). This absolutely singular space, peculiar to each work, is a visible or sonorous embodiment of that universal law of proportion through which creative reason manifests and veils itself in art as well as in nature.

All this appears in a pre-eminent manner when, as in the novel, the parts of the work are characters in mutual conflict, on whose inner depths the interest is concentrated. Then the poetic space becomes a world, and the number or harmonic expansion becomes the vital order—making diversity at its peak conspire in the unity of an enigmatic purpose —through which a creative providence governs a universe of free agents.

Yet, as we shall see, the proportion between the parts of the work and between them and the whole depends on, and originates in, a deeper and more primordial proportion, hidden in the spiritual fabric of the work.

6. At this point let us consider more closely the relationship of the three intentional values of the work we have just discussed with the creative intuition or emotion of the poet. I would say that there is for creative intuition three different states, in consequence of the spiritual spheres in which it acts.

In the spiritual sphere which is its own world—the creative night of the preconscious, nonconceptual life of the intellect—poetic intuition is in its pure, original, and native state, in its state of innocence and integrity, in its God-given state. And it passes into the work through the instrumentality of the *poetic sense*.

But in proportion as the exercise of the operative activity intensifies, poetic intuition makes headway in the "fourth dimension," which is neither breadth, height, or depth, but degrees of qualitative diversity in the specific perspective or angle of vision of the intellect. Thus poetic intuition penetrates into the world of the early morning vision of the intellect, or of nascent logos. There, it is no longer in its connatural state, but in an alien state, peculiar to *the work as mentally conceived, the work as thought*. And then a certain objective virtuality which was contained in poetic intuition is, as it were, detached from it and brought to the act: poetic intuition passes into the work through the instrumentality of the *action* and the *theme*.

Here it is all-important, as I already observed, to realize that the fundamental part played by the intellectual baggage of the poet, and his universe of acquired knowledge, refers to a pre-supposed condition in the order of "material causality." It is only through the poetic intuition and as integrated with it in its pure and original state that this intellectual baggage and this acquired knowledge take on a "formal" part in artistic activity. "The nature of a man's words, where he is strongly affected by joy, grief, or anger, must necessarily depend on the number and quality of the general truths, conceptions, and images, and of the words expressing them, with which his mind had been previously stored." [8] This is evidently and basically true. But what has been stored is but material, supply, food. However rich a soil may be, the juices of the earth must be assimilated by the living sap of trees. The deepest and most comprehensive conceptions, the diamonds of the most powerful reason and integrated knowledge, are of no use if they are not brought to a kind of intentional-experiential fusion with the subjectivity and to a state of fluid, simple, and entirely individualized emotive intuitivity in the preconscious night of poetic knowledge. Everything must pass through this creative night. Doubtless, as regards the material afforded, no great and consistent action or theme can emerge from creative emotion, however genuine, if the energies of the soul are divided or bewildered and its intellectual stuff threadbare or rotten. But action and theme are nothing in the work if they do not emanate from, and are not permeated by, the original spirituality of creative emotion and poetic intuition.

Finally poetic intuition penetrates into the sphere of the daylight vision of the intellect, or of the formed logos, I mean to say, of the virtue of art. Then it is in a still more alien state, peculiar to *the work in the making*. And then the working virtualities which were contained in it are brought to the act, by the fact that it quickens the virtue of art and controls the ways of execution. Poetic intuition passes into the work through the instrumentality of the *number* or *harmonic expansion*. Here again, all the laws and rules of proportion and arrangement are nothing if they are not permeated by the obscure fire of creative intuition.

But a new question arises. Does not the possibility of a certain division or split come about at the moment when poetic intuition passes from its first to its second state, and by the fact that the poetic sense of the poem is partially objectivized into the action? In other words, by the fact that the poetic work not only *is*, but also *does*? I do not think that "beauty is as beauty does," as Kenneth Burke puts it. I would rather say: beauty does as beauty is (a formula which is purely and simply valid for the poem or the song as such, but which must be qualified, as we shall see, when it comes to the drama or the novel). In every self-subsistent being the essence—even at the stage where (as in the drama and the novel, or in plastic arts) it is communicated by the poetic sense in a merely nascent and inchoative way—is a greater and more sacred mystery than the action, and the prime precept of the action is to do as one is. This precept, I believe, applies to the poetic work analogically. The action of a poem may happen to be false to its poetic sense. If there are so few genuine tragedies, it is because in tragedy the action is so prevalent that it risks outgrowing the poetic sense or superseding it. A bad tragedy, like Voltaire's tragedies, has only action, no poetic sense, that is to say, has no action at all, but only plot. The marvel with Sophocles, Shakespeare, and Racine is that the drama has by virtue of the poetic sense such radiant communicativity, such a charge of poetic knowledge, and such free and autonomous existence, that the action, all-animating as it may be, seems the pure motion, made visible, of the inner song of the work, through which the soul of the poet passes.

Let us say, then, that in the spiritual fabric of the poem, the difference in proximity to the creative source between the poetic sense on the one hand, the action and the theme on the other, implies a possibility that the action or the theme, escaping the hold of creative emotion, does not accord with the poetic sense and thus (since they are in interdependence) makes it degenerate or dissipate. Thus it appears that the primordial proportion which matters to the work is the proportion between the action and the poetic sense. It is from this primordial proportion that the number or harmonic expansion derives (as, in music, harmony from the original proportion of the theme to the melody), as well as all those other proportions, of parts between themselves and of parts with the whole, which fill the poetic space and of which I spoke above.

I would like to add, incidentally, that our present considerations may help us to make more precise the criterion to distinguish the "self-sufficient" or "autonomous arts" from the "subservient arts." In the subservient arts the work—a ship for instance—is merely "functional," uniquely determined by the requirements of its *action* (transitive action) or its use. But in the self-sufficient arts the work is "substantial" or self-subsistent, it is first determined by its poetic sense, and its action is first of all immanent action. When the work is a song, its action is a manifestation of its essence; when, as in painting, sculpture, or architecture (or in the novel), the work is given its poetic essence through its action and its harmonic expansion as well as its poetic sense, its action is involved in its very essence. And if it is also functional, as in architecture, this functional value appears itself as a consequence or property of the substantial value. In every great work of architecture the virtue of poetry is so powerful that the functional destination is absorbed, so to speak, in the self-subsistence and self-necessity of a man-made cosmos; all that which is directed—from the very start—to practical use and the service of human needs, appears only as a result and flowering of the inner requirements of such a self-subsistent cosmos.

I am aware of the tentative and exploratory character of the views put forward under the heading of this section. I hope, however, that they may be of some use for further inquiries, and may draw attention to central problems that are often passed over in the approach to the poetic work, whether in poetry or in painting, or in any other of the "self-sufficient arts."

To sum up, I shall say that the poetic sense or inner melody, the action and the theme, the number or harmonic structure, are the three epiphanies of poetic intuition or creative emotion passing into the work.

And I shall conclude that the analysis of the inner spiritual springs, in the poet's mind, in which the poem originates, and of the essential elements of which its own spiritual fabric consists, throws some light on the particular relationship of these three elements to the three components of beauty. *Radiance or clarity,* which is the absolutely prime property of beauty, and matters first of all, appears principally (I do not say uniquely) in the poetic sense or inner melody of the work; *integrity,* in the action and the theme; and *consonance,* in the number or harmonic structure.

Dante's Innocence

7. When we meditate upon the unique grandeur of the *Commedia,* its cosmic scope, and the joint superiority in it

of the inner melody, the action, the theme and the number, our admiration goes out to the genius of Dante, of course, but also to his luck.

A Frenchman has said that genius is a "long patience." He was probably right. But the *longue patience* and mad obstinacy in labor depend themselves on a deeper source. Complex as the obscure reality meant by this word may be, genius has essentially to do with the fact of poetic intuition taking shape in the inaccessible recesses of the soul at an exceptional degree of depth. When it comes to designating the particular quality which characterizes those creative regions, we are at a loss to find an appropriate name. The least defective term I am able to suggest is *creative innocence*. This creative innocence, which is one with unimpeded power and freedom of poetic intuition, is, I think, the most profound aspect of Dante's genius.

The word innocence has two connotations. The first is *naïveté*, that sort of total simpleness and confidence in gazing at things of which intelligence at the highest degree of its vitality or childish ignorance alone are capable, and which, like the charity spoken of by St. Paul, believes as one breathes, "believeth all things."

How could one utter if he did not believe? The native reliance, consubstantial with his own being, *"la bêtise,"* Baudelaire said (because he hid himself in the disparaging irony of nineteenth-century dandyism), with which any great poet *believes all things*—not only all things brought to him by poetic experience, but also everything in the world and in himself which is food or support for it, and every nod and wink that events give to him, and his own feeling, and his own urge to speak an unspeakable truth of his own —is carried in Dante to the point of an adamantine certitude. He has no doubt at all. He seems even immune from the doubt which troubles so many great poets about their own work.

And the feeling that every great poet has—be it in distressing obscurity—of a certain wound which has set free in him the creative source, and has separated him from other men (through the dreams and detachment of childhood, or some abiding despair) is carried in Dante to the point of a perfectly clear awareness. He knows his wound and believes in it; and cherishes it. Beatrice has made it. The best that we can do is to accept his testimony, just as it is given. Freudians may explain in their way the sublimation of the experience he underwent in seeing a girl of nine when he was nine. What matters to us is the fact that this trauma, penetrating to the very center of the powers of the spirit, has made of his relation to Beatrice the unshakeable personal truth on which his poetic intuitivity will live, the nest of his creative emotion, the basic *belief* through which all realities of the visible and invisible world will awaken his creative subjectivity. If by virtue of the magic of imagination and the symbol, Beatrice was to become, while remaining herself, a constellation of supreme spiritual lights, it is because everything revealed to Dante in the night of poetic knowledge was revealed to him in and through his love for her—captured itself by imagination but still keeping its original impact—and in continuity with the primordial intuition which had obscurely disclosed womanhood and desire to him.

Symbolically transmuted as she may be, Beatrice is never a symbol or an allegory for Dante. She *is* both herself and what she signifies. Dante's blessed naïveté is so profound that—at the preconscious level of creativity, in the deepest nocturnal recess of poetic intuition—he actually believes in this one and multiple identity. Without this central belief all his poetry would have quit him. His naïveté is such that he believes his love for Beatrice to be in itself and in the face of all men as important a thing as heaven and earth. This naïveté, which "believes all things," has such brazen audacity that nothing seems more natural to him than to have a certain girl, by the original fact that his flesh burned for her, exalted in paradise as the incarnation of theological knowledge, in whose eyes the humanity and the divinity of Christ are mirrored, and of faith illumined by the contemplative gifts, and of the inspired guidance in the regions of the beatific vision. Vergil and all the abysses of darkness and light were mobilized, the great voyage from hell to heaven was undertaken, the entire *Commedia* was written to glorify this woman. This was the first basic incentive. "Therefore," as he puts it in the last chapter of the *Vita Nuova,* "if it be His pleasure through Whom is the life of all things that my life continue with me a few years, it is my hope that I shall write yet concerning her what hath not before been written of any woman."

8. I would call *integrity* or incorruption, untouched original purity, the second connotation of creative innocence. If we remember what has been said in another part of this book about poetic experience and poetic intuition, we shall realize that the regions where they are born, when they are to possess the fullness of their nature, are regions of ontologic simplicity which are blissfully shielded from all the business of psychological interests. At the center of the Self self-research loses any sense. I have insisted elsewhere on the essential disinterestedness of poetic intuition. There is no merit in this disinterestedness. It is but an effect of the ontologic simplicity I just mentioned, some visible image of which the gravity of a child's gaze sometimes offers to us, who seems simply astonished *to be,* and condemns all our interests and their futility.

The creative emotion of minor poets is born in a flimsy twilight and at a comparatively superficial level in the soul. Great poets descend into the creative night and touch the deep waters over which it reigns. Poets of genius have their dwelling place in this night and never leave the shores of these deep waters. Here are the regions of integrity of which I am speaking.

We have no sign of this deep-seated integrity, except the work itself, or perchance the presence, in the visible regions of the soul, of some pure and lasting feeling, which is like a reflection on moving clouds of the sun fallen below the horizon. "What is God?" Thomas Aquinas asked when he was five. This question born in the creative innocence of a child's

astonishment developed into the multiform and single movement of his lifelong research. It is not unwise to assume that
in Dante something similar came about: not a prime question of nascent reason, but a prime wound of nascent sensibility and, in proportion as later on poetic experience
developed, a more and more profound (as this wound itself)
discovery by poetic intuition—an amazement without end
before the face of love unveiling its miraculous and terrible
ambiguity; and, then, across all the weaknesses and failings
of a human life, a pure abiding feeling of spiritual fidelity,
an unbroken process of deeper knowing and purifying of
love. Shelley states that Dante "understood the secret things
of love" more than any other poet. And did he not say
himself:

Tutti li miei pensier parlan d'Amore.

He never idealized carnal love, whose tricks he also understood, and he never forgot that any evil can "color as love
wills," as did the Siren's *smarrito volto*. He knew perfectly
the difference in nature which distinguishes the various
kinds of love, and especially divine love from human love.
He is frightened and ashamed when, at the appearance of
Beatrice in the Earthly Paradise, even before recognizing her
he suddenly feels "the mighty power of ancient love,"
"d'antico amor la gran potenza," "through hidden virtue
which went out from her." But he also knew that the lowest
forms of love bear in darkness and distortion the seal of a
higher origin, and that purified human love can be redeemed
by divine love, and serve it. While his love for God his Saviour, for "Him Who is the lord of courtesy," transfigures
the woman he once desired, his love for this transfigured
woman is the medium through which divine love penetrates
the creative center of his poetry. The entire *Commedia* was
written to bear testimony to the purification of love in the
heart of a man. This was the second basic incentive, and it
was one with the first.

How would this long movement itself of self-purification
have taken hold of the soul of the poet without the basic in-

tegrity of his creative experience, in which the "secret things of love" were gradually discovered to him?

9. Creative innocence is in no way moral innocence. It is, as I have indicated above, of an ontologic, not a moral nature. It has essentially to do with the intuition of the poet, not with his loves. And of the two things which alone make life worth living, love is more valuable than intuition when it transforms us into something better than we are, but intuition is not liable to all kinds of illusion and moral defilement, as love is: because intuition deals with knowledge (creative knowledge in the case of the poet) and, *qua* intuition, never misses the mark.

In every great poet creative innocence exists to some degree. It has its plenitude in the greatest. It exists in a place which is so deep-seated that no impact of the troubles, splits, vices, or failures which may undermine the domain of free will, passion, and instinct can spoil its ontologic integrity. In this place there is no conflict or break between senses and reason, because there is no division. All the powers of the soul are brought to unity in a state of habitual permanence, proper to a poetic experience which is not fleeting and transient, as it is usually, but lasting and steady, at least virtually. This place is the only one that is not wounded, I would say, by the old hereditary sin which wounds human nature. It is a kind of earthly paradise—but physical, not moral— concealed in nocturnal depths, in which nothing, to be sure, of the divine pageant described by Dante can be hoped for, but where the smile and the eyes of a Beatrice of beauty, not of sainthood, are mirrored in deep waters.

The inner world in the midst of which such a place exists may be filled with impurity; the moral experience of a great poet may be rotten; his thought and his passion may be stimulated by energies of illusion or perversity. When the things he has nourished in himself enter his earthly paradise of creative innocence, they keep their moral impurity—if they have any—which will also pass into the work. But they bathe in the ontologic purity of this place. In the waters of poetic knowledge they are dehumanized and made into mineral entities, transmuted into forms of the revelation of being through creative emotion; they receive a new nature, a poetic nature, a new principle of existence, which replaces in them the human one, and causes their moral impact and moral qualities, as well as the marks and stains upon them of a man's tics or vices, to become henceforth accidental and secondary in the particular sphere of this new state of existence, where only poetry and beauty are essential. To the extent to which moral deformity always involves some ontologic defect, some naught, there will be, if the things in question, the poet's intellectual and moral supply, are corroded by such naught, some lack or deficiency in their new nature as forms of the revelation of being through creative emotion. Yet inasmuch as they receive this new nature, and emerge from a poetic intuition proper to the great depths, this lack or deficiency entails only some comparative imperfection in the work into which they enter, and they are invested with the ontologic purity of creative innocence, they are possessed of a purity which is poetic purity.

Thus it is that a great poet can be corrupt, while his creative intuition never is. A purity remains in him, which of itself is of no avail for his soul, but which is a blessing for his work and for us. And if there are in this work poisonous human meanings and morally impure ferments, their impact on human minds will wear off in time, absorbed or superseded by another impact, more essential to the work, the impact of poetic purity and poetic energy. Time, as Shelley put it, will wash away all the sins of the poet in the eyes of those who receive from him the pure gift of a more profound discovery in the experience of beauty and the human soul.

10. Dante was not corrupt, and nothing morally impure went from his heart into his work. This is not, however, the fact with which our present considerations are concerned. They point to this other fact, that all things a poet puts in

his work must pass through the creative night of poetic intuition. Nowhere is Dante's great lesson clearer.

No poet has had to do with heavier equipment and am-
munition. Not to speak of his perfect craftsmanship, he knew
everything his time knew and took to heart all the conflicts,
whether social, political, or religious, in which his time was
engaged. His work is a *summa* laden with a world of divine
and human truths, yearnings, and violence. For ivory tower
he has the earth and heaven. He describes, he narrates, he
teaches, he preaches. Why such freedom? All his immense
materials, all the constellations of Christianity were carried
in the creative night of his poetic intuition to a state of im-
ponderable poetic existence. All passed through this intuitive night, by virtue of his extraordinarily profound creative
innocence. For creative innocence is the paradise of poetic
intuition, the existential state in which poetic intuition can
reach full power and liberty. (And another quality of the
entire soul concurred, but this is another point.)

In addition to the basic poetic incentives, all kinds of purposes, human, nonartistic in nature, played their part freely
in the productive effort of Dante. None entered his art and
his work as an extraneous element, interfering with, or
"bending," them. Being integrated in poetic intuition, all
were *in,* from the start, at each creative instant on which
each part of the work depended. As to the final end, it was,
so he wrote, "to remove those living in this life from the
state of misery and lead them to the state of felicity." In
fact, while the poet intended such a final purpose, poetry
was freer than ever, quickened from within in its very
liberty, and it was to make of the work, if not the great
instrument of salvation that the poet proposed, at least a
self-sufficient creation mirroring the wanderings of sinful
humanity in search of blessedness—simply a poem, in a
word, in which a host of readers most often deaf to its
preaching would look for the delights of beauty—not to
speak of the supreme delights afforded to scholars by the
puzzles of allegory, trope, and anagogy.

Dante teaches a great deal. Everybody teaches in the *Com-media*. Why do we never feel the tedium of didacticism? Nothing is more boring in a poem than philosophy or alle-gory. Why are we never bored with the philosophical lectures of Dante, and all his allegorical apparatus? Not to speak of his geographical contrivances and cosmological de-vices? The answer is always the same. If all these things are deprived of their natural weight, and become light and trans-parent, and have been made themselves *innocent*, it is be-cause, as a natural result of the poet's creative innocence, they have been seized hold of by his emotion, abstract as they may be, and have received from it an ingenuous soul, and an indefinite meaning which matters more than their own. May I suggest that Dante believes in his riddles and his cosmological and geographical sand castles with the ambigu-ous seriousness of childhood's imagination? As to allegory, he invests it with such visual melody that we already receive some intuitive pleasure from it—even from it!—before un-derstanding anything of it. As T. S. Eliot observes, it is enough for us to know that it has a meaning, without knowing yet what this meaning can be.

And perhaps it is not necessary to understand Dante's phil-osophical discourses either, to be allured by a pleasure of reason: so pure are their perfect economy and the intellec-tual sweep they delineate, like a dance movement, by virtue of some underlying music of emotion. Yet we enjoy them to the full, to be sure, when the marvelous precision of the in-telligible meaning appears also to us, adding clarity to clarity. Thus, in the *Purgatorio*, we are instructed in the existence of free will by Marco Lombardo:

> *Voi che vivete ogni cagion recate*
> *pur suso al cielo, pur come se tutto*
> *movesse seco di necessitate.*

> *Se così fosse, in voi fora distrutto*
> *libero arbitrio, e non fora giustizia*
> *per ben, letizia, e per male, aver lutto.*

Lo cielo i vostri movimenti inizia;
non dico tutti, ma, posto ch'io il dica,
lume v'è dato a bene ed a malizia

e libero voler, che, se fatica
nelle prime battaglie col ciel dura,
poi vince tutto, se ben si notrica.

A maggior forza e a miglior natura
liberi soggiacete, e quella cria
la mente in voi, che il ciel non ha in sua cura.[9]

Finally a point made by T. S. Eliot may be discussed, I think, in the light of our present considerations. Eliot observes that although the *Divine Comedy* could not have been written without Dante's religious faith, it is not necessary to share in this faith to understand the poem and assent to its beauty. You must be instructed, of course, about the things in which Dante believed, but you are not required to believe in them yourself. In reading the poem, Eliot says, "you suspend both belief and disbelief." Moreover, while being perhaps as remote as possible from Dante's own belief, you do not feel hurt by that imposition of the personal belief of a man forcing its way into another which other poets, Goethe for instance, do not spare us. I assume, as Eliot does, that the typical characteristics of the religious doctrine to which Dante adhered are not alien to the fact. "A coherent traditional system of dogma and morals like the Catholic . . . stands apart, for understanding and assent even without belief, from the single individual who propounds it." [10] More precisely, with the objective system of reference of a public revelation conveyed to all through the testimony of a visible Church, there is no need for the poet to push himself forward in speaking of what he believes more than in speaking of what everyone sees.

I hasten to say, nevertheless, that not with all Catholic poets does a non-Catholic reader feel himself protected from any intrusive assertion of an individual's belief. The reason for the fact mentioned by Eliot lies in the very purity of

Dante's poetic approach. It relates to the sovereign and native primacy of the poetic sense over the intelligible sense—even in a poetry which is splendidly clear. The ego of the man has disappeared in the creative Self of the poet. Theological faith itself, the most sacred belief, has entered the work through the instrumentality of creative emotion and poetic knowledge, and passed through the lake of disinterestedness of creative innocence.

And Luck

11. It is not enough to speak of Dante's genius. We must also take his luck into consideration. The extraordinary luck of Dante the poet was a result of the coincidence of an extraordinary variety of good fortunes. It had to do with the grace of God and the virtues of Dante the man, with centuries of culture and with a unique moment in time.

There was, first, the innocence of his heart. The subtle naïveté of the medieval man was all the greater in him as it was brightened but not yet corrupted by the dawning ardors of modern consciousness. Full of violence as he was, his passions, angers, and prepossessions, as well as the ventures of his life, all emerged from candor and ingenuousness. The purity of his eye made his "whole body lightsome." No fault leaves mud in a soul which knows itself in clarity and is steeped in the feeling of the mercy of its Redeemer. I do not believe that the creative innocence of Dante, and the transparency of his poetic experience, could have been so deep, had not the innocence of his heart established his entire soul in genuine connaturality with them.

Another luck for his poetry was the freedom of mind he received from the firmness of his religious faith. Because he was so perfectly sure of his faith, his poetry was able freely to play even with its tenets, and to fancy, without deceiving anybody, that condition of the "neither rebellious nor faithful," rejected both by heaven and by hell, which theology does not know. Because he was perfectly sure of his faith, he was eager for knowledge, whose consonance with his faith was for him divinely unquestionable, and he had such liberty in his appreciation of any effort of human reason, that he welcomed in his praise and paradise both Thomas Aquinas and Siger de Brabant. He was not afraid, as the Jansenists were later on, to do justice to the natural virtues of the pagans. He had none of the fears and complexes which paralyze our modern literary martyrs of freedom from truth. His undivided intellect was established in a state of general security by the all-pervading security of his faith. It is hard for our modern mind to imagine the simplicity in belief and firmness in adherence which characterized the whole thought of Dante, however refined, subtle, and learned, and his vision of the world and of himself. Here again a certain kind of innocence in man, an innocence of the intellect, which was in no way credulity, but integrity of the natural élan or eros, assisted creative innocence.

And so we are led to a different category of luck, which has to do not with a strengthening of the creative source itself, but rather with the prerequired conditions—depending on the general equipment of the mind and the harvest garnered in its granaries—of which I spoke with respect especially to the action and the theme, and which relate to creative intuition from the outside. I am thinking, here, of the heritage of culture received by Dante, and of the articulate universe of beliefs and values in which his thought dwelt. Dante wrestled with his time, which forced into exile the poet threatened with death. But as concerns the spiritual quality of the cultural heritage he was blessed by his time. Then the human mind was imbued with the sense of being, and nature appeared all the more real and consistent as it was perfected by grace. Being still turned toward wisdom, still permeated with rationality and mystery both of which descended from the Uncreate Word, still softened by the blood of the Incarnate Word, the universe of the late thirteenth century, with its ontological hierarchies mirrored in the hierarchies of intellectual disciplines, ensured to the intelligence and emotion of a poet, despite all the evil fevers, discords, crimes, and vices of the time, a state of integration and vitality that the modern man has lost. Dante participated with all his fibers in an organic order which already felt the first breaths of a newly born spring, and did not know it was already decaying.

I do not believe that the greater or less perfection in intrinsic truth of the universe of thought of a poet matters to his poetry save in quite a remote manner. The medieval universe, true as its highest metaphysical principles may be, was, on the other hand, lacking in a great many truths that the modern man has discovered at the price of his internal unity. Moreover, great poetry was to live in universes of thought quite different from that of Dante—already the universe of Cervantes, and still more that of Shakespeare, and still more that of Goethe, and still more that of Dostoevski, not to speak of what had been the universe of Homer or that of Sophocles, or that of the Upanishads. What matters to poetry in a close and direct manner are, I think, certain extremely simple but basic *presences* or existential certainties, assured by the universe of thought which constitutes the vital environment of poetic intuition: for instance a certitude both of the mysterious irrefragable existence and the exigency of intelligibility involved in things; a certitude of the *interiority* of the human being, and of its importance; a certitude that between man and the world there is an invisible relationship deeper than any material interconnection; a certitude that the impact of his freedom on his destiny gives his life a movement which is *oriented,* and not lost in the void, and which has to do, in one way or another, with the whole fabric of being. Such existential certitudes, and many others no doubt, existed in the mind of Baudelaire (at what cost—columns in what desert) as in that of Dante. The absence of some of them is responsible for the narcissism of Mallarmé. I submit that without them the prerequired conditions are lacking for any great poetry to reach full stature. Natural as they may be, these certitudes exist with greater force and stability if they are integrated in an articulate universe of thought. They cannot exist in us when the universe of thought that we have received—and accepted (in anguish or complacency, revolt or self-abandonment)—from our age of culture is a disintegrated universe which rejects or denies them, and has lost, together with the intellectual sense of being and truth, what Waldo Frank called, in the page quoted at the beginning of this chapter, the sense of the person (or of the interiority of the human being) and the sense of Time (or of the oriented movement of human existence). Dante's luck was to have all the *presences,* the existential certitudes which are the natural soil of poetry, integrated with absolute firmness in a consistent universe of thought rooted in reason and faith— and radiant to his emotion in the blissful innocence of the intellect. Never has creative innocence enjoyed so favorable a climate and such exceptional assistance. A whole cosmos could pass through the creative night of his poetic intuition.

12. Finally we have also to consider the fleeting uniqueness of the moment of human history which was the moment of Dante. As Allen Tate has pointed out, the luckiest periods for art and poetry are those where a great civilization is on the verge of decline. Then the vital force of this civilization meets with historical conditions which cease being appropriate to it, but it is still intact, for one moment, in the sphere of spiritual creativity, and it gives its last fruit there, while the freedom of poetry avails itself of the decay of social disciplines and ethos. Nothing less than age-old Christendom was singing its last song in Dante.

Yet the point with which I am concerned is much more particular. It has to do with the proper time of poetry itself. Considering the process of self-realization, through a work of words, of poetry as free creativity of the spirit, I would say that during the Middle Ages poetry (I mean in the vernacular) had remained in a pre-adult state. The diversity of generic forms (mystery play, romance, lyric, etc.) in which it expressed itself had only to do with a condition imposed by art or *technè*. Medieval poetry had not reached the stage where the inner growth of poetry demands a division of poetry itself into certain basic forms by virtue of an essential difference in its approach to the work. In other words art was differentiated; poetry, in its own ways of using the activity of art, was not. The virtualities of its energy of self-realization through the work of words were still united in indistinctness. Dante arrived just at the instant when medieval poetry touched its ultimate point of growth—on the verge of differentiation, but still undifferentiated.

Thus it is that the *Divine Comedy* breaks open the classical framework of the epic (it is in no way a simple Christian *Aeneid*) and cannot be classed in any literary genre. Here we are confronted with the central fact on which I wish to lay stress. The *Commedia* embraces in its substantial unity forms of poetic creation which demand of themselves to be separate, and which will separate after Dante—I say as specific types of *poetry,* apart from the more external division of the work (even if it happens to lack any poetry) into artistic or literary genres. The *Divine Comedy* is at the same time and with the same intensive reality poetry of the song, poetry of the theater, and poetry of the tale; the three epiphanies of poetic intuition compose together its single soul or entelechy.

The *Divine Comedy* is indeed a Song—a song to a woman who was loved (all poets think so) as no other woman ever was or will be, and a song to the purification of love in the heart of the poet. With its "lax and humble method of speech," as Dante put it, it is a sustained avowal, veiled under infinitely variegated external forms, of the subjectivity of the poet wounded by this woman, and through this wound awakened to its own depths and all things, in the transparent night of poetic knowledge. A long inner melody of feelings and meanings, running through the entire work, gives it its secret unity, and that pure freedom, satisfied only with being, which witnesses to the freedom in it of the poetic sense. The indefinitely vibrating echoes and overtones in intelligibility due to the multiplicity of allusive senses and to the "imaginative fusion of images and ideas" enigmatically convey in the tercets and sequences a singular impact of subjectivity in the act of intuitive emotion. The music of intuitive pulsions, prevented as it may be from direct expression by the requirements of intelligibility, passes despite all into the very intelligibility of the lines—translated into the infallible *cadence* of the intelligible and imaginative élan, which loads with pure emotion each particular unit or episode. Speaking of the third canto of the *Inferno*, "in this canto," Coleridge said, "all the images are distinct, and even vividly distinct, but there is a total impression of infinity; the wholeness is not in vision or conception, but in an inner feeling of totality, and absolute being"; and he noted the fundamental importance of "inwardness or subjectivity" in Dante's poetry. Everywhere, but especially perhaps in the *Paradiso*, the freedom of the song is a sign of the kind of "aseity" peculiar to the first epiphany of creative intuition.

> *Però che tutte quelle vive luci,*
> *vie più lucendo, cominciaron canti*
> *da mia memoria labili e caduci.*

> *O dolce amor, che di riso t'ammanti,*
> *quanto parevi ardente in quei flailli*
> *ch'avieno spirto sol di pensier santi!* [11]

But the *Divine Comedy* is also, indeed, a Drama. Scott Buchanan, in *Poetry and Mathematics,* and Francis Fergusson, in *The Idea of a Theater,* have remarked that "the deepest and most elaborate development of the tragic rhythm is to be found in the *Divine Comedy*." [12] The whole work and its three parts, and the whole and detail of each part, are animated by the intellectual élan, articulate and definite, proper to the action; and the unitary power of the theme is the meaning of a particularly powerful action. In the last analysis, it is by virtue of that objectivization of creative intuition which is the action that "the most wakeful reason" enjoys full freedom in the poem without threatening (because action and poetic sense are in perfect consonance) the spells of the night, and gently interweaves its threads with those of the myth and the dream. Thus could a theorist of the theater like Fergusson—I have already noted the fact—

find in the *Divine Comedy,* especially in the *Purgatorio,* an ideal exemplar of dramatic action. The *Commedia* is for him—with the drama of Sophocles and Shakespeare—one of the "cultural landmarks in which the idea of a theater has been briefly realized"; it shows us "not the contemporary possibility, but the perennial idea of a theater of human life and action." [13]

And the *Divine Comedy* is also, indeed, a Tale, or better, a Novel of the beyond and the here below. It is a continuous and complex narrative, in which the particular adventures of the two protagonists serve to put into existence and motion a world of adventures and destinies, so as to make of each human being involved a center of interest, looked at by the poet in its own singular ineffable reality. Though their fates are now sealed, and their lives have become only an object of memory, all these characters have life and existential interiority, because their author knows them, as every novelist does, from the inside, that is, through himself, or through connaturality. As the *Commedia* clearly shows, it is through his own inclinations, but especially through his love, that Dante knew his characters; love was the great medium, either pity or piety or fury (the reverse face of love). And although he nowhere indulged in any kind of connivance or complicity, he even loved, and even admired, certain of his sinners without being in any way hindered by their state of damnation—as in particular that master of his youth, his dear Brunetto Latini, who even in hell "seemed like him who wins, and not like him who loses":

> *Poi si rivolse, e parve di coloro*
> *che corrono a Verona il drappo verde*
> *per la campagna; e parve di costoro*
> *quelli che vince, non colui che perde.*[14]

At this point—just as the essence of the Song appears everywhere, but especially perhaps in the *Paradiso,* and that of Drama everywhere but especially perhaps in the *Purgatorio* —must we note that the essence of the Novel appears everywhere, but especially perhaps in the *Inferno?* [15] It has been said of Dante: "His eye is always directly upon the life of the psyche in its shifting modes of being, its thought, its sufferings, and its contemplation." [16] In other words he has the eye of a genuine novelist.

The Three Specific Types of Poetry

13. The *Divine Comedy* is Novel, Drama, and Song in indivisibility, and with equal plenitude. This fact—unique, I think, in our culture—does not depend only on the genius of Dante, it depends also on his extraordinary luck. Thereafter, the three types of poetry united in the *Commedia* divided from one another, by virtue of an irreversible process of differentiation—here again I do not speak of the differentiation (long since achieved) of the art of writing into various literary genres, I speak of the differentiation of poetry itself into three essentially distinct types: namely the Poem, the Drama, and the Novel, in so far as, in literary genres which often do without poetry, or betray it, poetry demands to make the work into a real, pure, and genuine expression of poetry itself.

As regards the Poem, I believe that this process of differentiation was fully achieved only in modern times, together with the self-awareness of poetry. During the classical age it did not proceed without trouble. One may wonder whether the example of Dante was always profitable to great poets anxious to compete with him in greatness, and the fact is that neither Milton nor Goethe completely escaped the kind of boredom inherent in any poetic work too big for its soul. As to *Faust,* whose general movement, curiously enough ("from Heaven, through Earth, down to Hell") is the opposite of that of the *Divine Comedy,* the action in it is poor and cold, and the philosophical expression owes its richness and warmth only to lyricism vivifying an alien matter, which comes from abstract reason.

Be that as it may, it is surely fair for us, when we think of poetry, to bear in mind the paradigm offered by Dante, but we may be unfair to modern poets if we use this paradigm as a too simple and univocal measure of comparison.

No poem, except for the unique case of the *Commedia,* can be poem, drama, and novel at the same time. The Poem, the Song, exists through its poetic sense, the first epiphany of creative intuition. Obviously it must also have action and harmonic expansion, but appropriate to its nature. When we say that the theme is weak in modern poetry, we are right in regard to those poets whose theme is frail or evanescent because they have nothing to say, even about an experience of their own. But it would be nonsense to require from modern poets a "greatness," an objective intellectuality and universality of theme comparable to those in Dante. With respect to the nature of a poetry whose prime virtue is to convey purely the intuitive night of subjectivity and the nonconceptualizable meanings caught in things through this night, modern poetry has shown that it is capable of greatness, as well as of any quality required in the action, the theme, and the harmonic expansion.

It has been observed that the modern poet is secluded in his own self: when it is a question of a great modern poet, this is true only on the condition that one adds that in this single self and its emotion unknown things grasped in the world are present, and some more than real reality is passing. Where in modern poems is that interest for a host of other human beings which fills the *Divine Comedy?* Is the modern poet unable to enter into creative communication with other selves than his own? As far as the Poem, or the Song, is concerned, it is not with other subjectivities, it is indeed with the world to be revealed together with his own subjectivity that all his creative knowledge has to be occupied. Yet modern poetry is capable of knowing through connaturality, and making live, a host of human beings. This is the business of the poetry of the Novel. Just as the Theater at the time of Lope de Vega and the Elizabethans, the Novel in modern times has allowed the Poem to free itself from functions which are alien to it and alienate it from its nature.

"A poem of any length," Coleridge said, "neither can be, nor ought to be, all poetry." But the modern poem is determined, and bound, to be all poetry. This is perhaps why Edgar Allan Poe considered a long poem "simply a flat contradiction in terms." If it relates to the length of a poem materially considered, the quantity of lines, this statement might be questioned. At least one would like to know at what number of lines a poem starts to be long. St.-John Perse's *Anabase,* which Poe would have admired, I assume, is a comparatively long poem. (As to Mallarmé, he could not finish *Hérodiade,* and I wonder whether greater length than that of "The Hound of Heaven," for instance, or of "The Wreck of the Deutschland," may be expected as a rule of a modern poem.) But Poe's statement is simply true, I believe, if it relates to the length of a poem in relation to its own inner measure, which is the poetic sense. The developed narrative, the description of characters, the exposition of a system, appear from this point of view as invested with incurable length. A great modern poem can be philosophical —why not?—or in the form of a tale. It must always be contained within the span of a free and pure conveyance of anything intuitively caught in and through the night of subjectivity.

T. S. Eliot remarks, in his essay on Baudelaire, that "many people who enjoy Dante enjoy Baudelaire." There must be some reason for this. In the strict order of poetry, Baudelaire appears in modern times, with his extraordinary depth in poetic intuition, his creative innocence surrounded by all the demons of impurity, as the most significant counterpart of Dante's extraordinary depth in poetic intuition, but blessed and lucky.

Baudelaire was wounded and destroyed by his time, as Dante was served by his. He waged within himself a hopeless spiritual war against his time, as Dante assumed his in exultation. He revealed the eternal and supernatural in man in man's perversity as Dante revealed it in God's justice and mercy. He was torn between God and the devil in his love for Beauty the idol as Dante was carried along toward his Saviour in his love for Beauty the sacrament. I am aware of his atrocious weaknesses. Yet in his frustrated dreams he also had his muse and guardian angel, a poor Beatrice of his own, powerless to save him. If we assume that he had perceived what kind of hell is our modern universe, and had descended into this hell, and looked at everything from there, we realize that, in distortion and cruelty, his vision of human love was the most profound—I do not say true—that the corrupt eye of a lost epoch was capable of; in darkness and division, his sense of the reality of sin and of the transcendent destiny of the soul, and his assertion of the necessity of Christianity —so thoroughly serious and personal, as Eliot emphasized —were the most gravely pressing, I do not say well-balanced, that the corrupt heart of a lost epoch was capable of.

Be all that as it may, what matters over and above all is the fact that Baudelaire had intelligence, and the creative innocence proper to the depths of poetry, to such an exceptional degree that the comparison with Dante forces itself upon us; and that in his despairing struggle with inspiration and with style, he succeeded in giving the poem, reduced to its pure essence, such inwardness and revealing power that what he did for poetry in concentration and intensity may be compared to what Dante did for it in sovereignty and immensity, while embracing in a unique work the joint virtues of a triple poetic essence.

When T. S. Eliot wrote that "in the adjustment of the natural to the spiritual, of the bestial to the human and the human to the supernatural, Baudelaire is a bungler compared with Dante," [17] I wonder whether he did not forget that Baudelaire, in the place where he was, and from which he looked at things, was precisely required by poetry not to perceive the adjustment, but to feel the split and derangement.

Allen Tate and Waldo Frank are right in pointing out the inadequacy of the theme in Hart Crane's poetry, and the tragic solitude and disintegration of the world in which his intellect and sensibility moved. But (apart from his moral weakness in the face of this world) the error of Crane, it seems to me, was to attempt a disproportionate task, and to look for a cosmic greatness which was but a cerebral ambition, a dream of a poet unaware of the limits of his own poetry. There was more soundness of theme—as a simple objective reflection of the poetic sense—there was more greatness, proportionate to the universe of the Song, in the admirable purity, less ambitious, and more deeply revealing, of Emily Dickinson's profound poetry. There was also more greatness, and genuine force, in Walt Whitman's verbal outpouring, because he innocently obeyed the impulse of a free fervor.

14. In quite another sense than when it was a question of Dante, the luck of the modern poet has to do with the time proper to poetry, and the moment at which he was born to poetry. The self-awareness, and the sense of its own freedom, that poetry has gained in modern times, place him from the very start at the center of the citadel.

His ill luck has to do with the time proper to culture, and the moment at which he was born to the world.

Modern poets, at least a number of them, may be reproached with many things—with the previously mentioned propensity to take upon themselves the part of the hero, and become the prophets and priests of the world; and with the lack of that quality which Matthew Arnold called high seriousness, and which is but an aspect, perhaps, of the naïveté of creative innocence; and with a futile submission to the demons of the time.

It is hard for any man, especially for a poet, to struggle against the streams of his world. Nevertheless the poet, though not in the manner of the saint, is also in this world without being of this world. If he wants to save his poetry, he must resist the world, at least to preserve or reconquer the basic *presences* or existential certitudes discussed above, and to keep and purify those aesthetic virtues whose kinship with Christian virtues Max Jacob stressed—in other words, to be the guardian of his Angel, as Cocteau put it. If he wants to save his soul, he must do more. Then he will be in a state of separation, and obliged, however, as a poet, to remain open and permeable to all that moves and ferments in his world and his time. He cannot escape being wounded. He may not be destroyed. All the troubles of the time may enter the soul of a man, and be mastered by creative innocence—that is the miracle of poetry. And they may enter the soul of man, and be mastered by the innocence of the heart—that is the miracle of sainthood. In both cases much suffering is involved; in the second, much love and contemplative experience.

The poet who endeavors to make a stand against the spirit of his time risks indulging in a certain stiffening of the intellect and the will which may impair his work—to the extent to which he is a minor poet or a beginner. He is helped nevertheless by poetic experience. It is certain that such a stand can be made without any detriment to the work—let us think of the spiritual attitude of William Blake with regard to his time, or of Léon Bloy or Chesterton, Falla, Lourié, Rouault, or T. S. Eliot, with regard to theirs. In this country Allen Tate has long maintained a similar independence, from which his work has not suffered—rather it witnesses to the possibility that modern poetry can gain a new intellectual firmness. I admit nevertheless that modern poets as a rule are but too eager for the ill-luck and the evil spells that their culture and their time bestow on them.

For all that, there is a thing with which modern poets can never be reproached. They can never be reproached with modern poetry.

15. Poetry, with which this book is fundamentally concerned, is the free creativity of the spirit, and the intuitive knowledge through emotion, which transcend and permeate all arts, inasmuch as they tend toward beauty as an end beyond the end. Then poetry, like Plato's *mousikè*, is taken in a primary, most universal sense.

This primary and universal sense can be restricted. Then we have poetry as using and quickening the particular artistic activity which creates a work of words: let us say poetry of verbal expression.

My point is that by virtue of the necessary differentiation

on which I have laid stress, poetry of verbal expression manifests itself in the three specific forms previously mentioned, whose distinction depends on an intrinsic difference in the spiritual structure itself of the work: the poetry of the Poem or the Song, the poetry of the Theater, and the poetry of the Novel—which, I hasten to observe, are not to be confused with the art of writing verses, the dramatic art, and the art of the novel. For just as not every piece of verse is poetry (not to speak of the fact that poems in prose may be) so not every play and not every novel are poetry—far from it. But between the many novels, plays, and poems which have no poetry, and those which have, there is so total a difference that the former are only nonexisting artifacts, fit at best to give the senses an instant of pleasure, and inflate the vanity or the purse of their author.

I would like to designate the poetry of the Poem or the Song as the *poetry of internal music.* I have spoken a great deal of this poetry. When I said that the poetic sense is the soul or the entelechy of the poem, I thought especially of the Poem properly so called, or of the poetry of internal music. It is only in regard to it that this statement is entirely true.

The poetic sense is the first epiphany of creative intuition. In it consists, as we have seen, the prime and basic intentional value in the structure of the poem. Through it the poem receives the intentional influx of the creative source in an immediate manner. The poetic sense is the immediate expression of poetic intuition, its native and purest expression—because still steeped in the intuitive night of subjectivity. It is therefore through the poetic sense that the poem receives its poetic essence and its existence before the mind. All this holds true for the three realms in poetry of verbal expression that we are discussing. But in the poetry of internal music, in the Poem strictly so called, the poetic sense *alone,* the inner melody *alone* (that is, the immediate expression of creative intuition, the meaning whose intentional content is purely a recess of the subjectivity awakened to itself and things—perceived through an obscure, simple, and totally nonconceptual apperception) gives the poem its poetic essence and its existence before the mind. The poetic sense is the inwardly constructive "form" or principle, the entelechy of the poem. The action and the number are essentially needed and necessary properties *in plus,* in which the poetic sense superabounds. The poem *does as it is.*

The poetry of the Theater is the poetry of the action. Then the poetic sense gives the work its poetic essence and its existence before the mind only inchoatively. It cannot achieve that except by virtue of the second epiphany of creative intuition, of that objectivization of poetic intuition in terms of motion—and still nonconceptual, but definitely engaged in the world of things—which is the action. It is through the action that the work receives, purely and simply speaking, its poetic essence and its existence before the mind. The action is, as Aristotle said (and as the authors of medieval mystery plays knew so well), the soul of the drama, its inwardly constructive "form" or principle, its entelechy. Only number or harmonic expansion is an essentially needed and necessary property *in plus,* in which the action superabounds. The drama *is in doing.*

The poetry of the Novel I would like to call the poetry of the picture of man. Then not only the poetic sense, but also the action—however basic, and prior in the order of intentional values—are insufficient to make the work exist, except by virtue of the final epiphany of creative intuition, the number or harmonic expansion that fills the poetic space with parts in mutual tension which are, this time, characters or free agents, human persons. It is through the number or harmonic expansion that the work receives, purely and simply speaking, its poetic essence and its existence before the mind. The number is the soul, the inwardly constructive "form" or principle, the entelechy of the novel. The novel *is (and does) in filling its space.* For obvious reasons the plastic arts—since their work exists only and totally in space—are with regard to the spiritual structure of the work in the same category as the novel,[18] while the dance is, I believe, in the same category as the drama, and music in the same category as the poem.

Great novelists are poets. They are few. In order for a novel to be poetry a particularly powerful creative intuition is required, capable of carrying its influx up to the inner recesses of other human selves living in the work. This is possible only because the creative intuition of a great novelist involves—starting with some primordial emotive awakening of his own self—that poetic knowledge of other subjectivities in and through his own, that knowledge through affective connaturality which makes him penetrate his characters and foresee their actions through the medium of his own inclinations, and which extends and develops all along the development of the characters and the production of the work, in such a way that the novel is made both by the poet and by his creatures.

The novelist is primarily concerned not with the action, but with the agents.[19] This principle, which stresses the essential difference between the novel and the drama, helps us understand certain characteristics of the novel: the *transposition*, the recasting of human nature into the fabric of the work, is less profound in the novel than in the drama; because of this, the "purgation of passions" is a privilege of the drama, especially the tragedy, where we contemplate our passions moving on a superior plane, both detached from ourselves and obeying their own fateful law; at the same time the inflexible necessity peculiar to the action in the drama gives room in the novel to a development in which contingency plays a greater part—the characters do sometimes more what they want than what the author wants. Finally one may say, as Mauriac likes to do, that "the aim of the novel is knowledge of the human heart"—and this has never been said of the drama, which implies such knowledge, no doubt, but does not *aim* at it.[20]

In Balzac or Dostoevski, Emily Brontë or Melville, Proust or Joyce—or in Cervantes, the greatest poet of the imaginary knowledge of man—the novel appears as a fruit of the slow process of revelation of the Self often alluded to in this book. While being a modern heir of the epic, the *chanson de geste*, the medieval romance, and more generally the story or the tale, it has carried the narrative to a point of spiritual interiority which is transcendent with respect to all preceding forms.

The fact remains, however, that the novelist is an artist, and that, therefore, knowledge of the human heart is involved for him in a primary aim which is of the order of the making—the production of a certain work into existence. And that work which is a novel exists only if it "fills its space"; it exists only by virtue of the consistency between the inner development and the evolution of events, and the composition of the reactions of the individual strands to one another. Henry James's theory of the "reflector" was but a particular application of this principle. Important as it may be in the drama, the *multiple plot* with the shifting perspectives it involves and the harmonic spaciousness it creates from clash and continuity, has still greater and more characteristic importance in the novel. When all the interest is concentrated on a single character, as in certain novels of Julian Green or Bernanos, his figure has such relief, and the movement of his internal life such amplitude, that he seems to fill the expanse of the earth. A novel, like the novels of Proust, may have almost no concern with action; it has all the more concern with the orchestral arrangement of the free units, each one a universe unto itself, which are its parts: the inner world of its agents, and the vicissitudes of the psyche, expand into a totality possessed of the intensive plenitude of the number. All this explains and confirms the idea that the soul or entelechy of the novel is the harmonic expansion of all that composes a whole of human agents, passions, events, and destinies.

16. There are, on the part of readers or listeners, three typically different kinds of poetic sensibility—lyrical sensibility, histrionic sensibility, as Francis Fergusson puts it,[21] and introspective sensibility—which correspond to the three specific forms of what has been called above the poetry of verbal expression. I have tried to describe these three spe-

cific forms, as I see them, and the spiritual structure of the poetic work typical of each one of them.

Great as the poetry of the Theater and the poetry of the Novel may be, the poetry of the Poem or the Song is by nature and will always remain the prime and most spiritual type of poetry, and the dearest to the human soul, because it is the closest to creative intuition.

As has been observed in another chapter, in connection with "obscure" or "clear" poems, the poem has always a certain clarity, at least some allusive and diffuse glimmer of logical or intelligible sense, because nothing can be conveyed to the spirit of man save through the intellect, and without some element of intelligible objectivity; and it has always a certain obscurity, at least a shadow of emotive content extending beyond the intelligible sense, because what it essentially conveys is born in the night of intuitive subjectivity, to which its very *raison d'être,* the poetic sense, refers.

Shall we turn now toward Homer, Vergil or Dante, Shakespeare, Racine, Pushkin or Baudelaire, looking for the testimony of the greatest poetry? There, in the fullness of the poetic sense the intelligible sense expands freely, and supreme clarity appears as the privilege of supreme mastery. Creative innocence is so powerful in them that it permeates with intuitive freedom the stoutest materials—things of nature and man perceived in all their rational objectivity, entanglements of instinct and passion, "store of clear and precise knowledge, as well as the most prosaic necessities of the language—and brings them to a state of fusion. Everything burns in those 'ravishers of fire,' and everything takes the form wanted by poetry's sweet will. Here we are confronted with unheard-of discoveries and pure poetry, intuition and understanding. And this poetry persuades us that the mystery of the sun and of a radiant day is no lesser than that of obscure night." [22]

Magic as a Free "In plus"

17. To conclude, I should like to touch upon a question I raised in another book,[23] in connection with music.

In this essay I tried to single out a particular quality present in certain great musical works, absent from others, which had something to do, I thought, with the Plotinian notion of grace, and which, for want of a better word, I designated by the name of "magic"—in a sense altogether different from that in which this word is used in the preceding chapters of the present book.

The point is that this quality seems to suggest a completely free element, a kind of separate "grace" superior to the poetry of the work as engaged or absorbed in the meaning and substance of the work. It is as if the soul of the work, acting on us, as it were, beyond its own capacity, became "an instrument of an alien spirit, a sign through which passes a superior causality, the sacrament of a separate poetry which makes a game of art."

"Fearing," I wrote, "to lay a parricidal hand on the greatest of musicians, dare I say that there is little of magic in Johann Sebastian Bach? Yes, I shall say that this most sublime of music, this mother-music, is a music without magic." This was probably too absolute a statement, neglecting some particular moments in the work of Bach, yet it holds true in the main, I believe. I went on to observe that in Bach (and this is perhaps the secret of his power and his fecundity) poetry is entirely integrated in the making and substance of the work, whose soul is not instrument but queen and goddess always. "That is why the music of Bach prays with a great vocal prayer that is elevated to the contemplation which theology calls 'acquired contemplation'; it does not pass the threshold of mystical or infused orison.

"The danger of magic arises from the fact that it is a gift of an order superior to art. He who has it without having sought it receives something from heaven or from hell— sometimes difficult to bear, and which exacts an art strong enough to obey. He who seeks it inevitably alters his art, fabricates counterfeit money. Wagner lived only for magic; if we except *Tristan,* there is no magic in his music, not even a ghost of black magic—only the frauds and the drugs of a head drunk with science and genius.

"The case of Satie is the reverse. Through the passion for probity, he detests, he excommunicates in himself all possible magic, he ferociously cleanses his work of it. Repressed, magic then disguises itself in the queer taste for mystification that disarms the enterprises of mystery, and that protects the ironic shows of a virgin music.

"There is no magic in Beethoven; and yet who makes himself loved better than he? Different indeed from Wagner, he does not seek for magic; how resist this great heart that gives itself, spirit and soul confounded, and which supplements a certain ungratefulness of the workman's invention by the generosity of his personal substance dispensed without measure?

"There is magic in Schubert, in Chopin, in Moussorgsky. Magic is not always white. The magic of Lourié rises from a sort of catastrophe of being whose tragic or desperate character remains so to speak in suspense, because of the face of God which passes through the walls. His music, when it prays, crosses the threshold of supernatural inwardness. The marvel with him, as with the other princes of magic, is that magic makes stronger and more intense the art through which it passes, which obeys without ever bending. The magic of the chief of princes is an angelic magic: I do not say that with Mozart an innocent angel is alone at work; in this miracle of heroic childhood the cruelty of the child and the angel, a murderous grace traverses at times the transparency and lucidity of infused knowledge, of the infallible skill."

18. May such suggestions be generalized, and extended to the whole field of *mousikè,* to all arts, and especially to the poem? Yes, I think, but to different degrees, the first rank in this connection belonging to music.

Let us try, first, to analyze things more closely in the case of music.

I think that the magic of the works I alluded to is only a free *surplus* of poetry. The "alien spirit" or "separate poetry" of whose presence and action magic gives the impression, is nothing but an inexhaustible intuitive emotion, diffuse in the composer's entire subjectivity, which has not been "caught" in the actuation of the free creativity of the spirit engendering the work through the instrumentality of art, and which, however, passes into music that has a magical quality. How does this occur?

Of every music it is true to say that the song begins where the word stops, as a bursting forth of a spiritual and emotional stir or exultation of the subjectivity—too deeply subjective, too existentially singular, too incommunicably affective to be possibly conveyed by any meaning of words.

Now I would say that in most cases this profound stir of the composer's subjectivity is entirely condensed, embraced, or caught in that deep and sovereign actuation, at the single root of the powers of the soul, which is poetic or creative intuition.

But in some cases the stir is, it seems to me, so imbued with intelligence or passion, so rich in intuitive virtuality or emotive power, that it cannot be entirely caught in this spiritual actuation. There is an *in plus* which remains—separate: the surplus, the inexhaustible intuitive emotion behind, to which I just alluded. This *in plus* passes nevertheless through creative intuition, but not as caught by it; it passes, on the contrary, as a free element, a free "spirit," which *overflows* the creative intuition through which it passes, and immediately moves and permeates, as a grace in addition, the working activity, without the composer's having the least awareness of it. Then there is magic, and we have the impression of an alien spirit, a separate poetry which freely makes a game of art, and gives more than any poetry engaged and absorbed in the making and the substance of the work can give.

This "separate" poetry—which overflows the creative intuition through which it passes, and which is not *caught*, but free—also overflows the making and the substance of the work; it is there, and it acts there, but as an element *in plus,* and free with the pure freedom of the nocturnal depths. And it overflows also the power with which the work attains intuitively the listener. More things that are unknown and unseizable stir in a deeper and more expansive way his energies of emotion, intelligence, and imagination, poetry strikes him in more obscure darkness, he is more completely and defenselessly taken hold of by it. It is because the work is thus endowed with greater power, born in night and operating in night, that the word magic seems appropriate, despite its ambiguity.

Such is the interpretation I submit in regard to the magic in music. If this way of understanding things is correct, we must conclude that the possibility of magic is not reserved only to music (for the process I have outlined can evidently take place in the other realms of poetry). But we must also say that the possibility of magic exists in music to a higher degree than in the other arts: since music, taken in its nature, even before any consideration of magic, has the peculiar privilege, as we have observed, of expressing—beyond any possible meaning of words—the most deeply subjective, singular and affective stirs of creative subjectivity, too deep-seated to be possibly expressed by any other art.

Yet poetry (the "poetry of verbal expression") is close to music in this connection, especially the first of the three types of poetry we have distinguished, the Poem—do we not say, moreover, Song as well? Did I not call the poem poetry of internal music? Though it uses words, there is in the poem, just after music, it seems to me, the greatest possibility of magic, because of the supremacy that the poetic sense enjoys in it over the intelligible sense, and because the soul or entelechy of the poem uniquely consists of the poetic sense, the first epiphany of creative intuition, in its native freedom. As in the case of composers, there are great poets who have little or no magic (say Ronsard[24] or Hugo, Byron or Goethe) and great poets in whom we immediately feel the presence of this free *in plus*. Taking some names at random, we may call as witnesses Racine and Dante, Keats, Coleridge and Pushkin, Baudelaire, Hölderlin and Rimbaud (especially the Rimbaud of *Une Saison en Enfer*), as well as, in an art less close to music. Watteau or Hieronymus Bosch, Rembrandt or El Greco. Dance and architecture, as any other "free" art, might also give evidence of a possibility of magic.

On the other hand—and apart from the natural kinship and attraction between music and poetry—the fact that music is eminently favored with respect to magic explains the singular ascendency that it exercises on those poets who look desperately for magic—for spurious magic,[25] thus betraying poetry, however adored, for the sake of power. Music leads them astray, though the blame is theirs. And they miss both spurious magic (with which poetry has nothing to do), and genuine magic, which shuns them because they seek after it.

Creative intuition is the only supreme gift that a poet, in any art whatsoever, ought to seek—in the way in which a gift can be sought: not in the sense that it might be acquired by any effort of the human will, but in the sense that it can be cared for, and protected, and assisted, when it is there. And it is there, perhaps in a humbler way than he believes, in any man who is inclined toward the workings of art by an inner necessity. Sometimes, and in the greatest artists, creative intuition may be at work in darkness and despairing agony. Then they may think of what Pascal felt about another kind of grace, and this holds true for them also: "Take comfort, thou wouldst not be seeking me, hadst thou not found me."

POETRY, MAN, AND THINGS

[1] Coleridge used the word *poesy* with the same universal meaning: ". . . poesy in general, as the proper generic term inclusive of all the fine arts as its species."

[2] The word *intentio,* in the Aristotelian-Thomist vocabulary, refers to an *esse* which is both immaterial and purely tendential. See infra, p. 87.

[3] I mean we modern Western people.

[4] "There, concrete reality itself is known as unreal and in this knowledge it is painted as it is known. It abides in the mind and is beheld by it." Stella Kramrisch, *A Survey of Painting in the Deccan* (Hyderabad: Archaeological Department, H.E.H. The Nizam's Government, 1937), p. 15.

[5] "There was something formless yet complete that existed before heaven and earth, without sound, without substance, dependent on nothing, unchanging, all-pervading, unfailing. One may think of it as the mother of all things under heaven. Its true name we do not know. Tao is the by-name that we give it." *Tao Tê Ching,* Chapter XXV.

[6] Chinese philosophy was quite aware of that. In the words of Chuang Chou, the Taoist philosopher of the fourth and third centuries B.C., "Without a *that* there would be no I; without an I there would be nothing to take hold of [the *that*]. This is near enough [to the truth], but we do not know what sets this acting." Quoted by E. R. Hughes, *The Art of Letters: Lu Chi's "Wen Fu,"* A.D. *302* (Bollingen Series XXIX; New York: Pantheon Books, 1951), p. 225.

[7] That was one of his answers to the Tribunal of the Holy Office, July 18, 1573. In *Artists on Art,* p. 106.

[8] Jared B. Flagg, *The Life and Letters of Washington Allston* (New York: Scribner, 1892), p. 15.

[9] Conversations with Vittoria Colonna, as recorded by Francisco de Hollanda (*Four Dialogues on Painting*) in Elizabeth Gilmore Holt, *Literary Sources of Art History* (Princeton University Press, 1947), p. 209.

[10] André Malraux, *Museum without Walls* (The Psychology of Art, Vol. I; Bollingen Series XXIV; New York: Pantheon Books, 1949), p. 60.

[11] Nature is a Thing-in-itself for the philosopher, inasmuch as through reason intent on being he attains in nature intelligible objects which transcend sense-experience. But for modern art nature is rather a Thing-in-man, inasmuch as through poetic or creative intuition the artist, as we shall see in Chapter IV, grasps in nature the reality of things as resounding in his own emotion and subjectivity. (And for modern science nature is rather phenomenon, inasmuch as through reason intent only on the observable and measurable the scientist draws from nature systems of symbols that are grounded on reality.)

As an application of views expressed elsewhere (*The Range of Reason*, New York: Scribner, 1952, Chapter IV), it might be suggested that Kant's prime insight in relation to the theoretical field finds its *locus naturalis*—after complete conceptual recasting—not in philosophy but in empiriological science; and that his prime insight in relation to the practical field finds its *locus naturalis*—after complete conceptual recasting —not in ethics but in art, which reaches transapparent reality not through any "postulate of practical reason" but through poetic knowledge.

[12] So as "to treat a flower *as his key*, not his model." James A. McNeill Whistler, from a letter dated at London, May, 1878; in *Artists on Art*, p. 348. (Italics mine.)

[13] The primacy of visual sensation in Cézanne's art gets clear of the rational grammar of painting (see infra, p. 54), especially of classical perspective, but in order to assert more forcefully the power of direct apprehension of corporeal existents, the realist (in the philosophical sense) knowledge-value which is inherent in sensation as such. Cézanne's painting strives obscurely after a reality in things which is deeper, more mysterious, and more significant than things themselves as offered in their logically interpreted appearances. So it is that this painting is intent on "the spectacle that the Pater Omnipotens Aeterne Deus spreads out before our eyes." On the other hand, the real incentive for Cézanne's fervor for sensation was in him the intensity of an emotion and concentration of the entire soul, and the inner pressure of subjectivity bent on grasping and disclosing itself through creative vision. Thus it is that Cézanne's painting conveys such a moving charge of humanity.

Those who, under the pretext that Cézanne's painting is a

painting of *reines Sehen,* fail to recognize these basic things —obvious as far as the sense of poetry is concerned—and who detect in Cézanne "chaotischen Raum" and the "Ausbruch des Aussermenschlichen" (cf. Fritz Novotny, *Cézanne und das Ende der wissenschaftlichen Perspektive,* Vienna, 1938; Hans Sedlmayr, *Verlust der Mitte,* Salzburg: Otto Müller, 1948), are biased doctrinaires who have fallen into a trap that a bit of intuition would have been enough to make them avoid. Mr. Sedlmayr may be right in pointing out the dehumanization of our age of culture (which has of course a repercussion on the weaknesses of our art and on mediocre modern artists). But he is seriously mistaken in seeking proofs and signs of that dehumanization of culture in great modern artists and in the very creativity of modern art (which, being spiritual creativity, transcends the cultural environment). There is no more misleading and unsound literary genus than ideological systematization of human history intent on disregarding the essentials of art, and its intrinsic laws of development, for the sake of a so-called cultural diagnosis and prognosis of art as a moral symptom.

In contrast to the above-mentioned blind judgments on Cézanne, see the excellent article by Theodore Rousseau, Jr., "Cézanne as an Old Master," *Art News,* April, 1952. The author analyzes the remarkable connection between Cézanne's pictures and those of the masters he ceaselessly studied, and he concludes with this quotation from the painter: "Our canvases are the milestones of Man—from the reindeer on the walls of caves to the cliffs of Monet—from the hunters, the fishermen who inhabit the tombs of Egypt, the comical scenes of Pompeii, the frescoes of Pisa and Siena, the mythological compositions of Veronese and Rubens, from all these the same spirit comes down to us. . . . We are all the same man. I shall add another link to the chain of color. My own blue link."

[14] As concerns van Gogh, no Self was more haunted by the reality seized in Things and Beings. To understand this it is enough to look at his pictures. And if we are not capable of such an obvious understanding, let us at least read what he wrote. (See infra, p. 97.) Meyer Schapiro points simply to the truth of the matter when he says: "In all the elements of his art we experience the force of his conviction and his exaltation before things. . . . In Van Gogh the opposites of reality and emotion are united and reconciled. The familiar objects he paints belong both to nature and to loving, desiring, suffering man. His art has helped to educate our eyes and to unloosen our feelings." Meyer Schapiro, *Van Gogh* (New York: The Library of Great Painters, Harry N. Abrams, n.d.).

On Malraux's views see the telling remarks of Huntington

Cairns in "The Artichoke and the Acanthus Leaf," *Virginia Quarterly Review,* summer, 1950.

ART AS A VIRTUE OF THE PRACTICAL INTELLECT

[1] Cf. G. H. Luquet, *L'Art et la Religion des Hommes fossiles* (Paris: Masson, 1926). The author insists in an illuminating manner on the genuinely aesthetic and poetic sense which permeated the art of the primitive man. But his vocabulary is sometimes confused, and he leaves blurred, in my opinion, the fact that this art, while being instinctively interested in beauty, was always and primarily, at the same time, subservient to the needs of human life. (I do not say limited to utilitarian aims in the too strict sense of this word in our civilized language. The truth of the matter is, I think, that the art of the primitive man was undifferentiated—more disinterested than our useful arts, and more subservient to human needs than our fine arts. We may safely assume, moreover, that this destination of satisfying the needs of human life was prevalent in the *consciousness* of the primitive artist.)

[2] As a rule the thing to be made, or the work to be done, refers to the realm of knowledge for the sake of action, not of knowledge for the sake of knowledge. That is why it is said in a general way that art belongs to the sphere of the practical intellect. Yet there are certain categories of works and, consequently, certain categories of arts which do not belong to this sphere, but to the speculative one; there are speculative arts, such as Logic is for instance. (Cf. *Sum. theol.* II-II, 47, 2, ad 3.) Such arts perfect the speculative Intellect, not the practical Intellect: but the kind of knowledge involved is still akin to the practical in its *mode,* and it constitutes an *art* only because it implies the *making of a work*—this time a work wholly within the mind, and whose sole object is the achievement of knowledge, a work which consists for instance in shaping an idea or a definition, in setting our concepts in order, in framing a proposition or a reasoning. The fact remains, therefore, that wherever we find *art* we find some productive operation to be contrived, some work to be made. Cf. *Art and Scholasticism* (New York: Scribner, 1930), Chapter II.

Given the abstractive and discursive nature of man's intellect, the part of the making, the manufacture of the tools of science, is (unfortunately) essential and necessary, and immense, in the immanent operations of knowledge and the inner life of the mind. But when all this is not vivified by intuition and actual knowledge, we are tempted to see in it, as Faust did, only "Skeletons of animals and bones of the dead."

³ "State of possession" renders *habitus* (ἕξις) better, it seems to me, than the expression "state of capacity" used by W. D. Ross in his translation.

⁴ Cf. *Art and Scholasticism*, p. 20.—In the Scholastic vocabulary "art" is synonymous with "practical science," in the sense that it is a kind of science which is practical in its very essence or its very way of knowing, and practical from the very start—science of the work to be made.

Practical science in this genuine sense is entirely different from applied science, that is, from a science which is theoretical in essence—and then particularized or applied (by art or practical science) in order to achieve a practical result.

A greater or less amount of theoretical science (the science of anatomy, for instance) is indeed involved in art (in medicine for instance) as *presupposed* by it, and *applied* by it. But it would be a fundamental error to mistake practical science for applied theoretical science: Medicine is not applied science of anatomy, it applies in its own way and in its own light the science of anatomy.

Sayings like "L'art c'est la science faite chair" (Jean Cocteau, "Le Secret professionel," in *Le Rappel à l'Ordre*, Paris: Stock, 1930) or "L'art ce n'est que la science humanisée" (Gino Severini, *Du Cubisme au Classicisme*, Paris: Povolozky, 1921) are therefore inaccurate if they relate to theoretical science as embodied in the work. Mathematics may be considered a basic *pre-required* discipline for the painter, yet painting is not humanized mathematics. Painting applies mathematics—it is not applied mathematics.

But such sayings take on fully true meaning if they relate to that knowledge which is implied in the very essense of fine arts, namely to poetic knowledge (See Chapter IV, §§ 6 and 7, and Chapter V, § 9). We must thus admit, if we get rid of our "scientist" modern prejudices, the existence of a poetic science which differs *toto coelo* from theoretical sciences, and which is however a real knowledge, attained through creative intuition. Its object is neither the essential structure of the object known nor the laws of phenomena; it is real nevertheless—the existential aspects and relations of things grasped through emotion and connaturality. Thus the painter has a real knowledge or "science" of "Nature," or the world of visible matter—a knowledge or "science" which has nothing to do either with mathematics or with physics, the theoretical science of nature (though the art of painting, in its ways and means of execution, has to apply certain mathematical and certain physical, especially optical, laws).

⁵ Be it noted, furthermore, that the truth of the creative judgment does not consist in judging of the work in conformity

with the rules (theoretically known); it consists in judging of the work in conformity with the appetite straightly tending to the production of this work through the appropriate rules. So art—*recta ratio factibilium*—is a virtue of working reason. But an element of knowledge through connaturality, a certain "instinct" developed in reason, is already involved in the basic notion of the truth of the artistic judgment, since this truth is conformity *with the appetite* intent on the use of the appropriate rules.

[6] *Cursus theol.*, t. IV, disp. 12, a. 6, § 21.

[7] The phrase "engendering in beauty" is Platonic in origin. Cf. *Symposium,* 206.

[8] *On the Limits of Poetry* (New York: The Swallow Press and William Morrow, 1948), pp. 9, 15.

[9] George Rowley, *Principles of Chinese Painting,* p. 80.

[10] Even, as we shall see further, the stock phrases "useful arts" and "fine arts," which I am using now to conform to the accepted vocabulary, are not, in my opinion, philosophically well grounded. I would prefer to say "subservient arts" and "free" or "self-sufficient arts." (See Chapter V, pp. 133-34.)

[11] "The Freedom of Song," in my *Art and Poetry* (New York: Philosophical Library, 1943), p. 72.

[12] Quoted by Etienne Charles in *Renaissance de l'Art français,* April, 1918.—Cf. *Artists on Art,* p. 308.

[13] "L'Œuvre et la vie d'Eugène Delacroix," in *L'Art romantique* (Paris: Calmann-Lévy, 1885), p. 13.

[14] *Lectures and Notes on Shakespeare and Other Dramatists* (New York: Harper, 1853), p. 54.

[15] "Richard Wagner et Tannhauser," in op. cit., p. 229.

THE PRECONSCIOUS LIFE OF THE INTELLECT

[1] One of these secrets, for instance, is irregularity. "If one examines the most famous plastic or architectural productions from this point of view, one quickly perceives that the great artists who created them, careful to work in the fashion of that nature whose respectful pupils they did not cease to be, took good care not to violate her fundamental law of irregularity. One realizes that even works based on geometric principles, such as St. Marco, the little house of Francis I in the Cours la Reine, as well as the so-called Gothic churches, contain no perfectly straight line, and the round, square, and oval forms that one finds, which it would have been easy to make exact, never exact. . . ." Renoir, project of a manifesto (1884); in *Artists on Art* (New York: Pantheon Books, 1945), p. 321.

"Ars imitatur naturam in sua operatione," St. Thomas said (*Sum. theol.*, I, 117, 1).

As regards the "fundamental law of irregularity," Renoir's observations on the workings of nature may be complemented by Baudelaire's remarks on beauty: "Ce qui n'est pas légèrement difforme a l'air insensible; d'où il suit que l'irrégularité, c'est-à-dire l'inattendu, la surprise, l'étonnement sont une partie essentielle et la caractéristique de la beauté." *Fusées,* XII; in *Journaux intimes,* ed. van Bever (Paris: Crès, 1919).

[2] Raïssa Maritain, "Sens et Non-sens en poésie," in *Situation de la Poésie* (Paris: Desclée De Brouwer, 1938), p. 14. [English transl.: *The Situation of Poetry,* (New York: Philosophical Library, 1955.)]

[3] *Paradise Lost,* Book V, 486-88.

[4] On Rouault, see my essay (written in 1924) in *Art and Poetry* (New York: Philosophical Library, 1943).

On Chagall, Raïssa Maritain writes: "[In his etchings inspired by the Bible] one sees that a genuine primitive demands little of nature (though he loves her with an ever young tenderness, and a mystical love) and much of himself; little of realism and much of transposition, or of what we call today abstraction, which is nothing but the upsurge of new forms mysteriously akin to natural forms, and rich with the spirit of the artist of whom they are born. And doubtless this is but one with the exigencies of art, if Baudelaire was right in saying that 'the first business of an artist is to substitute man for nature, and to protest against her,' but it is true above all of the great primitives who, under the thrust of their interior world, abstract from the natural universe, spontaneously, universal forms endowed with inexhaustible significance. . . . I asked him what had struck him in Impressionist, 'Fauves,' Cubist painters, when he first came into contact with their works in Paris—'Their realism,' he immediately answered with sorrow. . . . He does not avoid natural forms; he does not fly from them, on the contrary he makes them his own through the love he bears them, but by the same token he transforms and transfigures them, brings out and draws from them their own surreality, finding there the symbols of joy and life in their purified essence, their spiritual soul. . . . Surrealism came close to being called *surnaturalism,* in the person of its first representative. But the angels of the Sacred Vocabulary did not permit it. . . . Chagall's surrealism has both a spiritual and a plastic character. With no preconceived idea, through his art's magic, through the liberation of his internal world, Chagall has created forms signifying a spiritual universe entirely his own, whose traits cannot be found to such a degree in any other painter of our time. It was said of Rouault that he is the painter of original sin. But the universe created by Chagall is in ignorance of sin, hatred, and discord; he utters grace and joy, fraternity and love. The suffering of the world is also present, under the signs of a grave and melancholy contemplation; but the symbols of consolation are always near at hand. . . . A painting by Chagall is a tranquil, poised countenance; it is a presence which imposes itself even upon those who are deaf to poetry's voice. But to those who hear are told, not voluntarily, but through the very power of this art, a thousand dreams and mysteries which are, so to speak, the secret network of the arterial tree of the work: they secure life and they express life, the ineradicable images of childhood, the wishes of the heart, the joy of the eyes." *Chagall ou l'Orage enchanté* (Geneva-Paris: Editions des Trois Collines, 1948), pp. 126-127, 46-49, 94, 98, 83.

[5] Cf. Raïssa Maritain, "Sens et Non-sens en poésie," p. 27 (new ed., 1947, p. 28).

[6] That is why, in the nature of things, that absolute which is poetry (in the line of the free creativity of the intellect) tends of itself to make man more thirsty for *the* Absolute—the first Poet, the creator of being.

[7] "Surrealism" is, in itself, a quite apt word. But the great contemporary painter who best deserves the name, Chagall (as, among the old masters, Hieronymus Bosch), belongs in no way to the Surrealist school. See supra, p. 303 last part of note 4.

[8] "Absalom and Achitophel," Part I, 163. The interpretation of this line offered by Poe—"By 'great wit,' in this case, the poet intends precisely the pseudo-genius to which I refer" and which is "but the manifestation of the abnormal predominance of some one faculty over all the others" (*Fifty Suggestions*, XXIII; in *Complete Works*, New York: The Lamb Publishing Co., 1902, Vol. IX)—is more than questionable.

What Poe has in mind here is that requirement of unity and integrity in the poet which we shall stress in the next chapter. He also lays claim (thinking of himself, probably) to the possibility of "universal or even versatile geniuses," and to the right of the poet to pursue scientific studies; and he insists "that the highest genius—that the genius which all men instantaneously acknowledge as such, which acts upon individuals as well as upon the mass, by a species of magnetism incomprehensible but irresistible and never resisted,—that this genius which demonstrates itself in the simplest gesture, or even by the absence of all; this genius which speaks without a voice and flashes from the unopened eye, is but the result of generally large mental power existing in a state of absolute proportion, so that no one faculty has undue predominance."

In all this one can but agree with him. And who would not

approve of his impatience with the popular notion of the poet
as an abnormal scatterbrain, and of "genius" as "the state of
mental disease arising from the undue predominance of some
one of the faculties"? "The works of such genius are never
sound in themselves, and, in especial, always betray the general
mental insanity."

But Poe misses the real point, which has to do with that
element of "madness from above" which comes from the free
and intuitive creativity of the intellect and imagination start
ing in the spiritual unconscious, above logical reason, and has
nothing to do, except accidentally, with psychological un-
balance or "mental disease." Poe's and Baudelaire's desperate
pretension to make logical and calculating reason the supreme
creative power in poetry was but a process of defense to mask
and counterbalance the inner splits they suffered, and to protect in themselves that supremacy of the intellect for which
these superior minds had an invaluable feeling, but which they
mistook for the supremacy of logical reason—whereas it is that
of intuitive reason and creative intuition. By this fact they
risked misleading or confusing us in our notion of poetry.
There would be no more detrimental situation for modern
poetry than to be caught between madness from below—a
simple release of the automatic unconscious—and rationalistic
self-consciousness as a process of compensation. These points,
which I only mention here in passing, are elucidated in the
central chapters of this book, Chapters IV and VII.

[9] Novalis, *Schriften*, ed. Kluckhohn (Leipzig: Bibliographisches
Institut, n.d.), Vol. III, p. 349.

[10] *Ion*, 534, 536.

[11] Ibid., 534.

[12] *Phaedrus*, 245.—I think that in this passage ἄβατον (literally
"untrodden") is better rendered by "untamable" than by "virgin" as is usually done.

[13] Is not the purpose of the *Republic* to offer a picture of the
ideal requirements of reason—carried to the absolute— in matters of government? I cannot help thinking that, given such a
purpose, Plato delivered himself over to an intoxication of
pure logic all the more readily as, at the same time, knowing
that his picture was merely ideal, he indulged in laughing at
assertions made purposely extreme which he most seriously
proffered and actually held to be true on the level of that pure
logic. Hence a kind of transcendent irony. Thus it is, I think,
that in the third Book (389) he reproaches the poets for in-
fringing upon that privilege of lying which belongs only to
the rulers of the city. I would like to surmise that the same
kind of irony may be found in the *Laws*.

[14] *Symposium* (Discourse of Diotima), 205.

[15] The illuminating pages which Bergson wrote on the "deep-rooted mental healthiness" that is characteristic of great mystics, and the nervous disturbances which may nevertheless develop sometimes in them, but which are merely accidental with regard to mysticism, apply also, *mutatis mutandis,* to poets and poetry. "The truth is that these abnormal states resembling morbid states, and sometimes doubtless very much akin to them, are easily comprehensible, if we only stop to think what a shock to the soul is the passing from the static to the dynamic, from the closed to the open, from everyday life to mystic life. . . ."

The obscure depths of the soul are stirred in the poet. "We cannot upset the regular relation of the conscious to the unconscious without running a risk. So we must not be surprised if nervous disturbances and mysticism sometimes go together; we find the same disturbances in other forms of genius, notably in musicians. They have to be regarded as merely accidental. The former have no more to do with mystical inspiration than the latter with musical." Henri Bergson, *The Two Sources of Religion and Morality* (New York: Holt, 1935) , pp. 217-18. pp. 217-18.

[16] Cf. Ben Jonson, *Discoveries* (1641)—"how differs a poeme from what wee call poesy?"

[17] Cicero, *De Oratore,* II, 46.

[18] *A Midsummer Night's Dream,* V, i.

[19] This distinction between spiritual unconscious and automatic unconscious is altogether different from Jung's distinction between the *personal* and the *collective* unconscious—both of which are part of the spiritual unconscious inasmuch as they enter the sphere of the preconscious life of the intellect or the will, and are thus spiritualized, and both of which are part of the automatic unconscious inasmuch as they are shut up in a merely animal world, separate from the life of the intellect and the will.

Be it noted that, as will be pointed out infra (Chapter IV), all the sensitive powers of the soul (which are not "spiritual" in nature) and especially the imagination are involved in the spiritual unconscious, in so far as they participate in the preconscious life of the intellect or the will. The spiritual unconscious pertains primarily to the spiritual powers of the soul, but extends to the other.

[20] Recent studies in natural mysticism have opened a new and particularly fertile field of philosophical research. See in this connection: Olivier Lacombe, "Sur le Yoga indien," *Etudes Carmélitaines,* October, 1937; idem, "Un Exemple de mystique naturelle: l'Inde," *Etudes Carmélitaines,* October, 1938; Jacques Maritain, "L'Expérience mystique naturelle et le Vide," Ch. III

of *Quatre Essais sur l'Esprit dans sa Condition charnelle* (Paris: Desclée De Brouwer, 1939); Louis Gardet, "Recherches sur la mystique naturelle," in *Jacques Maritain, son œuvre philosophique* (a symposium; Paris: Desclée De Brouwer, 1948); idem, "Mystique naturelle et mystique surnaturelle en Islam," *Recherches de Science religieuse*, XXXVII (1950): 2; Lacombe, "La Mystique naturelle dans l'Inde," *Revue Thomiste*, 1951, 1; Gardet, "La Mystique avicennienne," Ch. V of *La Pensée religieuse d'Avicenne* (Paris: Vrin, 1951); idem, "Un problème de mystique comparée: la mention du Nom divin dans la mystique musulmane," *Revue Thomiste*, 1952, 3.—Olivier Lacombe and Louis Gardet are preparing a general survey of the subject, under the title *Mystique naturelle, l'Expérience du Soi*.

[21] The case of scientific discoveries, new ideas, or solutions that suddenly emerge from the unconscious (as was experienced by Poincaré and Gauss for instance) is well-known and particularly striking. Let us quote here the significant testimony of Marston Morse: "The first essential bond between mathematics and the arts," he writes, "is found in the fact that discovery in mathematics is not a matter of logic. It is rather the result of mysterious powers which no one understands, and in which the unconscious recognition of beauty must play an important part. Out of an infinity of designs a mathematician chooses one pattern for beauty's sake, and pulls it down to earth, no one knows how. Afterwards the logic of words and of forms sets the pattern right. Only then can one tell someone else. The first pattern remains in the shadows of the mind." Marston Morse, "Mathematics and the Arts," *The Yale Review*, summer, 1951, pp. 607-608.—And again: "Mathematics is the sister, as well as the servant of the arts and is touched with the same madness and genius." Ibid., 605. "The creative scientist lives in the 'wildness of logic' where reason is the handmaiden and not the master. I shun all monuments which are coldly legible. I prefer the world where the images turn their faces in every direction, like the masques of Picasso. It is the hour before the break of day when science turns in the womb, and, waiting, I am sorry that there is between us no sign and no language except by mirrors of necessity. I am grateful for the poets who suspect the twilight zone." Ibid., p. 612.

[22] It is not surprising that Freudian "explanations"—which deal only with the automatic unconscious, whose part in art and poetry, significant as it may sometimes be, is accidental, and which ignore completely what is essential, the spiritual unconscious—prove to be particularly unfortunate in this domain (as well as in the religious domain): a failure which has been disclosed by Jung in relation to art, by Malinowski in relation to the origin of morals and the theory of primitive patricide

which, as Roland Dalbiez says (*La Méthode psychanalytique et la Doctrine freudienne,* Paris: Desclée De Brouwer, 1936; English trans.: *Psychoanalytical Method and the Doctrine of Freud,* New York: Longmans, 1943), belongs to the realm of romantic anthropology.

Raymond S. Stites has clearly stressed this basic inadequacy of psychoanalytical theories of art in sifting Freud's own pseudo-scientific fancies about Leonardo ("A Criticism of Freud's Leonardo," in *College Art Journal,* summer, 1948). In the important studies he has pursued for years on Leonardo, and which will appear soon in a book to be entitled *The Psychology of Leonardo da Vinci,* Mr. Stites has been especially concerned with the role of the unconscious (the prescience, as Leonardo put it) in artistic activity. Such erudite researches provide philosophy with a remarkable confirmation of the fundamental distinction between the automatic unconscious and the spiritual unconscious.

²³ Gotthilf Heinrich von Schubert, *Geschichte der Seele.*

²⁴ The image of the sun, in Thomas Aquinas' vocabulary, was reserved for the Uncreate Intellect. Yet we can use it with respect to the *intellectus agens* without prejudice to the fact that its light derives from the supreme Sun, the Uncreate Intellect.

On the universally activating part played by the Illuminating Intellect in human intelligence, see my book *Les Degrés du Savoir* (Paris: Desclée De Brouwer, 1932), p. 244, note 1. For Thomas Aquinas the role of the Illuminating Intellect is in no way limited to the process of abstraction and formation of ideas; the Illuminating Intellect is rather the *activator* of intelligence in all its operations. We have a clear sign in this in St. Thomas' teaching (*q. disp. de Anima,* a. 15, ad 9; *Sum. contra Gent.,* III, 45) that the intellect agent will continue to activate and illumine the intellect in *souls separated from the body* (in which there is no longer any process of abstraction).

CREATIVE INTUITION AND POETIC KNOWLEDGE

¹ Edgar Allan Poe defined art as "the reproduction of what the senses perceive in nature through the veil of the soul." *Marginalia,* LXXXVI; in *Complete Works* (New York: The Lamb Publishing Co., 1902), Vol. IX.

² We may observe at this point, in regard to Coleridge's celebrated distinction between imagination and fancy, that what Coleridge called fancy relates to the "externals of imagination" (the second circle in our diagram) inasmuch as the streams and

associations of images are released from the actual service of sense perception and man's practical life ("Equally with the ordinary memory the Fancy must receive all its materials ready-made from the law of association."—*Biographia Literaria*, Ch. XIII).

What he called imagination relates to the imagination and the intuitive intellect *together*, as vitally united in the preconscious life of the spirit.

In forging—or rather borrowing from Schelling, as Huntington Cairns observes (*Invitation to Learning*, New York: Random House, 1941, p. 244)—the expression *esemplastic Imagination* (εἰς ἕν πλάττειν, "to shape into one"), Coleridge had in view the implied tendency toward creation, and the unifying power involved.

[3] "This thing which is in me *but* which no efforts of mine can slay!

"Wherefore time and again I stroke my empty bosom in pity for myself: so ignorant am I of what causes the opening and the barring of the door."

Lu Chi, *Wen Fu*, II, (o), 6-7, in *The Art of Letters: Lu Chi's "Wen Fu,"* A.D. 302, trans. and ed. E. R. Hughes (Bollingen Series XXIX; New York: Pantheon Books, 1951), p. 108.

[4] *Sum. theol.*, I, 1, 6, ad 3.

[5] See supra, pp. 6-7 and 8.—As I put it in *Art and Scholasticism* (New York: Scribner, 1930): "I will willingly suffer the domination of the *object* which the artist has conceived and which he puts before my eyes; I will then yield myself unreservedly to the emotion roused in him and me by one same beauty, one same transcendental in which we communicate. But I refuse to suffer the domination of an art which deliberately contrives means of suggestion to seduce my subconscious. I resist an emotion which the will of a man claims to impose upon me." (p. 66).

See also E. I. Watkin, *A Philosophy of Form* (rev. ed.; London and New York: Sheed and Ward, 1951), Chapter II, section IV.—In his remarkable analysis of aesthetic contemplation, Mr. Watkin rightly points out both the intellectuality and objectivity of artistic intuition, and its essential difference from the emotion or vital pleasure which normally accompanies it. These pages afford us the most correct philosophical approach I have read on the matter—except for the lack of the key notion of intentional emotion, as contradistinguished to ordinary or "vital" emotion.

[6] On the notion of intentionality, which is absolutely basic in the theory of knowledge, see my books *Réflexions sur l'Intelligence* (Paris: Desclée De Brouwer, 1924), pp. 59-68, and *Les Degrés du Savoir* (Paris: Desclée De Brouwer, 1932), pp. 221-24.

[7] The distinction made in this paragraph is basically important, and it is relevant to discuss in this connection certain views expressed by T. S. Eliot in *The Sacred Wood* (London: Methuen. 1920). Eliot, in his essays on "The Perfect Critic" and on "Tradition and the Individual Talent," points to valuable truths but at the price of serious equivocation, because he overlooks this distinction. He makes his point with regard to brute or merely subjective emotion (emotion as a simple psychological state), but glosses over what matters most: intentional or creative emotion (emotion as the proper medium of poetic knowledge).

It is quite true that, as he puts it in "The Perfect Critic," one who reads poets should not mistake for the poetry "an emotional state aroused in himself by the poetry, a state which may be merely an indulgence of his own emotions." (This deals with brute or merely subjective emotion.) It is quite true that "the end of the enjoyment of poetry is a pure contemplation from which all the accidents of personal emotion are removed"— that is, all the accidents of brute or merely subjective emotion. But this pure contemplation itself is steeped in the *creative emotion* or poetic intuition conveyed by the poem.

The emotions and feelings of which Eliot speaks in "Tradition and the Individual Talent" are, too, only brute or merely subjective emotions and feelings. Such affective states are indeed merely matter or material, as I have said, which poetry must "digest" and "transmute." "It is not the 'greatness,' the intensity, of the emotions, the components, but the intensity of the artistic process, the pressure, so to speak, under which the fusion takes place, that counts." That is perfectly right, but it is through the creative or intentional emotion that the fusion takes place. The pressure of the artistic process would be of no avail to poetry if it did not proceed from poetic intuition or creative emotion. "It is not in his personal emotions, the emotions provoked by particular events in his life, that the poet is in any way remarkable or interesting. His particular emotions may be simple, or crude, or flat. The emotion in his poetry will be a very complex thing, but not with the complexity of the emotions of people who have very complex or unusual emotions in life. One error, in fact, of eccentricity in poetry is to seek for new human emotions to express: and in this search for novelty in the wrong places it discovers the perverse. The business of the poet is not to find new emotions, but to use the ordinary ones and, in working them up into poetry, to express feelings which are not in actual fact emotions at all." All this deals with emotion as material, with brute or merely subjective emotion. It would mislead us if we forgot the essential, necessary part played by that emotion which *causes to express*, emotion as formative, emotion as intentional vehicle of reality known through inclination and as proper medium of poetic intuition. This creative emotion, moreover, distinct as it is from the merely subjective emotions or feelings of the poet as a man, lives on them, so that, while being bound to transmute them, he cannot "escape from them" as simply as Eliot seems to suggest. It would be misunderstanding Eliot in a most unfortunate manner to believe that self-restraint is enough for this, and finally to mistake poetic discipline for artistic skill *plus* desiccation of the heart. The escape of which he speaks cannot come about except through poetic knowledge and creative emotion, and in the very act of creating. And this is what he means.

"Poetry is not a turning loose of emotion, but an escape from emotion." An escape from brute or merely subjective emotion, yes! But, as I just said, through and in creative emotion!

One single sentence in this essay touches the core of the matter. "Very few," Eliot writes, "know when there is expression of *significant* emotion, emotion which has its life in the poem and not in the history of the poet." At last! At last we are told of the *significant* emotion, the intentional and creative emotion, without which there is no poetry. It deserved better than to be only alluded to in passing.

It seems also relevant to add at this point a few remarks about the indictment of Western art that Lionel de Fonseka offers us in the name of Eastern wisdom. The author has the merit of frankness in stating the issue in extreme terms. But he irremediably mistakes intentional emotion for brute emotion and the creative Self for the self-centered ego. In binding, moreover, art to utility, and making the artist an artisan at the service of human life, he simply disregards both the transcendental nature of beauty and the spiritual value of poetic knowledge and creative emotion.

"An obscene work to us [Orientals]," he writes, "is one wherein the artist lays bare his soul, and many of your modern artists we should consider spiritual prostitutes." *On the Truth of Decorative Art, A Dialogue between an Oriental and an Occidental* (London: Greening and Co., 1912), p. 56. This sentence typifies the philosophy of those *enemies of poetry* who hold forth on art without recognizing its deepest life-force, and who ignore the law of generosity proper to the spirit. For them, in the last analysis, any gift of oneself is prostitution. It is but natural that they regard as prostitution (which means no real gift but only making oneself into an instrument of pleasure) the gift of himself through which the artist discloses in his work his soul and the world, so as to become a free *creator* (through the work) of joy and delectation—of the spiritual delectation by which men are liberated from their material ego and raised to experiential knowledge and love of what is better than human life.

When Baudelaire spoke in his own way of art as prostitution (*Fusées*, I; in *Journaux intimes*, ed. van Bever, Paris: Crès, 1919, p. 4), he made just the reverse error, in the opposite direction, and used a perverse image to humiliate what he revered and to express the supreme law of the laying bare and giving of oneself which commands poetic creation.

[8] In the case of mystical contemplation, love of charity (which is much more than an emotion) becomes a means of experiential knowledge for the virtue of faith which already tends toward and knows (though not experientially) the reality with which to be united. And a special inspiration of the divine Spirit is necessary, because a supernatural object is then to be experienced in a supernatural manner.

In the case of poetic knowledge, on the contrary, no previous virtue of the intellect is already in the act of knowing when emotion brings the enigmatic reality which moves the soul, the world which resounds in it and which it suffers, to the bosom of subjectivity and of the creativity of the spirit. And the entire process needs no inspiration whatever from the outside—no more than the knowledge a mother has of her child through affection or connaturality—because the object as well as the mode of experience are simply natural.

[9] Thus it is through the notion and reality of poetic knowledge that the sentence of Novalis quoted in the preceding chapter (p. 61) takes on philosophical sense, and appears not as a pure élan of lyricism, but as a justifiable statement: "The poet is literally out of his senses—in exchange, all comes about *within him*. He is, to the letter, subject and object at the same time, soul and universe."

Rimbaud's saying "Je est un autre" is found in his letter of May 15, 1871, to Paul Demeny ("Lettre du Voyant"), first published by Paterne Berrichon in *La Nouvelle Revue Française*, October, 1912.

[10] Paul Eluard, *L'Amour la Poésie* (Paris: N.R.F., 1929).

[11] Apollinaire, "Zone," *Alcools*.

[12] Verlaine, in "L'espoir luit," *Sagesse*.

[13] Crane, in "Atlantis," *The Bridge*.

[14] Yeats, in "Two Songs from a Play," *The Tower*.

[15] Let us not be deceived by the language of painters. What they sometimes call the "original idea" is but the sketch itself in which poetic intuition first takes visible form. "The original idea, the sketch, which is so to speak the egg or embryo of the idea, is usually far from being complete. . . ." Delacroix, *Journal*, 1854, in *Artists on Art*, p. 234.

[16] "The Freedom of Song" in *Art and Poetry*, pp. 90-91.

[17] In his book *The Perfect Conductor* (New York: Pellegrini and Cudahy, 1951, pp. 101-102), Frederick Goldbeck stresses the direct line which relates the "unprecedented" symphonic works of Lourié to Monteverde—"a sort of al fresco polyphony of unrelated colors, as are piano, choir, brass, and double bass in his admirable *Concerto spirituale.*"

[28] I am afraid that T. S. Eliot, in his essay on "Tradition and the Individual Talent" (*The Sacred Wood*, pp. 47-53), missed the distinction between creative Self and self-centered ego, just as that between creative emotion and brute or merely subjective emotion (see p. 310, note 7). That is probably why, rightly stressing that poetry is not "expression of personality" in the sense of *individuality* or *self-centered ego*, but disregarding the fact that the poet is not only an individual, a material ego, but also (and, as a poet, much more essentially) a person, a creative Self, he uses the word "personality" where *individuality* is concerned, and conceives the poet as a mere "catalyst" and "only a medium, not a personality."

"The more perfect the artist, the more completely separate in him will be the man who suffers and the mind which creates." In reality the man who suffers *is in* the mind which creates—as creative subjectivity and to be given in the work—separated from the self-centered ego by the operation of poetic knowledge and creative emotion. In this sense only it is true that "the emotion of art is impersonal"—that is to say detached from the self-centered ego and one with poetic intuition, the most personal act of the creative Self.

"The progress of an artist is a continual self-sacrifice, a continual extinction of personality"—that is to say of individuality, of the self-centered ego with its natural claims and its deep natural, too natural entanglement with the activity of art. But at the same time the progress of an artist is an ever more significant assertion of personality, that is to say of the creative subjectivity—revealed in the work together with things.

In *Man and Superman,* Bernard Shaw condemned Shakespeare on the ground that his philosophy was "only his wounded humanity." Well, I do not complain of being taught by the *wounded humanity of a Shakespeare* about man and human existence, and many things which matter to me in the reality of this world.

TEXTS WITHOUT COMMENT

[1] *Grandes Odes* (*Œuvres complètes*, Paris: Gallimard, 1950, Vol I).
[2] English translation by Roy Campbell in *Poems of St. John of the Cross* (New York: Pantheon Books Inc. 1951).

[8] In *Poems* (New York: Oxford University Press, 1948).

[4] In *Les Amis Inconnus* (Paris: Gallimard, 1934).

[5] In *Complete Poems* (Boston: Little, Brown, 1924).

[6] In *Ferraille* (Brussels: Journal des Poètes, 1937); reprinted in *Main d'Œuvre* (Paris: Mercure de France, 1949).

[7] In *Lettre de Nuit* (Paris: Desclée De Brouwer, 1939).

[8] Cf. *Artists on Art* (New York: Pantheon Books, Inc.), p. 384.

[9] In *Les Amis Inconnus.*

[10] *Derniers Poèmes* (Paris: Gallimard, 1945).

[11] In *Poems* (New York: Scribner, 1907).

[12] In *Lettre de Nuit.*

[13] *Selected Poems* (New York: Knopf, 1945).

[14] In "Banalité"; *Sous la Lampe* (Paris: N. R. F., 1929).

POETRY AND BEAUTY

[1] Beauty, Dostoevski said, is the battlefield where God and the Devil contend with one another for the heart of man (*The Brothers Karamazov*).

[2] The definition offered by Coleridge seems to me to be less comprehensive; it fails to point out the element of radiance or clarity (*splendor formae*). "The sense of beauty subsists in simultaneous intuition of the relation of parts, each to each, and of all to a whole: exciting an immediate and absolute complacency, without intervention, therefore, of any interest, sensual or intellectual." Coleridge, *Selected Poetry and Prose*, ed. Stephen Potter (New York: Random House, 1933), p. 313.

[3] *Opusc. de pulchro et bono*, ascribed either to Albertus Magnus or to Thomas Aquinas.

[4] Contrary to Plato (as may be inferred from *Theaetetus*, 185-186, —cf. John Wild, *Plato's Theory of Man* (Cambridge: Harvard University Press, 1946), p. 260,—and from the *Symposium*, 211) Aristotle omits the beautiful in his enumeration of transcendentals. So did, following him, the traditional lists used in medieval schools. But there is no doubt either of the fact that beauty is in reality part of the transcendentals, or of the thought of Thomas Aquinas in this regard. Cf. *Art and Scholasticism* (New York: Scribner, 1930), note 63 b (French ed., Paris: Rouart, 1935, note 66).

[5] St. Thomas, Commentary on the Pseudo-Dionysius' *De divinis Nominibus*, cap. 4, lect. 5.

[6] Evil, it is true,—the wound of nothingness by which the freedom of a creature deforms a voluntary act—is ugly in the eyes of God. But no being is ugly, as Angelus Silesius (Johann Scheffler) repeatedly points out in his distichs:

Mensch nichts ist unvollkommn: der Kiess gleicht dem Rubin:
Der Frosch ist ja so schön alss Engel Seraphin.

Gott giebet so genau auf dass koaxen acht,
Als auf dass direlirn, dass ihm die Lerche macht.

Angelus Silesius, *Cherubinischer Wandersmann,* Book V,
no. 61, and Book I, no. 269 (Leipzig: Dieterich'sche Ver-
lagsbuchhandlung).

[7] Preface to *Nouvelles Histoires extraordinaires.* Baudelaire re-
produced this passage in "Théophile Gautier," *L'Art romantique* (Paris: Calmann-Lévy, 1885), p. 167. Cf. Poe's remarks
about the indefinitiveness inherent in true poetry, apropos of
Tennyson: "I am not sure that Tennyson is not the greatest of
poets. . . ." *Marginalia,* CCXV; in *Complete Works* (New York:
The Lamb Publishing Co., 1902), Vol. IX.

[8] Remark of Jean Cocteau.

[9] Our intellect produces its concepts by reason of both indigence
and abundance. On the one hand it needs to create all this apparatus of abstract ideas and logical tools, parceling out the
infinitely varied aspects of the intelligibility of things, because
it draws its objects from the senses, and must therefore spiritual-
ize them within itself in the concepts it forms. On the other
hand it manifests in and through the same concepts the knowledge and vision which are its inner and vital actuation. But the
motivation which comes from indigence is more basic and more
primary than the motivation which comes from abundance.

[10] The specifying end is that of *art*—of art quickened by poetry.
(Strictly speaking, the specification comes from the *object*. It is
because the end in question is at the same time object that I
use the expression "specifying end.")

[11] In this case the intellect, as in the Kantian system, creates its
own object—but an object *to be made,* not an object *to be
known.* Kant's system was wrong because it dealt with the
knowing activity of the intellect, and thus fancied that the
object known was a product of the creativity of the spirit, supposedly subsuming empirical appearances under the a priori
forms of the sensibility and of the understanding, and thus
knowing only "phenomena" it has manufactured.

[12] We may draw in this connection a particularly instructive lesson
from the great and noble illusion—and failure—of those masters
of the Renaissance, especially Albrecht Dürer, who believed that
a superior knowledge of the mathematical laws of forms and
of the world of geometrical proportions would enable the artist
to attain beauty in its unique and definite type (as if beauty
were not a transcendental) and to encompass its essence in

their work. As Edwin Panofsky put it, Dürer was "an artist-geometrician, and one who suffered from the very limitations of the discipline he loved. In his younger days, when he prepared the engraving 'Adam and Eve' [1504], he had hoped to capture absolute beauty by means of a ruler and a compass. Shortly before he composed the *Melancolia I* he was forced to admit: 'But what absolute beauty is, I know not. Nobody knows it except God.'" Quoted by Marston Morse in "Mathematics and the Arts," *The Yale Review*, summer, 1951, p. 606. Mr. Morse observes that "Dürer was a creative mathematician as well as an artist. He wanted his geometric theories to measure up to his art," and "his discontent on this account was unique among artists of all time."

[13] "It is no mere appreciation of the beauty before us," Poe says in "The Poetic Principle," which inspires the poet, "but a wild effort to reach the beauty above." And he adds, using a wrong simile, which exaggerates the distance to the point of making any real participation impossible: "It is the desire of the moth for the star." He also writes, nevertheless, that the poetry of words is "the rhythmical creation of Beauty"—a quite incorrect formula, and a program that, to be sure, no "moth" can implement. Poetry can produce or create a participation in Beauty, it cannot produce or create Beauty, any more than any other transcendental.

[14] Since the matter is particularly subtle (and important), I should like to make things precise even at the price of laying emphasis on points which, I think, have been clarified enough in my discussion.

I do not in any way make poetry independent of beauty. I insist, on the one hand, that, by reason of the inherent freedom of poetry, the need poetry has for beauty is a need born of love and connaturality, not of any submission to a specifying object; and, on the other hand, that, by reason of the transcendental nature of beauty, the ways in which we speak and think of the relationship of the work of art to beauty must never depart from that feeling of awe and always remaining distance which is due to transcendental things, however real the participation in them may be.

In the field of knowledge, when the mind conforms with a given reality, we may say that it *knows truth* (though never exhaustively), because in any true statement, in so far as it is true, the mind makes itself consonant with transcendental being (or ontological truth).

Yet in the field of art, the mind does not have to know, but to *make*. And it produces a work, a particular thing which is *contained in a genus*. That is why the proper and most primary requirement of this work as a work is to be *good* (in the particular, nontranscendental line of the *artistic* good), that is, to be done as it should be done, or in conformity with the rules of making and the inner necessities of the thing in question.

The work, no doubt, must also be beautiful. Yet it will be so through a kind of gift from above which permeates its generic properties as thing produced, and results from its participation in the transcendental order of beauty.

Once this point is understood, we may say, of course, that the fine arts (the self-sufficient arts) aim to produce beautiful things, but we should never say, in a rigorous terminology, that they aim to *produce beauty;* for the expression is equivocal, and risks leading the one who uses it to believe more or less obscurely that beauty in the work is produced as an object of making (a direct terminus of the process of production), that is, *a thing contained in a genus*—whereas, in reality, beauty in the work is produced as a participation in a *transcendental* quality, or in something which cannot be *made.* In other words the work is a product; but its beauty is not a product that impregnates it as with a perfume or invests it as with a garb or an armor; the beauty of the work, which inherently results from its very production, is in its very being a particular mirroring of a transcendental or an infinite, and a *gift* from the spiritual source—poetry—in which the production of the work originates. Let us say, then, that art engenders in beauty, or produces in beauty, not that it produces beauty.

[15] The object of making is a trap to catch a transcendental.

[16] In distinguishing aesthetic beauty from transcendental beauty (see supra, § 3) we have observed that aesthetic beauty is a particular determination of transcendental beauty but remains transcendental in nature.

[17] *L'Âme romantique et le Rêve* (Marseille: Cahiers du Sud, 1937).

[18] "My terrible struggle with that old and malignant plumage, fortunately crushed, God!"

[19] The need to create new myths, on which contemporary critics rightly lay stress, but to which they ascribe central importance, arises in reality from the above-mentioned experience of the void, which is the fundamental fact. The need for new myths is a secondary phenomenon, a sort of process of compensation. And it deals essentially, like the spiritual experience itself in which it originates, with the inner universe of the poet *as a man,* with the intellectual and moral foundations of his life, with his anguish and his crucial choices.

The fact of a poet laboring and straining to find new myths for the sake of his art, or considering the invention of new myths a direct requirement and a proper task of poetry itself, involves in my opinion a double and profound illusion.

For, in the first place, the myths in question—the myths

which are to ensure both the fundamental perspectives of a poet and his definite sphere of communication with men (be it exclusively self-centered, as in Joyce)—are not simply that symbolic approach of imaginative thought which characterizes for instance Platonic myths and which can never fail poetry, since it is part of its nature. (This kind of myth, say the *poetic* myths, poets ceaselessly renew.) The myths under discussion—let us accept the word, which emphasizes the imaginative impact proper to poetic thought, but which is wrong in its origin, for it was adopted as an anthropological substitute for something one deprived of any intrinsic truth while deeming it to be necessary—the *metaphysical* myths are the organic signs and symbols of some faith actually lived, be it by the primitive man; they are forms (either properly mythological or genuinely religious) through which a conviction of the entire soul nourishes and quickens from within the very power of creative imagination. Such myths have no force except through the faith man has in them. It is essential to them to be believed in. The effort of a poet to create new metaphysical myths of his own invention, for the sake of his work as a poet, is self-contradictory, since, having invented them, he cannot believe in them. A man lost in the night might as well invent an imaginary moon because he needs to have his way lighted. The only way for a poet to become inspired by a new metaphysical myth is his faith as a man; it is not to "invent a new myth," it is either to be the Mohammed of a new religious creed which has been revealed to him, or to adhere, soul and body, to some of the new religious creeds, however asinine, which the mysticism of sex so dear to D. H. Lawrence, or the occultist disciplines so dear to Yeats, or the state-totalitarianism so dear to Ezra Pound, or the black magic so dear to Surrealists, offer to modern man— or to adhere, soul and body, to some one of the ancient religious creeds (including the true one, the revelation of God through His own uncreate and incarnate Word) which becomes new to him—an always new "myth," an always new truth— in proportion as he believes in it with renewed and deeper faith. In any case it is not from the poet that the man has received a new myth, it is from the man that the poet has received a new vital belief (and a new incitation to create new poetic myths). Metaphysical myths are needed by poetry, but they cannot be provided by poetry.

In the second place, it is only *indirectly*, and so to speak extrinsically, that poetry depends on, and needs, the metaphysical myths (the symbols of vital beliefs quickening blood and imagination) which are present in the mind of the poet. These beliefs and metaphysical myths matter *directly* to him, not for his poetry, but for his human self, his own metaphysical situation in the mystery of being, and his way of working out his own destiny. Those poets who have rejected faith in Transcendence, and entered into the spiritual experience of the void, are bound—as men—to turn toward a substitute for what they have rejected: a new god of their own, or a system of revolt against and hatred for the celestial Intruder, as Lautréamont put it, or that "Profundum, physical thunder, dimensions in which We believe without belief, beyond belief" of which Wallace Stevens spoke—all this sought for in the place of God from Whom they had parted. Hence their nostalgia for "new myths." This nostalgia has directly to do, not with their poetic work, but with their humanity, with those substructures and preconditions on which poetry depends indirectly, in the order of "material" or "subjective" causality. Here it is a question of the soil on which poetry grows, not of poetry in its own essence. Yet because poetry is the only thing which remains to them, they shift this very nostalgia to poetry itself, and they labor desperately to make up for the soil which is lacking, and which poetry indeed needs, but which is not its own intrinsic life. And they expect from a new soil (if they were able to create it) the essential which can be given only by the spirit and grace of poetry. The notion that it would be enough to succeed in creating a new metaphysical myth for a poet to achieve the miracle of poetry for which he is striving can only sidetrack poetry. Give the most powerful new myth to a poet who lacks creative intuition, and he will remain a poor poet. In his very failure or despair to create the new myth he looks for, a real poet may produce his most genuine poems.

To sum up, the confusion between poetic myth and metaphysical myth, and the assumption that the invention of new metaphysical myths is the primary obligation imposed on a poet by poetry, cause what should be sought for as a material and indirect precondition for poetry, to be sought for as its very life and salvation; and cause what should be sought for—as a truth—for the sake of the poet's self, to be sought for—as a myth—for the sake of his poetry.

[20] Robert Lowell, "The Holy Innocents," in *Lord Weary's Castle* (New York: Harcourt Brace, 1946).

[21] Pierre Emmanuel, *Babel* (Paris: Desclée De Brouwer, 1951).

[22] Thomas Merton, "The Captives—A Psalm," in *The Tears of the Blind Lions* (New York: New Directions, 1949).

[23] Henri Michaux, preface to *Epreuves, Exorcismes* (Paris: Gallimard, 1945). The question is to *"tenir en échec les puissances environnantes du monde hostile."*

[24] I have noted (p. 301, note 4) that there is a genuine poetic

science, totally different from theoretical science, and conveyed by knowledge through connaturality and creative emotion. In the process I am now describing, this poetic science is completely perverted, because it is made into theoretical science confused itself with power, and into absolute (magical) science. —On the magical sign, see my essay "Sign and Symbol," in *Ransoming the Time* (New York: Scribner, 1941).

[25] R. P. Blackmur, "The Artist as a Hero," *Art News,* September, 1951, pp. 18-19. Blackmur illustrates his views on the matter with penetrating remarks on Joyce, Henry James, Gide, and Thomas Mann's *Doctor Faustus.*

[26] Ibid., pp. 19, 20.

[27] *Nouvelle Revue Française,* February 1, 1924.

[28] ". . . That idolatrous dissolution of language from the grammar of a possible world, which results from the belief that language itself can be reality, or by incantation can create a reality: a superstition that comes down in French from Lautréamont, Rimbaud, and Mallarmé to the Surrealists, and in English to Hart Crane, Wallace Stevens, and Dylan Thomas." Allen Tate, "The Angelic Imagination" (*The Forlorn Demon,* Chicago: Regnery, 1953).

BEAUTY AND MODERN PAINTING

[1] Since this time Severini has come a long way, and learned a great deal in the course of a constantly progressing effort. He has become one of the most powerful renovators of sacred art, and our greatest master in mosaic and fresco. In an essay written on him in 1930 ("Gino Severini," in *Peintres Nouveaux,* No 40, Paris: Gallimard, 1930; reprinted in *Art and Poetry,* New York: Philosophical Library, 1943), I observed, with respect to his decoration of the churches of Semsales and La Roche, in Switzerland, that "art is brought remarkably close to religious use by the most daring modern researches, requiring as they do as much formal purification. It is not the newness of their means, but rather the spirit from which they seek inspiration that often keeps them apart from such usage. It would need an essential purification, an interior renovation of this spirit—which does not happen without a sort of agony, and which the majority refuses. Semsales and La Roche show us the victory of a painter who has lived out the modern anxieties and discoveries, and has never renounced them, and who has been rendered master of his soul at the same time by a great inner deepening." During long years of tenacious labor the authority of Severini did not cease growing. By his meditation on the laws of number and the logic of abstract propor-

tions, and by his passionate attachment to all the concrete details of honest work, straightforward and rigorous, he affirmed more and more the natural kinship which relates him to the seekers of the early Italian Renaissance. While pursuing his research in pure painting, he decorated a number of churches in French-speaking Switzerland, and recently composed the great mosaic of St. Peter's Church in Fribourg, a masterwork of modern religious art, which was solemnly inaugurated on September 16, 1951.

Speaking of religious art, I would like to say how much we are indebted to Maurice Denis, who was an excellent artist and critic both, and to Alexandre Cingria. I would like also to point out the particular importance, in contemporary research, of André Girard's work, which unites to an exceptional degree science and inspiration, together with admirable imaginative richness and pictorial generosity.

[2] Marcel Duchamp is the youngest of the three Villon brothers. The most recent notice on him was written by Katherine Kuh for the Catalog of the Exhibition of the Arensberg Collection at the Art Institute of Chicago, in 1949.

[3] Except as regards his occasional collaboration with Hans Richter for some motion pictures.

[4] Kazimir Malevich, *Die gegenstandlose Welt* (Munich: Bauhausbuecher, 1927); in *Artists on Art* (New York: Pantheon Books, 1945), pp. 452-53. In 1913, Malevich had exhibited in Moscow a picture of a black square on a white field.

Cf. Mondrian: "The new art has continued and culminated the art of the past in such a way that the new painting, by employing 'neutral' or universal forms, expresses itself only through the relationships of line and color. While in the art of the past these relationships are veiled by the particular form, in the new art they are made clear through the use of neutral or universal forms. Because these forms become more and more neutral as they approach a state of universality, neoplasticism uses only a single neutral form: the rectangular area in varying dimensions. Since this form, when composed, completely annihilates itself for lack of contrasting forms, line and color are completely freed." Ibid., p. 427.

In his essay "Introduction to Abstract," in *Art News,* November, 1950, Thomas B. Hess remarks that today some American painters, Rothko for instance, who "like Mondrian refuse to invite recollections of nature," are trying to attain "the 'experience of objectlessness' which the pioneer abstractionist Malevich considered the supreme sensation in art" by doing "for color what the Cubists did for form" and endeavoring in this way to "project their deepest emotions into the canvas" (p. 158).

In the views that Kandinsky, the greatest representative, I think, of nonobjective art, offered (and which related to some sort of Platonic idealism blended with Mrs. Blavatsky's peculiar spiritualism), abstract painting appears as starting a kind of angelistic attempt to act directly on human souls through forms that are to be produced in accordance only with the "principle of inner necessity." (That is why he "enviously" looked at "the nonmaterial art of music," hoping to "reciprocate it with his own medium.") "[The] choice of object (one of the elements in the harmony of form) must be decided only by the corresponding vibration of the human soul." "The freer the abstract form, the purer and more primitive is its appeal. In a composition, therefore, where the material side may be more or less superfluous, it can be accordingly more or less omitted and replaced by the nonobjective forms or through abstractions of dematerialized objects. In any case the translation into the abstract or the employment of nonobjective forms, the artist's sole judge, guide, and principal consideration should be his feeling." For Kandinsky feeling—though merely subjective in the sense that it was neither dependent on the visible world, nor made intentional so as to disclose the transapparent meanings of this visible world—had nevertheless an ideal objective value, as a way to penetrate into the spiritual world of "the eternal truth embraced by art." Consequently, though "the artist may employ any form to express himself," and though the "expression of personality" is one of the "three mystical elements" of art, the expression of personality is destined progressively to lose importance, and to fade away before the final aim, the attainment of "pure and eternal artistry," "the main element of art, irrespective of time and space." "The process of development in art consists, so to speak, of the separation of the pure and eternal art from the element of personality as well as from the element of an epoch." Vasili Kandinsky, *On the Spiritual in Art* (New York: Hilla Rebay, 1946), pp. 20, 25, 35, 51-52, 55-56.

[5] Mondrian, 1937; in *Artists on Art*, p. 428.

[6] Ozefant likes to stress in this connection the presence, in the unconscious tendencies of our human nature, of "preforms" which are the preexisting "form of a need" (and which are only, I think, another name for the connaturality with logos or proportion inherent in our mind and senses).

[7] I might mention at this point Theodore Brenson, Clyfford Still, or Arthur Osver. But the production of contemporary American painting is so abundant and variegated that one hesitates to pick a few names among so many. While the strictly nonrepresentational current is still very strong, some artists are seeking their way in half abstraction. Many others—and this

is of greater interest for our present considerations—have set themselves free from the nonrepresentative system but remain close to modern abstractionism and owe to it either a firm geometrical substructure (e.g., Randall Thompson or Lamar Dodd) or a particularly refined and airy poetry (e.g., William Palmer, Lyonel Feininger, or Howard Cook). In sharp contrast with abstract painting, the effort that Edwin Dickinson has pursued for many years along the lines of the American Romantic tradition points to a personal reinterpretation of nature which corresponds, it seems to me, to a significant trend of our times. This Romantic tradition is being revived, prodded somewhat by Surrealist influences, in a number of young painters whose work deserves particular attention.

[8] And yet Leonardo was not ashamed to vindicate painting with such arguments: "A painting representing a father of a family happened to be caressed by his grandchildren, although they were still in long clothes: the dog and the cat of the household did likewise, and it was a wondrous sight to see. . . . I once saw a painting deceive a dog by its likeness to his master and the animal was overjoyed to see it. I have also seen dogs bark and try to bite other dogs in a picture; and a monkey frolic like anything before the painting of a monkey, and swallows flying about and alighting upon the painted railings depicted on the windows of buildings." In Péladan, *Textes choisis de Léonard de Vinci* (Paris: Mercure de France, 1907), pp. 175, 180.

[9] An observation made on Marin by Jerome Mellquist in his book, *The Emergence of an American Art* (New York: Scribner, 1942), seems to me particularly relevant here. "Once more," he says, "as certain of the critics have noted, Marin exhibited that strange gift of his for drawing from the atmosphere the signs and symbols by which, through his own graphic short hand, he can somehow summarize the essence of a place. He had learned this first, perhaps, from his etching. But here and throughout the works which have followed his first contact with the Cubists, it became a kind of calligraphic notation which put nature into the most compact and 'transportable' of forms. These are equivalents for its shapes and figures, with each hieroplyphic reminding us of the unchanging and ineluctable realities of nature." (pp. 400-401.)

[10] See infra, Chapter VIII, § 12. In painting I think that Chagall is now the greatest master of the "illuminating image." Certain early canvases of Chirico should also be particularly mentioned in this connection.

POETIC EXPERIENCE AND POETIC SENSE

[1] Poi chi pinge figura,
Se non può esse lei, non la può porre.
(Who paints a figure, if he cannot *be* it, cannot give form to it.)
Convivio, IV, Canz. 52-53. I do not claim that Dante spoke in the same sense as Rimbaud, yet both remarks stress in a striking way the fact of the identification between the poet and the *other*. Dante, moreover, was versed in Aristotle enough to be aware of the *intentional* character of this identification: "Onde nullo dipintore potrebbe porre alcuna figura, se *intenzionalmente* non si facesse prima tale, quale la figura essere dee." Ibid., IV, x, 11-13. (Italics mine.)

[2] See my essay "Sign and Symbol," in *Ransoming the Time* (New York: Scribner, 1941), Chapter IX:

". . . In our logical state, sensations, images, ideas, are bathed *in sunlight,* bound up with the luminous and regular life of the intelligence and of its laws of gravitation.

"In the magical state, all these things were *of the night,* bound up with the fluid and twilight life of the imagination, and with an experience which was of an amazingly powerful impact, but entirely lived and—to the extent that is was an object of reflection—dreamed.

"The same is true of the sign and of the relationship between the sign and the signified.

"Truth being a relationship of the cognitive faculty to the thing, and being possessed only by the judgment of the intelligence which seizes upon it as such, it must be said that among primitive men this relationship is lived, but is not winnowed out for its own sake. Doubtless it is known, since the intelligence is there present, but known in a nocturnal fashion, since the intelligence is there immersed in the powers of the imagination.

"Reflecting upon primitive man, we can say that in him the relationship of the mind to the thing is ambivalent. The same relationship is 'false' (in the eyes of our evolved consciousness) to the extent that it, for instance, asserts the existence of composite ancestors for the tribe: duck men or kangaroo men. It is 'true' to the extent that it asserts the living union of man with nature, whereof this myth is the symbol. But for primitive man such a distinction has no meaning. It is because his very consent to truth is not the same as ours (the idea of truth not having for him been winnowed out for itself).

"He adheres *en bloc,* at the same time and indistinctly, to the symbol and the symbolized: here is for him, in indivisible fashion, an image or a likeness of truth, an equivalent, an *als ob* of truth, without his having winnowed out the idea of truth for its own sake. In similar fashion a child believes in a story, in the adventures of Alice in Wonderland; awaken the child, withdraw him from the world of the imagination, and he knows very well that a little girl cannot enter a rabbit hole. But primitive man does not wake up, he is not yet withdrawn from the motherly bosom of the imagination, which for him makes all nature familiar and without which he could not face the dangers, whereby he feels he is surrounded on all sides, and (if we are dealing with true primitive man, with man of prehistoric times: today's homonym thereof is doubtless merely a distorted reflection of the original) the pitiless hardship of his existence as a dweller in caves, struggling among the wild beasts. He inhabits the land of *seeming truth.* . . .

"Since we are by hypothesis dealing with the nocturnal regime of the imagination, and since for the imagination as such (as dreams bear witness) the principle of identity does not exist; and then again, since the intelligence is still present, bound up with and clothed in the imagination, it is easy to understand that for primitive man the identity of things is constantly unmade and made again. It is altogether too hasty for us to say that with him there is simply an identity between the sign and the signified. No, there is an oscillation, there is a going and coming from distinction to identification. When children play by building sand castles, these castles are truly castles for them. If you trample them, the children will cry with rage and indignation. But once their play is at an end, what were castles is only sand. Primitive man believes to be identical (through the living power of the imagination) that which he obscurely knows to be different (through his intelligence, bound up in the imagination). It is impossible to understand anything about his thought if it be conceived from the point of view of the logical or daylight state of intelligence, taken as the rule and measure of all thought. It is the thought of an awakened dreamer, wherein the role of *play* (and the allowance of *play*) is tremendously great."

[*] See the observations made on this score by Allen Tate in his remarkable essay on "The Angelic Imagination" (*The Forlorn Demon,* Chicago: Regnery, 1953) especially with regard to "The Colloquy of Monos and Una."—"Poe understood the spiritual disunity that had resulted from the rise of the demi-religion of scientism, but by merely opposing its excesses with equally excessive claims for the 'poetic intellect,' he subtly perpetuated the disunity from another direction."

As concerns the search for magic, I think that there is only a seeming disagreement between Allen Tate and Raïssa Maritain. The latter holds [*Situation de la Poésie,* Paris: Desclée

De Brouwer, 1938, p. 58; *The Situation of Poetry* (New York: Phil. Libr., 1955), pp. 25-26] that Poe never intended to make, in his own work, an instrument of magical power out of poetry. The former holds that he dreamed of, and longed for, the possibility of a magical *power of words* ascribed to the angels of his dialogues.

⁴ Cf. Raïssa Maritain, "Sens et Non-Sens en Poésie," in *Situation de la Poésie*, pp. 22-24. (English transl., pp. 6-8.)

⁵ "Of our thinking, we might say, it is but the mere upper surface that we shape into articulate thoughts; underneath the region of argument and conscious discourse, lies the region of meditation; here, in its quiet mysterious depths, dwells what vital force is in us; here, if aught is to be created, and not merely manufactured and communicated, must the work go on." "Characteristics," in *Essays* (Boston: Brown and Taggard, 1860), Vol. III, p. 9.

At this point we may understand, I think, the true meaning of the tranquillity of which Wordsworth spoke ("emotion recollected in tranquillity")—though T. S. Eliot is right, on other scores, in his criticism of this celebrated formula: "Tradition and the Individual Talent," *The Sacred Wood* (London: Methuen, 1920), p. 52. One might perhaps try to rescue Wordsworth's formula by saying that in it "recollection" has more to do with *recueillement* than with memory, and "emotion" means the intuitive emotion inseparable from concentration; but this interpretation does not square with the context of the formula in the Preface to the *Lyrical Ballads*.

⁶ T. S. Eliot, *The Use of Poetry and the Use of Criticism* (Cambridge: Harvard University Press, 1933), pp. 137-38. Cf. René Char, *Seuls demeurent* (Paris: Gallimard, 1945), p. 81: "Etre poète, c'est avoir de l'appétit pour un malaise dont la consommation, parmi les tourbillons de la totalité des choses existances et pressenties, provoque, au moment de se clore, la félicité."

In another essay ("Tradition and the Individual Talent," in *The Sacred Wood*, p. 52), Eliot writes also, in relation to the state peculiar to the poet: "It is a concentration, and a new thing resulting from the concentration, of a very great number of experiences which to the practical and active person would not seem to be experiences at all; it is a concentration which does not happen consciously or of deliberation."

⁷ There was, I think, as much good as bad in Romanticism, or even more. As T. S. Eliot puts it, "Romanticism," moreover, "is a term which is constantly changing in different contexts, and which is now limited to what appear to be purely literary and purely local problems, now expanding to cover almost the whole of the life of a time and of nearly the whole world. It

has perhaps not been observed that in its more comprehensive significance Romanticism comes to include nearly anything that distinguishes the last two hundred and fifty years or so from their predecessors, and includes so much that is ceases to bring with it any praise or blame." *The Use of Poetry and the Use of Criticism,* p. 121.

8 John St. Thomas, *Les Dons du Saint-Esprit,* French translation by Raïssa Maritain (2nd ed., Paris: Téqui, 1950), p. 3.

9 T. S. Eliot, "Tradition and the Individual Talent," *The Sacred Wood,* p. 52.

10 Benjamin Fondane, *Baudelaire et l'Expérience du Gouffre* (Paris: Pierre Seghers, 1947), p. 29.—"En art," Léon-Paul Fargue said, "il faut que la mathématique se mette aux ordres des fantômes." *Sous la Lampe* (Paris: N.R.F., 1929).—John Crowe Ransom's statement may be recalled here: "Science gratifies a rational or practical impulse and exhibits the minimum of perception. Art gratifies a perceptual impulse and exhibits the minimum of reason." *The World's Body* (New York: Scribner, 1938), p. 130.

11 "La grande poésie est essentiellement *bête,* elle *croit* et c'est ce qui fait sa gloire et sa force . . ." Baudelaire, *Œuvres posthumes* (Compte-rendu du "Prométhée délivré" de M. de Senneville) (Paris: Mercure de France, 1908), p. 167.

Baudelaire played a dangerous game in masking himself with feigned cynicism, and calling *bêtise* what is *innocence.* Ironical disparagement in the form of understatement may be misleading. Valéry did not want to be *bête,* and was afraid to seem so. This had perhaps a part in the show he made of being ashamed of inspiration.

In a more general way, a certain self-consciousness or modesty may prevent a poet from daring enough. I wonder whether some excellent poets, like Miss Marianne Moore, do not restrict themselves to an almost purely visual or perceptual poetry for fear of avowing the subjectivity of their poetic experience, from which they fly at the very moment when they receive from it the fortunate spark of creative incitement and perception. In an interesting article ("The Symbol and the Rose," *New York Times Book Review,* January 20, 1922) Miss Kathleen Raine rightly emphasizes the remarkable achievements of the "poetry of pure perception" which she considers (in quite an oversimplified manner, to my mind) characteristic of contemporary American poetry. She quotes in this connection Marianne Moore's fine description of a camellia:

> . . . *Gloria mundi*
> *with a leaf two inches, nine lines*
> *broad, they have; and the smaller,*

> Camellia Sabina
>   with amanita-white petals; there are
>   several of her
>
>   pale pinwheels, and pale
>   stripe that looks as if on a mushroom the
>   sliver from a beet-root carved into a
>   rose were laid . . .

And she observes that "this elaboration refines the sensible image by association with other sharp and precise sensible images, to produce a highly sophisticated and delicate way of looking at the visible world." Yet she also observes that "perceptual images, however intense or refined, lack a dimension without which we soon begin to feel an intolerable claustrophobia," and she wishes for "a synthesis of the symbolic and the contemporary." I would say that the kind of modesty to which I have alluded—which causes a poet to fly from the inwardness of poetic experience toward the world of sensory perception, and to conceal the vastness of his soul in the colors of a lizard or a tulip—should some day yield to the pressure of what *exists* in him.

[12] *The Prophecy of Dante.*

[13] René Char, *Seuls demeurent,* p. 70.

[14] Thomas Aquinas, *Comment. in Psalm.,* Prolog.

[15] Letter to Clara, April 13, 1838, in Schumann, *On Music and Musicians,* ed. Konrad Wolff (New York: Pantheon Books, 1946), p. 260.

[16] *Frederic Chopin,* ed. Stephen P. Mizwa (New York: Macmillan, 1949), p. 51. (Accepting the authenticity of the Potocka correspondence.)—Mozart's famous letter to Baron V. (Edward Holmes, *The Life of Mozart,* Everyman's Library, pp. 254-58) has too little authenticity to be used as a document here.

[17] Arthur Lourié, "De la Mélodie," *La Vie intellectuelle,* December 25, 1936, pp. 491-99.

[18] T. S. Eliot, *The Use of Poetry and the Use of Criticism,* p. 138.

[19] Cf. R. P. Blackmur, *The Double Agent* (New York: Arrow Eds., 1935), Chapters III and V.

[20] "L'Art chrétien," in *Art poétique* (Paris: Emile-Paul, 1922), pp. 63, 69, 56.

[21] Raïssa Maritain, "Sens et Non-sens en poésie," *Situation de la Poésie,* p. 14.

[22] Raïssa Maritain, op. cit., p. 16 (English transl., p. 3).

[22a] "Ars Poetica," in *Collected Poems 1917-1952* (Boston: Houghton, Mifflin, 1952).

[23] Raïssa Maritain, op. cit., pp. 19-20 (English transl., pp. 4-5).

"Par l'intonation pleine de sous-entendus, par la gesticulation rythmique, par une certaine démarche ordonnée durant toute cette longue lecture, il donne une signification apparente à des textes affranchis de toute liaison logique. Signification qui dépend ici tout entière du nombre, du débit, de la sensibilité et de l'intelligence de celui qui lit. En somme, le lecteur a joué ici le rôle de l'intelligence dans les rêves. Bien que liée par le sommeil, et c'est pourquoi le principe de contradiction y paraît aboli, elle ne dort pas, elle pénètre, elle entoure d'une mystérieuse atmosphère de clarté les suites d'images les plus incohérentes."

[24] Ibid., p. 25 (English transl., p. 8).

[25] In *Collected Poems of W. B. Yeats* (2nd ed., New York: Macmillan, 1950).

[26] In *Alcools* (Paris: N.R.F., 1920).

[27] I confess that when trying to illustrate my discussion with appropriate examples, I found the task significally more difficult with the material offered by American and British modern poets than with that offered by French modern poets. This fact may be related, I think, to the above-mentioned observations (pp. 189-90) about French and British poetry.

[28] From Dylan Thomas, "Poem," in *Selected Writings* (New York: New Directions, 1946).

[29] Henri Michaux, "Les Craquements," in *Epreuves, Exorcismes* (Paris: Gallimard, 1945).

[30] The distinctions I am making here point only to ideal directions. I have no desire to enclose poems in categories. I thought that even the fact that the reader might question my particular choice would indicate the validity of the ideal distinction.

[31] From Hart Crane, *The Bridge*, V (Three Songs: "Virginia"). (In *Collected Poems*, New York: Liveright, 1933.)

[32] From Wallace Stevens, "Six Significant Landscapes."

[33] From Jean Cocteau ("Dimanche Soir," in *Opéra*).

[34] From John Peale Bishop, "Perspectives Are Precipices" (in *Collected Poems*, New York: Scribner, 1948).

[35] There is something similar in the experience alluded to by Wordsworth:

> . . . *the soul*
> *Remembering how she felt, but what*
> *she felt*
> *Remembering not, retains an ob-*
> *scure sense*
> *Of possible sublimity.*
> (Prelude, *Book II.*)

[36] In another connection, it would be of particular interest to examine the cases where the symbol *exists before* the meanings

with which man's poetic instinct will fill it. This is what came about, as a rule, with old myths whose primitive meaning had been forgotten and which received new meanings in the course of subsequent centuries. But the instance in which the students of poetry could find the most striking and richest implications is, I think, the Arthurian legend. In his remarkable book *La Légende Arthurienne et le Graal* (Paris: Presses Universitaires, 1952), Jean Marx has demonstrated, by dint of clear-sighted erudition, the Celtic origin of this legend, and elucidated the complex—and natural, irrepressible—process of its further Christianization. He has made clear, by the same token, the extraordinary polyvalence and plasticity of the forms that the primitive themes, characters, and marvelous objects of the romance progressively took, all the while penetrating into the collective unconscious of the Western world.

We are also confronted here with a typical process of *poetic internalization*. Pre-existing symbols—primitively characterized by the sheer exteriority either of the properties and enchantments of a fairy world, or of the various obligations and trials incurred by the characters, or of their adventures—were to become signs of abiding dreams and realities of the human soul. It is enough to think for instance of the charge of poetic meaning, henceforth invested in our cultural heritage, with which the *Geis* was to be laden as regards woman's mysterious initiative in the *fatalité* of love—or the character of the Fisher-King as regards the inherent melancholy of wounded greatness —or the character of Perceval as regards the miraculous power of simplicity of heart and intrepid candor.

[87] In T. S. Eliot, *Collected Poems 1909-1935* (New York: Harcourt, Brace, 1936).

[88] Lecturing on January 7, 1668, at the Royal Academy of Painting, on Poussin's *Eliezer and Rebecca,* Philippe de Champaigne expressed regret that the Master had not seen fit to depict "the camels mentioned in Holy Writ." Lebrun thereupon replied that "Mr. Poussin, in a constant endeavor to purify and disencumber the subject of his paintings and to portray attractively the main action he was dealing with, had rejected *any bizarre object likely to debauch the eye of the beholder and amuse it with trifles* (les objets bizarres qui pouvaient débaucher l'œil du spectateur et l'amuser à des minuties)." In Henry Jouin, *Conférences de l'Académie royale de Peinture et de Sculpture* (Paris: A. Quantin, 1883), pp. 93-94.

THE INTERNALIZATION OF MUSIC

[1] Albert Béguin, *Gérard de Nerval, suivi de Poésie et Mystique* (Paris: Stock, 1936), p. 110.

[2] The word "pulsion" is not commonly used in English or in French, although it is listed in *The Shorter Oxford Dictionary*. I am taking the liberty of appropriating it for my own ends, because I cannot find a better word to designate the kind of mental wave or vibration, charged with dynamic unity, of which I am speaking here.

[3] Wallace Stevens, "Peter Quince at the Clavier."

[4] Interesting indications in this regard can be found in Allen Tate's remarkable reflective analysis of his own "Ode to the Confederate Dead" ("Narcissus as Narcissus," in *On the Limits of Poetry*, New York: The Swallow Press and William Morrow, 1948).

[5] Francis Thompson, "Essay on Shelley" (*Works*, London: Burns and Oates, 1913, Vol. III, p. 16).—In relation to Henri Bremond's *Prière et Poésie*, T. S. Eliot wrote: "My first qualm is over the assertion that 'the more of a poet any particular poet is, the more he is tormented by the need of communicating his experience.' This is a downright sort of statement which is very easy to accept without examination; but the matter is not so simple as all that. I should say that the poet is tormented primarily by the need to write a poem. . . ." *The Use of Poetry and the Use of Criticism* (Cambridge: Harvard University Press, 1933), pp. 130-31.—See also the telling remarks of Cleanth Brooks in *The Well Wrought Urn* (New York: Reynal and Hitchcock, 1947), chapter IV.

[6] The disregard for the intrinsically intellectual character and *knowledge value* of poetic intuition, and of the essential distinction between simple or "brute" emotion and the intuitive, spiritualized emotion which is the proper means of poetic knowledge, is responsible, I think, for the theory that the "one final cause of poetry" is to act "as a safety valve tending to preserve" the poet "from mental disease" (Keble), or that poetry is essentially *"ein Heilungsprozess durch Autoanalyse"* (W. Stekel), as Frederic Clarke Prescott relates in *The Poetic Mind* (New York: Macmillan, 1926), pp. 271-77.

I do not deny, to be sure, the *vis medica* of poetry, both with respect to the poet and the reader, and the effect of *catharsis* it produces. What I maintain is that all that is a secondary result, not the essence nor the "one final cause."

[7] C. E. M. Joad, *Matter, Life and Value* (Oxford University Press, London: Humphrey Milford, 1929), Chapter IX, p. 396.

[8] The music of the intuitive pulsions has been repressed and

superseded *in the expression.* This, of course, is not incompatible with the fact, which I pointed out at the beginning, of the fundamental part played by the intuitive pulsions *in the soul of the poet,* in his preconscious activity, especially, as we shall see further, at the source of the poetic image.

9 Walter Savage Landor, "Rose Aylmer."

10 Shelley, "When the Lamp Is Shattered," first strophe.

11 In T. S. Eliot, *Collected Poems 1909-1935* (New York: Harcourt, Brace, 1936).

12 Of course I am thinking of good or truly representative modern poets.

13 Both poems in *Collected Poems* (2nd ed., New York: Macmillan, 1950).

14 I Cor. 7:32-33.

15 *Le Secret professionnel* (1922: in *Le Rappel à l'Ordre,* Paris: Stock, 1926), p. 213.

16 This was the case with the poems I described above (Chapter VII, p. 197) as poems in which the conceptual utterances either have disappeared or are reduced to a minimum or are merely allusive.

17 T. S. Eliot, "The Perfect Critic," *The Sacred Wood* (London: Methuen, 1920), p. 7.

18 John Crowe Ransom, *The World's Body* (New York: Scribner, 1938), p. 115.

19 Corneille, *Polyeucte,* IV, ii.

20 "Maid Quiet."

21 "the lion's ferocious chrysanthemum head seeming kind by/ comparison." In "The Monkey Puzzle" (*Collected Poems,* New York: Macmillan, 1951). Cf. R. P. Blackmur, *The Double Agent* (New York: Arrow Ed., 1935), p. 137, note, and p. 161.

22 Pierre Reverdy, "Sur la Ligne" (*Ferraille,* Brussels: Journal Des Poètes, 1937; reprinted in *Main d'Œuvre,* Paris: Mercure de France, 1949).

23 "What Being," in Unfinished Poems (*Poems,* New York: Oxford University Press, 1948).

TEXTS WITHOUT COMMENT

1 In *Works* (London: Burns and Oates, 1913), Vol. III.

2 New York: Scribner, 1938.

3 In *Vers et Prose* (Paris: Perrin, 1935).

4 Fragment cxi.—Trans. anon., from *The Limits of Art,* coll. and ed. Huntington Cairns (Bollingen Series XII; New York: Pantheon Books, 1948), p. 55.

5 Fragment xlviii.—Ibid., p. 53.

6 Trans. Louis Untermeyer in his *Heinrich Heine: Paradox and Poet* (New York: Harcourt, Brace, 1945), Vol. 2.

[7] *Poems* (New York: Oxford University Press, 1938).

[6] In *1939-1945, Poèmes* (Paris: Gallimard, 1946).

[9] *Collected Poems* (New York: Liveright, 1933).

[10] In *Le Chant des Morts*, 1944-1948; reprinted in *Main d'Œuvre* (Paris: Mercure de France, 1949).

[11] *Poems 1922-1947* (New York: Scribner, 1948).

[12] In *Lettre de Nuit* (Paris: Desclée De Brouwer, 1939).

[13] *Collected Poems 1909-35* (New York: Harcourt, Brace, 1936).

[14] In *Alcools* (Paris: N. R. F., 1920).

[15] "Nord-Sud," N° 13, March, 1918.—Cf. André Breton, *Manifeste du Surréalisme* (Paris: Sagittaire, 1924), pp. 58-59.

[16] In *Vers et Prose* (Paris: Perrin, 1935; "Crise du Vers," in *Divagations*, Paris: Fasquelle, 1949).

[17] *Collected Poems* (New York: Macmillan, 1951).

[18] Trans. H. R. Fairclough, in the Loeb Classical Library (Cambridge: Harvard University Press, 1932).

[19] Trans. Thomas Okey (The Temple Classics; London: J. M. Dent and Sons, 1946).

[20] *Collected Poems* (New York: Liveright, 1933).

[21] *Le Forçat Innocent* (Paris: Gallimard, 1930).

[22] In *Nightwood* (New York: New Directions, 1937).

[23] *L'Œil écoute* (Paris: Gallimard, 1936).

[24] In *A Witness Tree* (New York, Henry Holt, 1942).

[25] *Four Quartets* (London: Faber and Faber, 1944).

[26] Op. cit. Lautréamont had said: "Beau comme la rencontre fortuite sur une table de dissection d'une machine à coudre et d'un parapluie." In both cases we have to do, I would say, less with an illuminating than with an intelligence-born and intelligence-titillating image.

[27] "What Happened, a Five-Act Play," in *Selected Writings* (New York: Random House, 1946).

[28] Op. cit.

[29] Ibid.

[30] *Poèmes* (Paris: N. R. F., 1919).

[31] Ibid.

[32] *Anabasis*, with a translation into English by T. S. Eliot (New York: Harcourt, Brace, 1938).

[33] Ibid.

[34] *Lettre de Nuit.*

[35] *Portes de l'Horizon, Poèmes, with an English version by the Author* (Bethlehem, Connecticut: Regina Laudis, 1952).

[36] *Ferraille.*

[37] *Le Chant des Morts.*

[38] *Vocabulaire.*

[39] *Chanson complète* (Paris: Gallimard, 1939).

[40] *L'Amour la Poésie.*

THE THREE EPIPHANIES
OF CREATIVE INTUITION

[1] New York: Liveright, 1933.

[2] Cleanth Brooks and Robert Penn Warren, *Understanding Poetry* (New York: Henry Holt, 1938), pp. 141, 489, 581, 640.

[3] Francis Fergusson, *The Idea of a Theater* (Princeton University Press, 1949), pp. 4-5, 36-37, 229-34.

[4] The action plays as necessary a part in painting as in poetry. "There are," Poussin said, "two instruments for influencing the minds of an audience: action and speech. Action is by itself so potent and effective that Demosthenes assigned to it the primacy among rhetorical devices: Marcus Tullius called it the language of the body, and Quintilian attributed to it such vigor and force that he deemed thoughts, proofs, and emotions ineffective without it. In like manner, if in a painting there is no action its lines and colors are ineffective." *Artists on Art* (New York: Pantheon Books, 1945), p. 155.

[5] Brooks and Warren, op. cit., p. 521.

[6] Be it noted that in the things of nature, because they are material, quantity is the first accident of substance. In the spiritual structure of the poem, on the other hand, harmonic expansion is the ultimate (in the order of nature, of course, not of time) constitutive actuation, complementing both the poetic sense and the action.

[7] When the sense of the number is lost, we have what Nietzsche called the "anarchy of atoms." "How," he said, "is decadence in literature characterized? By the fact that in it life no longer animates the whole. Words become predominant and leap right out of the sentence to which they belong, the sentences themselves trespass beyond their bounds, and obscure the sense of the whole page, and the page in its turn gains in vigour at the cost of the whole—the whole is no longer a whole." *The Case of Wagner*, trans. A. M. Ludovici (London: Allen and Unwin, 1911).

[8] Coleridge, *Biographia Literaria*, Ch. XVII.

[9] Ye who are living refer every cause up to the heavens alone, even as if they swept all with them of necessity.

Were it thus, Freewill in you would be destroyed, and it were not just to have joy for good and mourning for evil.

The heavens set your impulses in motion; I say not all, but suppose I said it, a light is given you to know good and evil,

and Freewill, which, if it endure the strain in its first battlings with the heavens, at length gains the whole victory, if it be well nurtured.

Ye lie subject, in your freedom, to a greater power and to

a better nature; and that creates in you *mind* which the heavens have not in their charge.

Paradiso, XX, 10-15. (Trans. Thomas Okey. The Temple Classics, London: J. M. Dent and Sons, 1946.)

[10] T. S. Eliot, "Dante," in *Selected Essays* (New York: Harcourt, Brace, 1932), p. 219.

[11] Because all those living lights, far brightlier shining, began songs which from my memory must slip and fall.

O sweet love, smile-bemantled, how glowing didst thou seem in those flute-holes breathed on only by sacred ponderings!

Paradiso, XX, 10-15. (Trans. Thomas Okey, The Temple Classics.)

[12] Francis Fergusson, *The Idea of a Theater,* pp. 39-40. The author goes on to say: "The *Purgatorio* especially, though an epic and not a drama, evidently moves in the tragic rhythm, both as a whole and in detail. The daylight climb up the mountain, by moral effort, and in the light of natural reason, corresponds to the first moment, that of 'purpose.' The night, under the sign of Faith, Hope, and Charity, when the Pilgrim can do nothing by his own unaided efforts, corresponds to the moments of passion and perception. The Pilgrim, as he pauses, mulls over the thoughts and experiences of the day; he sleeps and dreams, seeing ambivalent images from the mythic dreaming of the race, which refer, also, both to his own 'suppressed desires' and to his own deepest aspirations. These images gradually solidify and clarify, giving place to a new perception of his situation. This rhythm, repeated in varied forms, carries the Pilgrim from the superficial but whole-hearted motivations of childhood, in the Antipurgatorio, through the divided counsels of the growing soul, to the new innocence, freedom, and integrity of the Terrestrial Paradise—the realm of *The Tempest* or of *Oedipus at Colonos.* The same rhythmic conception governs also the detail of the work, down to the *terza rima* itself—that verse-form which is clear at any moment in its literal fiction yet essentially moving ahead and pointing to deeper meanings."

[13] Ibid., pp. 227, 228.

[14] Then he turned back, and seemed like one of those who run for the green cloth at Verona through the open field; and of them seemed he who gains, not he who loses.

Inferno, XV, 121-24 (Trans. Thomas Okey, The Temple Classics).

[15] Speaking of the *Inferno,* there is a far-reaching observation of Mark Van Doren about the punishments inflicted by the poet on those he puts in his Hell which I should like to cite here, though it deals with a question extraneous to my subject. "It is proper," Mr. Van Doren said, in a discussion of the

Divine Comedy, "to understand as Dante's meaning that all these persons have punished themselves. They are getting what they wanted. They died in life. They are the only persons in the poem who are really dead."—"Capaneus, one of the heroes of *The Seven Against Thebes,* says: 'What I was living, that I am in Hell,' " Mr. Tate added. Huntington Cairns, Allen Tate, Mark Van Doren, *Invitation to Learning* (New York: Random House, 1941), pp. 300-301.

[16] Francis Fergusson, op. cit., p. 227.

[17] "Baudelaire," in *Selected Essays,* p. 343.

[18] This passage from Marin's letters is a remarkable illustration of the requirements and prime importance of harmonic expansion in painting:

"To get to my picture, or to come back, I must for myself insist that when finished, that is when all the parts are in place and are working, that now it has become an object and will therefore have its boundaries as definite as that the prow, the stern, the sides and bottom bound a boat.

"And that this my picture must not make one feel that it bursts its boundaries. The framing cannot remedy. That would be a delusion and I would have it that nothing must cut my picture off from its finalities. And too, I am not to be destructive within. I can have things that clash. I can have a jolly good fight going on. There is always a fight going on where there are living things. But I must be able to control this fight at will with a Blessed Equilibrium." In *Artists on Art,* p. 467.

The following passages refer also, more or less directly, to the laws of harmonic expansion in painting: "The elements of this [the logical connection of parts to the whole], therefore, are solidity of objects and transparency of shadows in a breathable atmosphere through which we are conscious of spaces and distances. By the rendering of these elements we suggest the invisible side of painting, and the want of that grammar gives to pictures either the flatness of the silhouette or the vulgarity of an overstrained objectivity or the puddling twaddle of Preraphaelism." Inness, ibid., p. 344.—"A drawing must have a power of expansion which can bring to life the space which surrounds it." Matisse, ibid., p. 410.—"When, in Italy, I learned to understand architectural monuments I had at once to chalk up a remarkable advance in knowledge. Though they serve a practical purpose, the principles of art are more clearly expressed in them than in other works of art. Their easily recognizable structure, their exact organism, makes possible a more fundamental education than all the 'head- nude- and composition-studies.' Even the dullest will understand that the obvious commensurability of parts, to each other and to the whole, corresponds to the hidden numerical proportions that exist in other artificial and natural organisms. It is clear that these figures are not cold and dead, but full of the breath of life; and the importance of measurement as an aid to study and creation becomes evident." Paul Klee, ibid., p. 443.

The emphasis put by Severini on the "aesthetics of number" and "the laws of harmonic relations" comes from his deep realization of the essential part played by harmonic expansion in painting. A similar realization is the reason for Rouault's primary concern to have his picture perfectly *fill its space*. I think that Rouault would be in special agreement with Marin's views quoted at the beginning of this note.

The notion of harmonic expansion, as I see it, seems to me to be quite close to the Chinese concept of *K'ai-ho* or "unity of coherence." "From the revolution of the world to our own breathing," Shên Tsung-ch'ien, a writer of the eighteenth century, said, "there is nothing that is not K'ai-ho. If one can understand this, then we can discuss how to bring the painting to a conclusion. If you analyze a large k'ai-ho, within it there is more k'ai-ho. Even down to one tree and one rock, there is nothing that does not have both expanding and winding up. Where things grow and expand that is k'ai; where things are gathered up, that is ho. When you expand (k'ai) you should think of gathering up (ho) and then there will be structure; when you gather up (ho) you should think of expanding (k'ai) and then you will have inexpressible effortlessness and an air of inexhaustible spirit. In using brush and in laying out the composition, there is not one moment when you can depart from k'ai-ho."

As George Rowley observes at this point, "ch'i, the basic principle of rhythmic abstraction, has become k'ai-ho, the basic principle of rhythmic relationship." And after having indicated the essential importance of this "unity of coherence" in the writing of ideographs, he concludes: "From this analogy of the ideograph we can understand why, in painting, when you expand (k'ai) you must think of the gathering up (ho), 'or else the composition will fly apart through the explosive tendency of creativity, and the structural unity of the whole will be lost'; when you pull the parts together (ho) you should think of the vital force which gave them birth (k'ai), 'or else the result will be a dead mechanical adjustment and the whole will have missed the life breath of the spirit.' " Rowley, *Principles of Chinese Painting* (Princeton University Press, 1947), pp. 48-49.

Chinese theorists elucidated the notion of k'ai-ho in the particular perspective of Taoist philosophy, and Chinese painters put it into force in their own particular way. But this notion—let us say the notion of harmonic expansion—has of itself universal value because it has to do with the very essence of painting as quickened by poetic intuition. In looking at all great Occidental as well as Oriental painters we can verify the fact that harmonic expansion, the ultimate epiphany of creative intuition, is the entelechy, the definitely existence-giving "form" of a work made up of space-extended tensions.

[19] In tragedy, Aristotle said, "the agents are imitated mainly with a view to the action." *Poetics*, ch. 6, 1450 b 3-5. We may say that in the novel *the action is imitated mainly with a view to the agents.*—"Without action there is no tragedy, Aristotle also said, but there might be one without character" (ch. 6, 1450 a 24).

[20] The sole defect, to my mind, in the interesting discussion on Aristotle's *Poetics* related in *Invitation to Learning* (pp. 222-23), was the assumption that Aristotle's theory of tragedy covers the novel as well as the tragedy. Had the specific distinction we are stressing here been recognized, such excellent remarks as the following ones would have been given their full bearing:

"Van Doren: We get in many modern novels the whole life of a man, beginning perhaps in his childhood and going on through his marriage and through his professional or business career.

"Tate: Aristotle provides for that too, does he not? He says that unity of character does not mean unity of plot. That is, if you have a man named John Smith running through a novel, it does not mean that the novel has unity in terms of the plot. Smith remains a unit, but the plot is disorderly.

"Van Doren: The biography of a man is not necessarily a plot.

"Cairns: He goes even further. He says that dramatic action is not developed with a view to the representation of character; character comes in as subsidiary to the action. The incidents and the plot are the end of a tragedy and without action there cannot be a tragedy; there may be tragedy without character.

"Tate: We get that principle in Homer. Aristotle says that Homer omits certain characters that were traditionally attributed to the *Odyssey*. They would not fit into the plot.

"Van Doren: A famous novel of our time which is biographical in form, namely, *Of Human Bondage,* by Somerset Maugham, follows the hero from the time he is a little boy until he is married and has settled down in his profession of doctor. It might be Aristotle's point that Maugham's novel might be more interesting if the events in which we find Philip Carey, the hero, had a greater unity. At the end, you may remember, Philip Carey looks back over his life so far and says:

'I can find no meaning in it except insofar as the pattern of any life has meaning if we are absorbed as we follow the intricacies of that pattern.' Maugham has there very conveniently referred us back to Aristotle. A tragic hero, according to Aristotle's definition, would be capable of looking back over his life—Shakespeare's tragic heroes always did—and saying, 'It was this or that.'

"Tate: There is James Joyce's *Portrait of the Artist as a Young Man.* We know that it is largely, though not strictly, autobiographical. And it is significant that at the end of *The Portrait of the Artist,* the hero, Stephen Dedalus, says that he is going on to other things. He is going to have a new life elsewhere.

"Cairns: In other words, it is not a complete action. . . ."

[21] Op. cit., pp. 10-11.

[22] Raïssa Maritain, "Sens et Non-sens en poésie," in *Situation de la Poésie* (Paris: Desclée De Brouwer, 1938), p. 33 (English translation, p. 13).

[23] "The Freedom of Song" in *Art and Poetry* (New York: Philosophical Library, 1943).

[24] I wonder that Humbert Wolfe could write of Ronsard's famous line: *"Quand vous serez bien vieille, au soir, à la chandelle,"* "Is there any single line in all English poetry more subdued to magic?" This line is beautiful indeed, and has deep human resonance. There is not the least trace of magic in it.

[25] Spurious with respect to poetry, but not with respect to the original sense of the word magic, since it is a question of acting directly upon things and transforming them, and mastering reality through the power of words.